Why Keep Us Divided?

Colette D. Orr

Orr Novels Trademark

Copyright© 2014 by Colette D. Orr
Orr Novels Trademark
Edited by: Diane T. Owens

All rights reserved. No part of this book may be distributed, posted, or reproduced in any form without written permission from the author, except for the inclusions of brief quotes in a review. This is a book of fiction. Any names, events, and places herein are from the author's imagination. Any resemblance to individuals, living or dead is purely coincidental, unless author has obtained permission from individual(s).

Although my editor and I have gone through great lengths manually and electronically to ensure there are no grammatical errors within this book, we cannot guarantee that you will not find any, and we sincerely apologize in advance if you do. However, any errors found will be very minor and will not take away from the content of the book. Thank you so much for your undying love and continued support for Orr Novels. It is so greatly appreciated.

ISBN-13: 978-0615994598
ISBN-10: 0615994598

Website: http://www.ornovels.wix.com/colettedorr
Facebook: https://www.facebook.com/orr.novels
Twitter: https://twitter.com/orr_novels
Email: orrnovels@yahoo.com

Dedication and Thanks

First, I must thank you, Lord. This has been such an amazing and exciting journey. I pray that I will always keep you as the center of my novels. I couldn't have done it without your strength and guidance, and I am eternally grateful.

To everyone who supported my first novel, *It's Okay, You Loved Him...and you looked like a fool*, words cannot express how much appreciation I have for you. You've been so supportive in wanting to see me succeed. Thank you for coming out to my book signings and for all your uplifting cards and emails. Thank you for volunteering to sell copies of my book, spreading the word about my book, asking for my autograph and pictures, and bringing your precious kids and grandbabies to meet me. This has been an incredible experience; it's one I will never forget.

To Diane Owens, my editor and friend, you are a jewel and I'm very grateful for the sacrifices you've made to help me pursue my dreams.

To my three babies, Janessa, Katlyn, and Chaiden, who are not so little anymore, you are my rock! You have been my biggest fans. You listen to my ideas and give me your honest opinions; you have truly become my unpaid advisors and I'm so grateful for you. No matter what, I will always be your mother first; everything else comes second. My heart is forever with you. Thank you!

To everyone who has fallen in love with someone of a different race, and to those who are adamantly against interracial dating, this book is dedicated to you! I hope it inspires you to see that happiness, not skin color, should be the determining factor for entering into and/or supporting interracial relationships.

Ultimately, love will conquer all and if two people are meant to be together, nothing and no one will be able to keep them apart. Freely love whomever you choose to love…

Blessings Always,

Colette D. Orr

CHAPTER

"I've had it with this place! There's nothing but a bunch of fake, racist, bigots here, Mel! If I'm ever going to get promoted, I have to move away from here!" Daniel said angrily, to his girlfriend, Melah.

"I don't understand why you didn't get the promotion, baby. They pretty much promised it to you. They trained you for it and everything," Melah said sorrowfully.

"Baby, I could do that job with my eyes closed. I was the most qualified person in the organization, but they gave it to some kid down the hall, then he had the nerve to ask me if I would train him. I said, 'Nope, sure won't! You can learn it on your own just like I did.' Mel, I don't know if I can keep working for this company. I've got to move baby, that's all there is to it!"

"Well, what about—"

Just then, Daniel's phone rang; it was his mother.

"Hold on, babe. My mom is calling."

"Tell Mrs. Sarah I said hello," Melah responded, but Daniel was so glad to hear from his mom, he didn't hear Melah.

"Hey, ma," Daniel said, answering the phone as if a call from his mother was all it took to make everything better.

"Hey, baby son, you were on my mind and I decided to give you a call. How are you doing?"

"I'm okay, ma. I'm making it."

"You don't sound okay. What's wrong, Daniel?"

Daniel paused. He decided to go into the other room so Melah couldn't hear him, but it didn't matter, because Melah put her ear to the door and listened anyway.

"Ma, I didn't get the promotion. That job was supposed to be mine, but the minute they found out about Melah, everything changed. Of course I can't talk to her about it because it's only going to cause problems between us; she'll get offended and start acting all funny! It's just better to keep it to myself!"

"Aww, baby! I'm so sorry to hear that, but I can't say that I'm surprised."

"Well, I am! Ma, I think I need to move somewhere else. I don't think I can stay here much longer."

"Yeah, maybe so. You know Kirsten is doing very well in Atlanta. Maybe she can help you find a job up there!"

"Hmmm, Atlanta may be just the change I need. Do you have Kirsten's number?"

"Nah, I have her mom's number, though. You can give her a call; she'll be glad to give you Kirsten's number."

"I haven't talked to Mrs. Jan or Kirsten in years. Ma, you and Mrs. Jan have been friends a long time, huh?"

"Yeah, we sure have and it wasn't always easy with all the racial tension going on back in the early sixties, but our friendship prevailed. If you care enough about Melah, then your relationship will prevail too."

"Yeah, I guess you're right."

"Just hang in there, son. It'll work out for ya. You know Kirsten just got married? Oh, it was a lovely wedding, Daniel. They seemed really happy together."

"Oh yeah? Ma, you went? Why didn't you tell me? I would have loved to see everybody."

"Sorry, son. I didn't even think about it, but if you come home to see your momma more often, you'll know what's going on."

"Okay, ma. I hear you. I'll do better with that."

"Good! I look forward to seeing how well you do," she said, giggling. "Now here's Jan's number. Go on and give them a call. Call me later and tell me how it went."

"Okay, I will. Thanks, ma."

Daniel walked back into the room where Melah was.

"Where do you want to go eat, baby?" Melah asked, as if she didn't hear any of Daniel's conversation with his mother. "It's my treat."

"You're treating me to dinner?" he asked, surprisingly.

"Yes, anywhere you want to go. It doesn't matter if you got the promotion or not; we both know you deserved it, so I think we should still celebrate."

Daniel smiled.

"And that's why you've managed to steal my heart in this small amount of time," he responded.

Melah gave Daniel a big smile. They had only been dating four months, but Daniel loved how Melah treated him. She made him feel like he could rule the world. Melah didn't make much money, but she was very thrifty and always spent her money wisely. Everything was an investment. Even taking Daniel to dinner was an investment for Melah. She needed to know what happened at work that day and the only way to find out was through his stomach.

A full stomach and a glass of wine will get anyone talking, she thought.

Another thing Daniel loved about Melah was that she never raised her voice, even when she was upset. Being around Melah was always very peaceful and calming to Daniel, who'd been in quite a few rocky relationships in his lifetime.

Daniel grabbed his jacket while Melah locked up her apartment, then they jumped in the car and headed downtown for dinner.

The restaurant they went to was nice and quaint, chosen by Daniel for his "not getting my dream job/promotion" celebration.

Since Melah was being so thoughtful, Daniel tried not to ruin it with his bad mood. They sat there chatting while they waited for their food to come. Daniel did everything he could to avoid talking about what happened at work, and Melah did everything she could to try and coax it out of him. Daniel had never seen Melah act so determined and persistent before. Up until now, he thought she was as gentle as a lamb, but another side of Melah was rapidly creeping up and Daniel wasn't sure if he liked it.

"Daniel, do you trust me?" she asked, unexpectedly.

Daniel looked at her like she had grown a horn in the middle of her forehead.

"Yeah, of course I do. Why would you ask that?"

"Then tell me why I was the reason you didn't get that promotion."

He closed his eyes, took a deep breath, then looked back at Melah.

"Baby, they are stupid, don't worry about them. I'll get another promotion."

"Where, Daniel? Atlanta?"

"Wherever I can get a job, wherever that takes me."

"Us?" Melah asked.

"Huh, what do you mean?"

"You mean wherever that takes us, right?"

"You would go with me?"

"Would you want me to?"

"Well, yeah, but we've only been dating four months, Mel. I don't think we're at the point of picking up and moving together, do you?"

"So, how long does it take to get to that point?"

Daniel laughed, "I think it takes more than four months and surprisingly enough, I just learned today that my wonderful, sweet girlfriend is an eavesdropper, so I don't quite know how all that factors into the picture either."

Melah huffed. "Well, if it was something you were planning to tell me, you wouldn't have gone into the other room to talk on the phone."

"My point exactly, Mel. My point exactly!"

Melah gritted her teeth.

"All women eavesdrop, so stop acting like it's a big deal because it's not."

"Oh, do they now? That's very good to know."

"Daniel, don't avoid the question. I think we have something great and I'm not ready to give that up."

"No one said we have to give it up, Mel, but I'm not going to jump into a live-in situation after only four months of dating either. And it's very interesting how my sweet, loving, laid back girlfriend is starting to show me an aggressive and persistent side of her that I never knew existed. Is there anything else I need to know?"

"Don't patronize me, Daniel," Melah snapped.

"I'm not trying to patronize you and I'm not trying to avoid the question, but this is a lot to think about, Mel. Besides, my family is very religious; my momma don't play that living together without being married stuff."

"Really, Daniel? Your momma don't play that? You're a grown man, you can make your own decisions."

"Okay, well, I don't play that. Is that better?"

"No. Actually, it's not," Melah said, sounding aggravated.

"Listen, Mel, I do care about you, but I don't even

have a job anywhere yet. I don't know where I'm going or what I'm going to be doing. I can't make a permanent decision based on my current situation. I'm going to call Kirsten tonight and see what the job market is like in Atlanta. If all goes well, I will be able to get a job there and we can see where we are then. They call it the melting pot, so we shouldn't have some of the same issues there that we have here."

"Issues? I didn't know we had issues here. Do you care to share?"

"No, Mel. Actually I don't care to share," Daniel responded intensely.

"Okay, well can you at least tell me who Kirsten is?" she asked.

Just then the waitress walked up with their food. "Hi, sir! Would you like to try a glass of wine?" she asked, placing the food on the table, and leaning in front of Daniel, giving him a good view down her blouse. Melah's mouth dropped open and Daniel tried very hard not to look.

"No, thank you," he said, gazing straight at Melah.

"Ummm, I would like some, please," Melah responded, "But preferably without the extra side of chicken breasts in my face."

The waitress looked at Melah, slightly gasping as if she was offended, quickly poured Melah a glass of wine and walked away.

"You're so wrong for that, Mel," Daniel said, laughing.

"I don't care! She acted like I wasn't even sitting here."

"It's just the culture down here, Mel. People don't like seeing us together."

"That's not true, Daniel. No one cares about that stuff anymore. That girl was just attracted to you, that's all. She's what my grandma would call a fast-tail skank!"

Daniel let out a huge laugh and several people looked over at their table to see what was going on.

"What's a fast-tail skank?" Daniel asked, still laughing.

"That is a woman who's always flirting and trying to get some man to notice her. They are the ones you have to hide your man from. You can't even compliment your man around this type of woman, because the next thing you know, she'll be in his face trying to take him from you. You can't ever trust a fast-tail skank!" Melah said, sounding super country and southern.

Daniel was laughing so hard that his face was turning red.

"Do you know your accent changed when you were giving me that description?" Daniel asked, still laughing.

Melah sat there with a serious look on her face, as if she was ready to pull out a dictionary and prove to Daniel that such a word existed and the definition was exactly as she had described.

"Okay, Mel, our waitress is a skank, but people still care more about interracial couples than you think, so don't be naive."

"I said she's a fast-tail skank, Daniel, and I'm not naïve. Why do you feel that you have to protect me? Just tell me what happened at your job. Tell me why you think people care about us being together. If things are affecting you, then they also affect me and they affect our relationship, so I think I should know about them, don't you?"

"Mel, what's with you tonight? Why are you being so GRRRRAAAHH?" he asked, holding his fingers in the air like bear claws.

Melah looked down at her food.

"I just feel like I'm losing you. You're keeping secrets from me, you're talking about moving, and now our waitress is trying to give you a personal strip show right in front of me. I just feel like we're falling apart."

Daniel laughed. "Women are all the same. If a man seems distant, you guys automatically go into panic mode and think the relationship is in danger. I wish women wouldn't be so emotional about everything. Just because I don't want to talk about something, doesn't mean I don't want to be with you anymore."

Melah smiled. "That's nice to know, because I want to be with you forever."

Whoa! Forever is a long time, Daniel thought, but then again, spending forever with Melah didn't seem like such a bad idea.

"I actually like the sound of *forever* with you, Mel."

Melah smiled and gave Daniel a wink, accentuating her dreamy slightly slanted cat eyes that Daniel never seemed to be able to resist.

"You are so beautiful! We should probably eat now before I get sidetracked and pull you underneath this table,"

Daniel said, smiling.

"Uh Uh! You're not putting me on this dirty floor. But yes, please let's eat because I'm starving."

Daniel gave Melah a half grin like he was still fantasizing about them being underneath the table. Melah decided to leave him right there in his fantasy world while she gobbled down her food.

"Oh, this is so good!" she said, finally pulling Daniel away from his dirty thoughts. He eventually came back to himself and joined in on the feast.

After dinner, they decided to go back to his place. Melah flopped down on the couch and wrapped herself up in a blanket. Daniel came over and snuggled up next to her.

Melah kissed his forehead.

"So, what did you say was the reason your boss didn't honor his word about the promotion?" Melah asked softly, as if she was going to somehow trick Daniel into spilling the beans.

"I am not Samson, and there will be no secrets shared here, Delilah," Daniel answered.

"Huh? Who is Samson and Delilah?" Melah asked, with a confused look on her face.

"Melah, you've never heard of the Samson and Delilah Bible story?

"Don't judge me! I told you I wasn't religious."

Daniel laughed!

"I'm not judging you. I just thought everyone had heard of Samson and Delilah. That's all. Okay, here's your bedtime story so close your eyes and listen," Daniel said to Melah.

"Just tell the story," she said.

"Don't ruin the mood, Mel! Okay, so Samson was very strong; he actually had the strength of several men. No one could defeat him in battle, but like most guys, his weakness was beautiful women. Poor Samson," Daniel interjected. "So, he fell in love with this beautiful girl named Melah, I mean Delilah."

"Quit playing, Daniel, and tell the story. I'm actually interested."

"So, the men from Delilah's town wanted to know what made Samson so strong. They promised to give Delilah some money if she could find out where Samson got his strength from. For days she asked him to tell her, but he wouldn't, then she tried to make him feel guilty like women always do, saying, 'Samson, if you love me, you will tell me what makes you so strong,' and eventually she wore him down. He gave in and told her that if someone cut his hair, he would lose all of his strength."

"Ooooh, this is good!" Melah responded, like she was in a children's Sunday school class.

Daniel continued the story.

"So, when Samson was asleep, Delilah cut off all of his hair and then called the men in to capture him. That was pretty much the end of Samson," Daniel said, shaking his head like he was disappointed. "You can't trust these beautiful women! But, I'm not Samson, and I'm not giving in," he said, looking over at Melah like he was tough.

"Oh good grief!" she replied. "I bet you left out half the story. I'm gonna read it myself to see what else happened."

Daniel laughed. "Whatever! I can't believe you've never heard that story, Mel. I thought everyone knew about Samson and Delilah."

"Everyone doesn't have parents that take them to church or read the Bible to them, Daniel."

"Yeah, you're right," Daniel responded, then he and Melah started chatting about whatever was on television.

About thirty minutes later, Melah looked over at Daniel, rubbed his hair and whispered into his ear, "Samson, please tell me all your secrets."

Daniel could feel Melah's lips on his ear. He glanced over at her.

"Delilah, you have no idea what you do to me. I suggest you stop before you get into something you can't handle," he said, picking her up and tossing her on the couch. Melah laughed, but Daniel did not.

"It was just a joke, don't get distracted," she yelled, but it was too late. Things got very heated, very quickly. When Daniel looked into Melah's eyes, he felt shivers down his spine. He was so transfixed on her that he couldn't even think clearly. Everything was moving so fast and clothes were flying off at the speed of lightning. Being with Melah was always breathtaking for Daniel, but this time it seemed more incredible than ever. This time, everything seemed magical and they both seemed to be in another world.

Moments later, he laid on the couch next to Melah. He kissed her shoulder.

"Mel, I think I'm—"

"OH MY GOSH, DANIEL! WE DIDN'T USE ANY PROTECTION! HOW COULD WE FORGET TO USE PROTECTION?" Melah screamed, holding her head, interrupting what Daniel was about to say."

"Calm down, Mel. I didn't really forget; I just didn't have any more condoms and we were so caught up in the moment, I just said to myself, 'Forget it! Let's get it on.' You're on the pill anyway, so it doesn't matter. Besides, you're the only—"

"I'm not on the pill, Daniel! I never told you that! Why didn't you just ask before making a huge assumption like that?"

"What? Why are you not on the pill? What grown woman is not on the pill?"

"It's not like I'm out here sleeping with the whole United States or anything. If I'm not in a relationship then I don't just have pills laying around at my disposal. I was going to college to earn my degree, not to have freestyle sex, and then you came into my life out of nowhere, with that sneaky grin, saying, 'Melah, I have a sensitive stomach and I know you can cook really good. If you make me some home cooked meals, I'll make you a straight 'A' student in math.' You knew I was darn near flunking math, so of course I cooked for you. The next thing I knew, you were coming over for more than a home cooked meal," Melah said, giving Daniel an evil look. "I bet you planned the whole thing, didn't you? You don't even have a sensitive stomach do you? And you're probably a great cook too, aren't you?"

Daniel laughed really loudly. "No, I'm not a great

cook and you weren't great at math either; we needed each other. You know I was allergic to that cafeteria food."

"That doesn't even make sense, Daniel. Who's allergic to everything in the cafeteria? You tricked me!"

"It worked out, didn't it? We're like two peas in a pod, Mel. We're meant to be together."

"Yeah, yeah," Mel said, nonchalantly. "And I didn't become a straight 'A' student like you promised."

"Well, I can't work miracles, Mel," Daniel said, laughing, "But you did pass, didn't you?" he asked.

"Whatever! So why don't you have any more condoms?" she asked, trying to get back to the original conversation.

"Well, as soon as I buy some, we use them all up; the factory couldn't make'em fast enough. You're too wild for me, Mel. You're just too wild."

"That's not funny, Daniel, and that's not true either. You should always make sure we're protected," she responded.

"No, I shouldn't! That's a woman's job. Women are supposed to make sure they're on the pill."

"What? Don't tell me you're one of those guys that think it's solely the woman's responsibility to not get pregnant. I have never understood the rationale behind that," Melah responded, irritably.

"Why are we even talking about this, Mel? You don't think you're gonna get pregnant, right?" Daniel asked, nervously.

"I SURE HOPE NOT!" Melah yelled. "You just graduated from college six months ago and you're working an entry-level job and I'm still in college, working a part-time job. We are nowhere near ready for marriage."

"Marriage? Who said anything about marriage?"

"Uhhh, if I got pregnant, you wouldn't marry me?" Melah asked, jumping off the couch and putting her hand on her hips.

Uh Oh! Daniel thought. He looked down at the couch like he didn't see Melah standing in front of him, patiently waiting for an answer. He was sure that whatever he said next wasn't going to go over well.

He stretched his hands in the air and pretended to yawn. "Whewww, I'm getting sleepy," he said, "Let's finish this conversation in the morning, babe."

"Oh, stop faking, Daniel. I'm going home," Mel said.

Daniel sat up on the couch.

"Come on, Mel. You know I care for you, but we've only been dating four months and seeing how this was only a hypothetical question, I really don't see why you're getting so worked up about it."

"Well, let's just hope that your sperm is hypothetical too," Melah said, as she threw on her clothes and left, slamming the door behind her.

Daniel took a deep breath. "Okkkkkaaaaayyyyy, that's not how I saw the night ending," he said, looking at the door.

How could she get mad at me over a hypothetical question? I'll never understand women! He thought.

He wanted to go after Melah, but that was the first time she'd ever been angry with him, so he wasn't quite sure how to react. There was no doubt that he cared about her, but Daniel had a lot going on in his head and seeing how his relationship with Melah just caused him his dream promotion, he definitely felt this would be a good time to be alone so he could process his thoughts.

"I'll just get some rest and try to tackle everything in the morning," he said, turning out the lights and snuggling up in the blanket that smelled just like Melah's perfume.

CHAPTER

The next morning, when Daniel got to work, he tried very hard to forget about the promotion he didn't get.

"I'm going to act like nothing happened," he said to himself. "If they don't want to give me the promotion, then I'll go find another job. I'm not going to allow them to mistreat me just because I fell in love with a black wom—"

Daniel stopped himself in the middle of his sentence. "Did I just say, 'I fell in love?' Nah, nah, nah, that's not what I meant, that's definitely not what I meant," he said, trying to reassure himself that he was in control of his feelings.

"Are you talking to someone, Daniel?" his supervisor asked as he walked by Daniel's cubicle.

"Nah, I wasn't talking; did you hear something?" Daniel asked in a concerned tone.

"Well, I could have sworn I heard you talking, but you know I'm getting old, so my hearing isn't as good as it used to be."

"Yeah, you may want to get it checked out," Daniel

said, trying to sound supportive.

"You're right. I just may do that. You wanna go to lunch today, Daniel? I heard they have great sandwiches at that new restaurant downtown."

You gotta be kidding me. I'm not going anywhere with you. I know you could have helped me get that promotion and you didn't. Now you're asking me to hang out for lunch like everything is cool between us. I HATE fake people!

"No thanks, I can't do lunch," Daniel responded, cordially.

"Okay, well maybe another day then," his boss said, sounding disappointed.

Daniel didn't bother to respond. He started typing on his computer like he was really busy. His supervisor continued to stand there, so Daniel typed faster, hoping he would get the hint and leave, which he did.

Daniel worked hard all morning, trying to keep his mind occupied. After a few hours passed, he decided to go into the break room to get something to drink.

"Hey, Daniel," he heard a girl say as he headed towards the vending machine. He looked up at her and she gave him a subtle smile.

"Hey, how are you?" Daniel said, slowly, not recognizing who the girl was.

"I heard about what happened and I'm sorry," she said, putting her hand on Daniel's arm.

Daniel shrugged his shoulders.

"Oh, it's cool. I don't sweat the small stuff, but thanks for being concerned," he responded, as he grabbed his drink out of the vending machine, and started walking towards the door.

"So, are you still with her, or did you learn your lesson like a good boy?" she asked, giving Daniel a seductive grin.

Daniel made an abrupt stop. "Excuse me?" he asked, turning around towards the girl.

She threw her hands up.

"C'mon, Daniel! You can't be serious about her. She cost you a well-deserved promotion."

Daniel looked into the eyes of this tall, slender, blond-headed girl, whose pink v-neck shirt with sequins on it showed just enough cleavage to tempt any man. She wore a black skirt that came just above her knee, which was conservative, yet still sexy. Her pale pink lip gloss made her lips look soft and perfect for kissing, and her four-inch heels put the finishing touches on her flamboyant attire. She stared back into Daniel's eyes and slightly bit the corner of her bottom lip. He walked closer to her. He could smell her flowery perfume. He looked at her silky blond hair, noticing how nice her highlights were. He smiled and said, "No offense, but unless I ask for your opinion, I'd really appreciate it if you kept it to yourself."

The girl let out a small gasp. She couldn't believe he said that to her, but she quickly regained her composure, flipped her hair to one side, and said, "I'm just trying to help. You should stick with your own kind, Daniel. God never meant for different races to mix together. There are plenty of wonderful white women who would love to be with you. Besides, don't they have Affirmative Action or something to make sure blacks are treated well? You don't owe them anything."

Daniel frowned.

"Affirmative Action?" he asked.

She can't be serious! It's a travesty that a woman so beautiful can be so ignorant.

"For the record," he whispered, softly, "Yes, I am still with her and yes, I am very serious about her. And until you can show me in the Bible where it says God doesn't want me to date a black woman, then no promotion or woman with her chest hanging all out in the workplace will be worth me losing my relationship over." Then he popped his drink open, took a sip, and walked out of the room.

Although Daniel tried not to show it, he was very angry by the conversation. When he got to his desk, his face was blood red.

I have to get out of this place. I can't deal with narrow-minded people.

For the rest of the day, Daniel stayed to himself. At this point, he wasn't sure who was for him or against him.

When he left work that evening, he knew he needed to patch things up with Melah, but he also needed to work on finding another job. He grabbed the piece of paper with Ms. Jan's number on it and gave her a call. They talked for about thirty minutes, then she gave him Kirsten's number. He waited for a few hours to get his thoughts together, then he called Kirsten.

"Hey, Kirsten, this is Daniel Stine. Remember me?"

"Daniel, I haven't talked to you since I graduated high school. How are you?"

"I'm good, how are things in Atlanta?"

"Everything is great. I just got married!"

"Yeah, my mom told me. I wish I had known; I would have definitely come to the wedding. It's sad when old neighbors lose contact with each other."

"Well, Daniel, you're not exactly one who stays in one spot very long."

"Yeah, you're right about that, but I'll make sure you know how to reach me next time. Is he treating you good? I'd hate to drive to Atlanta to give him the Daniel beat down."

Kirsten laughed. "He's really awesome, Daniel."

"Any kids yet?"

"No, we just got married two weeks ago."

"Oh, wow! Just two weeks ago? Well, you should still be on your honeymoon."

"Actually, we were. We just got back this morning."

"Oh, where did you go?"

"Jamaica. It was so nice. I could have stayed there forever."

"I bet it was."

"So what about you? Are you married with kids, yet?"

"No, not yet. I think I'm going to leave those kids where they're at. I have way too much that I want to do with my life before I think about any of that."

"Yeah, my husband and I are enjoying our quiet

time alone. No little people running around getting into everything."

Daniel laughed. "I know what you mean. My sister, Roslyn brings her bad kids to my house and I count down the time until they're all gone. I love'em, but Kirsten, those crumb-snatchers touch everything. I mean, EVERYTHING! Once, Jeremy, her middle son put a whole jar of Vaseline all over his face and hair. The whole jar, Kirsten! Roslyn was running around trying to clean him up before he touched the walls. Then the baby girl started taking her first steps, so Roslyn stopped chasing Jeremy and started looking at the baby. While all of this was going on, Leon, her oldest son, got a step stool, climbed up on the cabinets, and was eating sugar straight out of the bag. Roslyn started fussing at him, I had to chase Jeremy before he destroyed my house with Vaseline, and I don't know who was watching the baby anymore. It was crazy, Kirsten. Roslyn is like Mother Goose; she's got too many children and she doesn't know what to do."

Kirsten was laughing so hard that her husband, Everett, came in to see what was going on. "What are you laughing so hard about, woman?"

"I'm sorry, baby," Kirsten said, still laughing. "This is my neighbor, Daniel, from back home."

"Well, you and your neighbor, Daniel, need to keep it down because the game is on. Everybody knows that a man shouldn't be disturbed during football season, and why isn't he watching the game? Real men watch football," Everett said, as he let out a loud *GRRRRRR* noise.

Kirsten put Daniel on speaker so Everett could hear

his response.

"Tell your husband that I don't like people growling at me, but since he's in the family now, I'll let it slide. But real men have man caves to block out all the noise, so where is his man cave?"

"Oh, no! Please don't mention a man cave, Daniel. Everett can build anything; he'll turn our entire house into a man cave if I let him," Kirsten said.

"Yeah! A man cave?" Everett chimed in. "That's exactly what I need. Tell Daniel he's finally talking with sense. Hey Daniel, I may need some help building this man cave, so come on up after you and Kirsten are done with all that laughing and I'll teach you a little bit about football and carpentry while you're here."

Kirsten laughed at how Everett and Daniel were going back and forth like they had known each other for years.

"No problem!" Daniel yelled back. "I may be moving up there soon anyway."

"Oh really?" Kirsten interjected. "When?"

Daniel reverted back to his conversation with Kirsten. "Well, that's why I'm calling. I'm thinking about moving to Atlanta and I might need some help getting settled."

"That's awesome Daniel. I'll ask Everett if you can stay in our guest bedroom until you can get settled."

"Nope!" Everett responded. "I don't know him like that."

"Everett!" she yelled, but Daniel just laughed it off.

"I kinda like him, Kirsten, but no, I don't want to

move in with you guys. I know you're in the construction business, and I'm hoping you can give me the names of some companies up there, so I can see if they're hiring. I just need to move somewhere that's more accepting of me."

"Oh, sure, I can help with that, but what do you mean by 'more accepting of you?' Why would someone not accept you?"

"It's not that they won't accept me, they won't accept me being with my girlfriend."

"What is wrong with your girlfriend?"

"She's black, Kirsten. All people need to see is a white man holding a black woman's hand and it ticks them off. It ticks off white people, it ticks off black people, and as far as I know, it may tick off the Indians, Asians, Italians, and Hispanics too. I don't know anymore."

Kirsten wanted to laugh, but she knew Daniel was serious, so she just listened.

"Kirsten, the same people who loved me so much, paraded me around their business conferences, and told everyone how wonderful I was, were the same people that treated me like I was the devil once they found out I was dating a black girl. I am a hard-working man, Kirsten. I go to work on time, I do my job, and I pay my bills. I made straight A's in college, I've never done drugs and I've never gotten into any trouble with the law, but for some reason, I still can't choose to date who I want? Blacks look at me like I've stolen something from them and whites look at me like I'm a disgrace to the white race. I can't take all this crazy, ignorant thinking anymore."

"Kirsten, I was up for a promotion. My boss

promised it to me when I first started working there and they groomed me for it for months. I was already doing the job, and doing it quite well, I might add. The day before they announced their selection for the job, Melah stopped by the office to take me to lunch. When I introduced her as my girlfriend, the manager, who was the chairman of the promotion panel, looked like he was going to vomit. After that, everything changed. When I came back from lunch, my boss started acting funny and making excuses for why they were moving me to another project, then he stopped talking about the new position all together. The next day came and went and there was no word on the promotion. Then one day, a guy in a different division told me that the boss came down and congratulated his co-worker on getting the promotion. He wasn't even qualified for the job, Kirsten! Do you think my boss said anything to me about what happened? Not one word! He didn't even have the decency to come and talk to me like a man!"

"I work my butt off for this company, and simply because my girlfriend is black, they passed me over for a promotion that they had told me I deserved. They didn't even try to get to know her. Sometimes I feel like we're back in the fifties, but it's not just white men and it's not just white people, it's both sides of the fence. Black men hate seeing me with Melah, yet they love white women. I don't get that, Kirsten. I need to move to the melting pot, so I don't have to deal with all of that craziness."

Kirsten laughed, "Yes, I think you will really enjoy the melting pot, Daniel, but you may still have to deal with a little racism up here too. Definitely not like you just described, but a lot of people are just not ready to see races intermingling like that."

"But, it's not any of their business. If two people are happy together, then that's what should matter."

"Yeah! That's very true, Daniel! Well, come on up, I'll be glad to introduce you to some people. Just let me know when you're coming."

"That's great, Kirsten. How does next Monday sound? Not this upcoming Monday, but the Monday after that?"

"Okay! Hold on," she said, taking the phone away from her ear. "Everett, Daniel is coming to visit us next Monday," she yelled to Everett, who had gone back into the den to finish watching football.

"Alright," he yelled back, not paying any attention to what Kirsten actually said.

"Okay, Everett is good with it, so come on. I'd love to see you again and I'd love to meet your girlfriend too."

"Well, she's still in college; it's her last few months before graduating, so she can't miss any classes. Besides, she's mad at me right now, so she probably wouldn't want to come anyway," he said, laughing.

Kirsten laughed too.

"Well, go call her and fix it," she said.

"Yeah, I need to do that. It was great talking to you, Kirsten. See you next week."

"Okay, Daniel. I can't wait," she responded just before hanging up the phone.

CHAPTER

♬ ♪ ♬ Pitter, patter, pat, tat, tat. ♬ ♪ ♬ Pitter, patter, pat, tat, tat ♬ ♪ ♬ was the sound of the drumbeat playing on Melah's ringtone.

"Who's calling?" she said, reluctantly putting her schoolbook down and running into the kitchen to answer the phone. "Okay, I hear it ringing, but where is it?" she asked herself, trying to find her phone. Meanwhile, Daniel, on the other end couldn't help but wonder if Melah was still upset with him and just refusing to answer. Just when he got his *I'm sorry* speech ready to leave on her voicemail, he heard her voice.

"Hello," she said, finally picking up the phone.

"Hey, Mel. What are you up to?"

"Studying."

"Okay. Well—"

"I have three finals coming up this week. I'm so stressed, Daniel."

"Oh! That's too bad. I wanted to take you out to dinner tonight," he responded, trying to smooth things over from the night before.

"I can't. I'm swamped with schoolwork and I don't—"

"I'm sorry about last night, Mel. The whole conversation was too overwhelming for me and I didn't know how to respond."

"Don't worry about it, Daniel. It was all hypothetical and we have a long time before we have to think about any of those things."

Well that didn't go so bad, Daniel thought, letting out a sigh of relief.

"I really wish I could see you tonight," he said, "But I know you're busy. Maybe we—"

"I don't know why I got so upset like that," Melah continued, cutting him off. "Hormones, I guess," she added, laughing and closing her car door. "I'm definitely going to get on the pill, though," she said.

"Oh! That'll be great. Are you going somewhere? I thought I heard a car door close."

"What?"

"Nothing. I just thought I heard a car door slam. So I guess we won't be able to see each other this week, huh?"

"Ummm, hold on."

"Mel, what are you doing?"

After a minute or so, Melah returned to the phone.

"Sorry! That was my aunt calling. She's been calling all day. I had to answer," Melah said to Daniel.

"Okay, so I probably won't see you th—"

"No, probably not, babe. It's going to be crazy for

me over the next two weeks."

"Okay, well, you know I have to go up to D.C. for this stupid conference next week," Daniel replied.

"Oh, yeah! I forgot about that. That means, I won't get to see you until you get back from D.C. Booooo!" Melah said, making a sad face. "I have so much going on this week and all of next week as well, including the weekends. Maybe we can do something the following week, though," Melah said. "JERK!" she screamed.

"Beep, Beep!"

"What was that?" Daniel asked. "Melah, what are you doing?

"What? I didn't hear anything."

"Mel, I heard a horn blowing."

"A horn, Daniel?"

"Yeah, Mel! I heard a horn. I'm not crazy."

Melah shrugged her shoulders.

"The jury is still out on whether or not you're crazy, Daniel," she said, laughing.

"Not funny!" he responded with a stern voice.

"Daniel, I think I want a cat for my graduation present. Do you want to go to the pet store with me and help me pick one out?"

"A cat? Yeah, sure. So anyway, I'm going straight to Atlanta after my trip to D.C., but when I—"

"Are you moving?" she asked, suddenly, giving Daniel her full attention.

"Oh, so now you're paying attention to me?"

"I always pay attention to you," Melah said.

She and Daniel chatted a little while longer, then

she asked, abruptly, "So, are you moving?"

"BAM, BAM, BAM, BAM!"

Daniel jumped off the couch.

"Hold on, Mel. Someone is at my door. I don't know who it could be!" he said, looking out of the peep hole. He smiled and opened the door.

"I asked you a question," Melah said, letting herself into the house and hanging up the phone.

He gave her a hug and kiss.

"It's good to see you, babe and no, I'm just going up to see if I can find a job," he responded, hanging up the phone too.

"Oh," Melah said, disappointedly, returning his hug and kiss. "I guess that means you are moving, but that's good, baby. I'm happy for you."

"You don't have to pretend to be happy, Mel."

"I am happy for you," she said, grabbing her favorite cheetah blanket off of the couch. "I just don't want to lose you," she added, as she wrapped up in it like always.

"Here we go again. I told you that's not going to happen. I'm just going to look for a job, not another woman," he said reassuringly, as he sat down beside her.

"That's very good to hear," she replied, letting out a small laugh. "I can't stay long, Daniel. I just came to get one of your world famous hugs to help me get through all this work I have to do."

"I can give you more than that if you'd like."

"Nobody has time for all of that, Daniel. I don't feel like taking off my clothes. I just want a hug. So when are you coming back?" she asked, with a cute grin on her face.

"That's really too bad, Mel. Really too bad! I will be in D.C. until next Monday, then I'll fly into Atlanta and will probably stay up there until Wednesday or Thursday."

"Aww, I won't see you for almost three weeks!" she complained. "That makes me sad, but by the time you return I'll be done with all of this schoolwork and I can start preparing for graduation! Yippie!" Melah said, excitedly.

"That's why you need to love on me now," he said, leaning against Melah's face. "Three weeks is a long time for us not to see each other."

"Daniel, I just told you I'll be graduating, but all you heard was an opportunity to have sex?"

"I said 'congratulations,' didn't I? Then I said, 'Baby, that's awesome.' You didn't hear me?"

Melah smacked her lips. "Whatever! You didn't say any of those things and you know it."

"Mel, you know I can't wait to see you strut across that stage. I'll be on the front row with a big orange sign that says, 'There goes my baby' on it."

Melah let out a huge laugh.

"I bet you will," she responded. "Daniel, although I don't want you to move, I know you will be a great asset to anyone's company. You are so smart and gifted. They would be crazy not to hire you!"

"Dang, babe! You really make me feel like I can rule the world. I love that about you. You always act like you believe in me."

"I do believe in you. You can do and be anything you want and I will never get in the way of you trying to advance your career."

"Okay, stop before you make me go crazy over you," he said, rubbing his forehead.

"Well, that is the goal," Melah responded, with a smirk.

Melah and Daniel sat and watched a movie for about ten minutes, then Melah had to go so she could get back to studying. Daniel was sad to see her leave, but he was very happy for the surprise visit.

*Normally, a woman just popping in unannounced like that is grounds for getting kicked to the curb, but this girl has me breaking all the man-rules. I can't let the fellas see me like this. Man-up, Dan! Man-up, h*e thought, as he gave Melah a kiss goodnight.

The week went by fast, with Daniel and Melah having very little time to even talk to each other, then soon came time for Daniel to head to D.C. and then to Atlanta.

His trip to D.C. was uneventful; just a whole lot of people trying to network and get others to buy their products. When the conference was over, he was very happy to get on the plane and head to Atlanta. As soon as his plane landed, he gave Kirsten a call.

"Hey, Kirsten, this is Daniel. I just made it to Atlanta. Do you want to grab lunch?"

"Yeah, that'll be great, but can you come to my office first? I am knee deep in a project and I've got to get it finished before I can goof off," she said, giggling.

"No problem. What's the address? I'll put it in my

GPS."

Kirsten gave him the address and rushed back to her project. When Daniel pulled up, he immediately noticed the reserved parking spots.

"Reserved for Kirsten Larson. I know Kirsten doesn't have her own parking spot," Daniel said, with a shocked look on his face. "I wonder if that's her new last name," he added, breaking out into a song.

♫ ♪ ♫ Moving on up, to the east side, in a deluxe apartment in the sky. Kirsten's moving on up. She's finally got a piece of the pie ♫ ♪ ♫

Daniel laughed at himself as he thought of George and Weezie from The Jefferson's show. He got out of the car and headed into Kirsten's building.

"Hi, I'm here to see Kirsten Jabard, I mean Kirsten—"

"Larson?" the receptionist chimed in.

"Yes, Kirsten Larson."

I sure hope this is the right Kirsten, Daniel thought, nervously.

"May I tell her your name, sir?" the receptionist asked.

"It's Daniel Stine. She's expecting my visit."

"Well, why wasn't I expecting your visit, Mr. Stine?" she inquired, flirtatiously. "Don't you think the receptionist needs to know who's coming into the building?" she asked, with a very serious look on her face, then she let out a haughty laugh. "I'm just playing. My name is Mandy," she added, reaching out to shake his hand. "Please have a seat. I'll let her know you're here."

Daniel looked like he had a delayed reaction to Mandy's joke, but he managed to let out a small chuckle as he shook her hand and sat down in the waiting area.

"Mrs. Larson, you have a Daniel Stine waiting to see you," Mandy said, as she buzzed Kirsten's intercom.

"Daniel, it's so great to see you!" Kirsten said, running out of her office and giving Daniel a big hug. They were so happy to see each other, they hugged three times.

"Mmmmm, must be nice to have all kind of good-looking men to hug on," Mandy whispered, sarcastically.

Mr. Wayne, the CEO of the company, and several others came out to see what all the commotion was about.

"Everyone, this is Daniel Stine. He was my neighbor back home and he's thinking about moving to Atlanta. He's up here job hunting. We haven't seen each other in years. Mr. Wayne, can I possibly get him on your calendar sometime today?"

"No can do," Mr. Wayne replied. "I will be out of the office most of the day, but I am totally free tomorrow afternoon. He's welcome to come see me then."

"No, sir, he cannot because your wife called and said she made you a dentist appointment for tomorrow at 2:00," Mandy stated.

"A dentist appointment? I don't need to go to the dentist," he said, grinning.

Kirsten and Mandy both gave Mr. Wayne a frown.

Oh, gosh. He can't be serious, Kirsten thought. *I've never seen teeth so disgusting in all my life.*

"You really should go to the dentist, Mr. Wayne,"

Mandy said, encouragingly.

"Okay, fine!" he grumbled, like a school boy who was just told that recess was over and it was time to go inside. Mr. Wayne glanced over at Daniel who was respectfully trying to hold in his laughter.

"What are you laughing about, Daniel?" Mr. Wayne asked.

Daniel threw his hands in the air.

"Nothing, sir! Nothing at all."

Mr. Wayne chuckled.

"These girls are always trying to keep me straight, Daniel. They should know I'm a lost cause, but they won't give up, and that's including my wife."

He gave Daniel a grin. "I tell you what, Daniel. I'll have Mandy move some appointments around for me in the morning so we can chat a little bit. How does that sound?"

"That sounds great, sir. Thank you," Daniel responded excitedly.

"Okay, come see me first thing tomorrow morning and we'll talk."

"Okay, thank you, sir. I appreciate the opportunity."

"No problem," Mr. Wayne said. "Lord knows Kirsten is not the nicest person in the world, but I don't know what I would do without her, so if I can help, I will."

Kirsten cut her eyes at Mr. Wayne and gave him a *how dare you* stare. She wanted to roll her eyes and say something smart, but since he was willing to help Daniel, she decided to just give him lots of dirty looks inside of her head.

"Thank you, Mr. Wayne," Kirsten said as nicely as she could, trying to focus on the positive, but he didn't respond. He just walked off chuckling.

Daniel gave them a funny look.

"Oh, don't mind those two, they love each other like brother and sister," Mandy said to Daniel.

"Daniel, are you ready to head to lunch?" Kirsten asked.

"Yeah, sure. Let's go."

"Where are you two going for lunch?" Mandy asked. "I would love—"

"You're not going with us, Mandy, and Daniel is taken," Kirsten said, cutting her off.

Mandy made an ugly face at Kirsten.

"Mrs. Larson, I was just trying to look out for you. You are a married woman now, so you need another woman there just in case someone sees you and wants to start rumors about you cheating on your husband. Now, do you see why you need me there?" Mandy asked, laughing like someone had convinced her that she was funny.

"I'll just take my chances without you," Kirsten responded. "Let's go, Daniel. I'll drive."

Mandy gave Kirsten another nasty glare.

"Where is your ring, Mr. Stine?" Mandy asked Daniel. "Your wife lets you leave the house without it? Brave woman!"

"I'm not married, but I have a—"

"Bye, Mandy," Kirsten said, pulling Daniel out the front door.

"We will finish this later, Mr. Stine," Mandy said,

as she tapped her fingers on her desk and waved goodbye to Daniel.

CHAPTER

"Oh, this is a nice ride, Kirsten!" Daniel said, as he sat down in her black Camaro.

"It's Everett's. He had to take mine to the shop this morning. I hate driving this car. It's too fast and too sporty for me. If you put just a little weight on the gas pedal, the next thing you know, you're zooming down the highway. Everett loves it, though, so what can I say? What do you want for lunch?" she asked.

"Kirsten, if you can take me somewhere that has good lemon pepper chicken wings, I will be in hog heaven."

Kirsten laughed. "The food court in the mall has excellent wings. I'll take you there."

"Yummm! I've been wanting some wings for weeks, maybe even months, Kirsten, but there are no good places to eat in that hole-in-the-wall town I live in. I hate it there! Everyone is fake! I don't mean to start on my rampage again, but I have got to get out of that place,"

Daniel said.

"Why is it so bad?" Kirsten asked.

"The stupidity and narrow-mindedness of people gets depressing. As long as I was dating a white girl, everybody was fine, but as soon as I met Melah, now all of a sudden I'm different. How am I any different? I am the same guy that I was when I had a white woman on my arm. I didn't change, but they act like I'm of a lower caliber now. It's insane! I guarantee that I won't be worthy to attend their seminars anymore, I won't be worthy to go to their high society luncheons, and we all know I'm not worthy of their promotions."

"Come on, Daniel. It can't be that bad. Why do you think you won't get invited to seminars and luncheons anymore?"

"Because last week both of my bosses received an invitation to the Chiefs of America's Workforce luncheon and not one of them mentioned it to me. They have this luncheon every quarter. Since the day I got there, they have paraded me around like I was a golden child, but last week the invites came out for the upcoming event and no one has said a word to me. They don't want me there because everyone brings their wives and girlfriends and they don't want me to bring mine."

"Are you sure, Daniel? You may still get invited."

"Ummm, no I won't! They don't want me and my black girlfriend there. It's just a fact. I'm a good man, Kirsten, and it just so happened that I fell in love with a good woman who, by the way happens, to be black. If a white woman meets a black guy who treats her good, I will be happy for her. People should be with the person who makes them happy, regardless of what race they are. People would rather I date someone who's the same color that I am because it makes them more comfortable when they're around me. It's not about my happiness, it's about their comfort."

"That's an interesting perspective, Daniel. I'm sorry that this has happened. You'll love the A.T.L. It's truly the world's melting pot. There are so many mixed couples here and people of so many different nationalities. I love it," she said as she pulled into the mall parking lot.

"What? No reserved parking space for you here?" Daniel asked.

Kirsten laughed really loud, almost letting out a holler.

"That was hilarious, Daniel, but no. I have to walk through the parking lot like everybody else."

"Oh, that's a bummer!" Daniel said, as if he was really disappointed.

Kirsten and Daniel went inside, got their food, then grabbed a seat. Daniel immediately noticed how he didn't catch anyone staring at them. After all, Kirsten was a black woman too. They sat there chowing down on wings and catching up on old times and how much fun all the kids had in the neighborhood when they were growing up. Daniel was younger than Kirsten, but all the kids used to play together.

"We grew up when neighbors were your extended family members," Daniel said to Kirsten, "But it's not like that anymore, I tell ya!"

Kirsten laughed out loud.

"You sound like an old man, Daniel, but you're right," she agreed.

"Kirsten, do you remember when you used to wear those two pigtails in your hair with those big red ribbons? I thought you were the prettiest thing I'd ever seen," he said, laughing.

"So you have always loved chocolate meat, huh, Daniel?" Kirsten asked as she laughed some more.

"Oh, I don't discriminate, madam," Daniel responded and they both laughed.

"I see," Kirsten said, giggling.

As she looked around, still laughing, she looked right into the face of her ex-fiancé, Jason, who seemed to be heading her way.

Jason wasn't just any ex-fiancé; he was once the love of Kirsten's life, her soul's addiction, the only man that could make her heart sing and make all time stand still. Jason was everything Kirsten loved looking at and although she loved Everett very much and knew that he was the man she was supposed to marry, she also knew life would be so much better if she never had to lay eyes on Jason's beautiful face, triceps, and biceps again.

"Kirsten! How are you?" Jason asked, as he walked up to her table, totally disregarding the fact that she was sitting there laughing with another man.

Kirsten's laughter came to an immediate halt and she responded to Jason with a very faint "Hello."

Just then, Daniel stood up and introduced himself.

"Hi, I'm Daniel Stine. Kirsten and I grew up

together," he began to blabber. "I'm up in the Atlanta area job hunting. We're catching up on old times," Daniel said.

When Daniel looked over at Kirsten she was staring at him like she wanted to cut off both of his ankles and make him crawl back to the car the best way he could.

Did he ask you for any of that, Daniel? Kirsten thought.

Jason glanced at Kirsten and back at Daniel.

"Is that so?" Jason said, with a smirk on his face. "Well, here's my card. Maybe we can all meet up for dinner later tonight and discuss what kind of skills you have, then I'll see what I can do for you."

"Oh, God! No!" Kirsten said really fast, without realizing she was thinking out loud.

"Huh?" Daniel said, giving her a cruel look like she was intentionally trying to sabotage his job opportunity.

Jason gave Kirsten another quick glance, but her head was down and she was trying to envision herself in some far away land where old boyfriends didn't pop up out of the woodwork and make your life miserable.

"Mr. Stine, any friend of Kirsten's is a friend of mine. I'll definitely find you a job in my company," he said, as he put the card in Daniel's hand.

"Ummm, I was actually planning to introduce him to some people as soon as we left here," Kirsten interjected.

Daniel gave her a buck-eyed look like he was really getting fed up with all her interruptions and she gave him a dirty look right back.

"No need, Kirsten. I'll take care of Daniel," he said, turning back to Daniel. "Daniel, make sure you bring a resume so we can find the right fit for you, okay?"

Kirsten put her hand on her forehead.

Please tell me this is not happening. Please, somebody, tell me that this did not just happen!

"Kirsten are you okay?" Daniel asked. "You don't look so good," he said, in a worried tone.

Kirsten wanted to reassure Daniel that she was okay, but there was no reassurance to give. She was simply not okay.

"I don't feel good," she said, looking like she was about to faint.

"Here! Drink some of this water," Daniel said, handing her a bottle of water he'd just purchased.

"And here! You can have this fan. I picked it up from one of those kiosks down there," Jason said as he was handing the fan to her.

"You stole the fan, Jason," Kirsten asked, giving him a strange look.

Jason laughed. "They were giving them away, Kirsten."

As Kirsten reached out to grab the fan from Jason, he noticed the huge ring sitting on her wedding finger.

"You're married, Kirsten?" he asked, snatching the fan out of her hand.

"Oh, I guess you didn't get an invitation to the wedding either," Daniel said, staring at Kirsten with his mouth tooted out.

"No, I didn't," Jason responded sorrowfully. "Kirsten, you got married? Why didn't you tell me?"

Daniel looked over at Jason, who looked like he

was about to cry.

Oh, man! Does this mean he's not going to help me get a job now? Daniel thought.

"Do I need to leave you two alone for a minute?" Daniel asked, suspiciously.

"NO!" Kirsten said, abruptly.

"No, there's no need to leave, Daniel," Jason said. "I just had no idea Kirsten got married on me. Since we go way back, I figured I would at least get a phone call, if not an invitation. Nevertheless, Daniel, are we good to go for tonight?" Jason explained, trying to gather his composure and reassure Daniel that everything was okay.

"I'll be there. And don't feel bad about not getting an invite. I've known Kirsten since I was five years old and I didn't get an invite either," Daniel said, letting out a big laugh, as if he actually believed everything was okay between Jason and Kirsten.

"Ummm, I'm right here," Kirsten said, sounding irritated. "I'm sorry that I didn't give either of you an invitation. It happened really fast so we didn't have time to invite all the people we wanted to come."

Daniel and Jason both looked at Kirsten with a *yeah, right!* stare.

"I have a feeling that I still would not have gotten an invitation," Jason countered.

"Exactly!" Daniel said, giving Jason a high five like they were good buddies.

"Well, Kirsten, you and your husband are welcome to come to dinner as well. I'd love to meet him," Jason said, knowing he'd already met Everett and had an edgy encounter with him once in the mall. He figured Kirsten didn't know about that, so he decided to pretend it didn't happen.

Kirsten gave Jason a blank stare, and a, *you must be crazy* look was written all over her face.

"Well, I've taken up too much of your time," Jason said. "Daniel, I'll see you tonight. Kirsten, it is always a pleasure to see you, and congratulations on getting married. I'm very happy for you, really I am," he said, walking off, not waiting for a response from either Kirsten or Daniel.

"What a great guy!" Daniel chimed in immediately. "I feel really good about this move, Kirsten. I got a job without even trying! How cool is that?" Daniel said.

Kirsten sat there with her arms folded. She really wanted to be angry, but Daniel seemed so happy. She knew Jason was only using Daniel to get back into her life. She hated how manipulative Jason was. She hated she'd ever gotten involved with him and she hated how she was never going to get rid of him.

I obviously need to move too, because EVERETT IS GOING TO KILL ME! she thought.

Kirsten sat there in a daze, while Daniel went on and on about working for Jason. He soon realized that Kirsten wasn't listening and suggested that they head back to the office.

Thank goodness! I thought he'd never shut up! Kirsten thought, as she packed up her things and headed for the exit.

CHAPTER

When they got back to the office, Mandy was anxiously waiting to pick up where she and Daniel left off. This time Kirsten didn't care.

"Mandy, do you mind showing Daniel around the building? Take him to each section and ask if they're willing to tell him a little bit about what they do."

"Oh, I'd be very happy to escort Mr. Stine around the building," Mandy answered, eagerly.

"That's great. Thank you, Mandy. I have a headache, so I'm going to go get some medicine. You two have fun."

Daniel gave Kirsten a weird look for her drastic change in attitude about Mandy being near him.

"Come on, Mr. Stine, this will be a wonderful tour," Mandy said, grabbing Daniel's arm.

Kirsten shook her head and went to the snack store to see if they had something for her headache.

As soon as Kirsten got back to her desk, her husband, Everett, called.

Why Keep Us Divided?

"Hey, babe. How are you feeling?" he asked as if he could sense something was wrong.

"Hey! I have a headache, but other than that I'm fine. How's your day going?"

"It's good. I'm sorry about your headache. I was just calling to see if you wanted to do dinner tonight?"

"Well, Daniel is here, but he's going to dinner with a potential boss of his, so sure, we can go out. I'm not sure what time he'll be coming back to the house, but we can give him a key."

"First, Kirsten, no man is getting a key to my house and second, who is Daniel and why is he coming to our house?"

"EVERETT!!!! We talked about this last week, remember?"

"Nope!"

"Everett, stop it! Daniel is my neighbor from back home. He's moving to Atlanta and he's here doing some job hunting. Everett, you talked to Daniel two weeks ago. I told you he was coming to stay with us while he looks for a job."

"Yeah, I remember the conversation, but I don't remember agreeing to let him stay with us. I don't let men stay at my house, Kirsten."

"Everett, I asked you and you said it was okay. You were in the den watching football and—"

"Well, that's the problem right there. If I'm watching football, I'm not listening to anything else. You should know that about me. Why do women want to come and talk about important stuff when men are watching football? We are listening to the game."

"Bye, Everett! You are unbelievable!"

"Wait a minute, woman! So where is he gonna stay?"

"Everett, I told him he could stay with us."

"Okay, well he can't, so where else is he going?"

Kirsten let out an aggravated sigh and Everett let out a loud laugh. "I'm just kidding, he can stay with us, but tell him don't make it a habit, because homey don't play that," he said, laughing some more. "For future reference, if you have something important to say, please wait until the game is completely over because I watch the commercials too."

"Whatever! But thank you for letting him come and thank you for making my headache worse."

"I'm sorry, but you can't be springing strange men on me, and if I sense that he has bad motives, he's gonna have to leave. For his sake, I better not catch him looking at you sideways."

"Everett, stop it! We grew up together; he's practically like family to me. Our mothers are best friends."

"I don't care!"

"Bye, Everett!"

"Love you, mean it!" he said, chuckling.

"Everett, you play too much."

"Oh, I'm not playing. Okay, I'll see you and our guest later this afternoon."

"Okay, bye, baby."

"Bye."

Why Keep Us Divided?

A few minutes later, Mandy and Daniel had returned from their tour, but Kirsten's headache wasn't any better. Matter of fact, it was worse, and the last thing she wanted was to see Mandy desperately flirting with Daniel and Daniel acting like he was clueless about Mandy's motives. It had become more than Kirsten could bear, so she did what anyone would do in this situation; she hid under her desk. She knew it was wrong, but that was the only thing she could think of on such short notice.

"Oh, Mrs. Larson isn't back yet," Mandy said, as she walked in Kirsten's office. "Well, I guess that means you'll have to spend some more time with me, Mr. Stine, but that wouldn't be so bad, would it?"

Daniel chuckled, "Nah, you did a great job showing me around. I appreciate your help."

"It was my pleasure. Do you want some chocolate? Mrs. Larson keeps the best chocolate in her jar; you've got to taste it," Mandy said, pointing to Kirsten's candy jar. "Come sit down, she won't mind if you wait for her in here."

Kirsten's eyes got big. *Oh, no! Don't wait in here!*

"Okay, if you're sure she won't mind. This is a nice couch," Daniel mentioned."

"Yes, we can take a nap if you want. I mean, you can take a nap," Mandy said, charmingly.

"That's not a bad idea, actually. I mean, for me to take a nap."

Mandy laughed. "Well, it's your choice, whichever you'd prefer."

That little hoochie! If I ever catch her laying her

nastiness on my couch, I will strangle her, Kirsten thought!

Kirsten hated that she was stuck under her desk, with no way of escaping. She never thought they would stay in her office. At least her desk was big and it was very roomy underneath.

"Mandy, you seem like a nice girl, but I'm in a relationship and—"

"Oh, I don't want you to get rid of your girlfriend. Maybe we can hang out and enjoy each other's company whenever you're in town," Mandy said, as she rubbed her finger along Daniel's pants leg.

You have got to be kidding me! Kirsten thought!

I will never let her around Everett! Not for a second!

"Nah, I'm good, Mandy! My girlfriend would kill me and she would kill you too, if she found out."

"Well, let's not let her find out then."

"I'll just wait for Kirsten out here in the lobby," he said, standing up. "You should probably get back to your desk. Folks may be looking for you," Daniel said, firmly.

"Well, can we at least exchange numbers, just in case you guys don't work out?"

"No, no! I can't give you my number," he said.

"Well, take my number then," Mandy said, reaching in her pocket and pulling out a piece of paper that already had her number on it."

"You keep your number handy, just in case you see someone you're interested in?" Daniel asked in a turned off tone.

"No! I wrote this down just for you," she said,

tucking it in his pocket.

Daniel threw his hands up, "Nah, I'm good, Mandy. I'm good!" he said, walking out of the room.

Mandy smiled and went back to her desk. Daniel went into the lobby to watch television while he waited for Kirsten to return, and Kirsten crawled out from underneath her desk. She managed to pull herself up, fix her clothes, and walk out to the lobby, giving Mandy an evil glance as she passed by her desk.

Mandy's eyes became enormous and her mouth fell open when she saw Kirsten coming out of her office.

"Yeah, I heard it all," Kirsten whispered, rolling her eyes at Mandy.

Mandy didn't say a word.

"Hey, Daniel! Are you ready to go? There are several other people I want to introduce you to. That way, when you meet with Jason tonight, you can have other options," Kirsten said, praying that Daniel would get a job with anyone else but Jason.

"That's great!" he said, and they both walked out the door, neither saying goodbye to Mandy.

Kirsten took Daniel around to several companies that she had already arranged meetings with. He was very impressed with every place she took him, but he was still more excited to work for Jason. He just sensed that Jason would be fair and he would take care of him. Besides, Jason also seemed to have a thing for Kirsten, so Daniel wanted to capitalize on whatever favor he could get out of that. In his eyes, that could potentially mean more money.

Sorry Kirsten, he thought, as he did an inward

chuckle.

When the day ended, Daniel jumped into his car to follow Kirsten home. When they got there, Everett was outside cleaning off his lawn equipment. Daniel got out of his car and went over to shake Everett's hand.

"I don't shake hands with men that don't watch football," Everett said, jokingly.

Daniel laughed.

"I'm just playing, man. Come on in. Kirsten and I are glad to have you."

Everett looked back at Kirsten and gave her a wink. She rolled her eyes.

"You look very nice, baby," Everett said, as he gave Kirsten a kiss.

"Thank you, sweetie!"

"Hold on! Daniel, you might need to wait outside a little while, so I can take my wife in the house and give her a proper welcome home."

"EVERETT!!!!" Kirsten shouted, embarrassingly.

"I'm just joking, baby! Geez, I'll wait until Daniel goes to sleep to welcome you home."

Daniel burst out in laughter. "I see that she does to you what my girlfriend does to me. I can't keep my hands off of her. I knew she would be mine the first day I saw her."

Everett gave Daniel a high-five. "That's right man! We know a good thing when we see it."

"Thing? It?" Kirsten chimed in.

"Woman, Kirsten. We know a good woman when we see her," Everett said, giving Kirsten a smile, showing off his beautiful deep dimples.

Kirsten loved seeing Everett smile. For some reason, it always made her smile, even if he was getting on her nerves with all of his joking around.

They went inside and Everett showed Daniel the guest room, while Kirsten went to her room to take off her shoes.

Everett said to Daniel, "Kirsten and I are going out to dinner tonight, but she told me you already have dinner plans with a potential boss. That's pretty awesome, man! I'm happy for you. I hope you get the job."

No, no, no, no, no! Please don't tell him who you're going to dinner with, Kirsten thought, as she ran into the room to try and change the subject.

"Daniel, how's your mom doing?" Kirsten asked, interrupting the conversation.

"Oh, she's doing great!" he answered, turning back towards Everett. "Yeah, Everett, I'm going to dinner with—"

"How's your dad?" Kirsten asked, frantically.

"Ummm, he—"

"And your sister, Roslyn? How is she...and her kids? And your grandmother? Everybody, tell me about everybody? I want to hear about everybody."

Everett and Daniel both looked at Kirsten like she was crazy.

"They're all good, but you know I lost my grandma a few years ago?"

"Oh, no! I didn't know that. How'd she die?" Kirsten asked, hoping not to sound excited that the subject was changing.

"I still don't like talking about it but maybe later I'll tell you what happened." He turned to Everett, "I'm going to dinner with an awesome guy. His name is—"

"AAAHHHHCCCCCHHHHHHUUUUUUU," Kirsten said, letting out a huge sneeze.

"Bless you," Everett said, giving her a strange look.

Daniel grabbed Jason's card out of his pocket.

"Jason B. Glaznyte. Yeah, that's his name. He said you and Kirsten are welcome to come to dinner with us too. We're just going to talk about my skills and how he can help me get a job. You should come."

Everett looked over at Kirsten and Kirsten looked down at the floor, nervously wiggling her leg. The room was completely silent. Then all of a sudden, Everett let out a boisterous laugh.

"HAHAHA! HAHHHHHHHHAHAHAHA! HAHAHAAAAAAHAAAAAAAAAAAA! HA!"

Kirsten twisted her lips at Everett's nonsense, but at this point Daniel didn't know what to think of Kirsten or Everett's strange behavior.

Everett abruptly cut off his laughter. "Nah, that's not gonna happen, but hey, go out and have a great time. Please tell Mr. Glaznyte that I said hello."

"Ummm, okay," Daniel said, hesitantly. "I think I'll go ahead and take a shower so I can get my mind right for my meeting tonight. Can I have a bath cloth and towel?"

"Sure, man! Everything you need should already be on the shelf above the toilet," Everett said.

Kirsten scurried out of the room in hopes that Everett wouldn't follow her, but she would have no such luck, because he immediately took off after her with his arms out.

"Hello, Mrs. Larson! You care to tell me how this happened?"

These people are crazy, I might need to get a hotel, Daniel thought as he closed the bedroom door. *I think I'll just lock this door.*

Just then, Melah called.

"Hey, babe. How was your day?"

"Mel, I'm so glad to hear from somebody who is sane. Kirsten and her husband are both loony."

"What?"

"I'm not kidding, baby. I think they are bipolar. One minute they're cool and the next, their behavior is totally bizarre. I may have to cut my trip short."

Melah laughed. "Well you know I would love for you to come home. So did you talk to anyone today that may be able to give you a job?"

"Yeah, actually I have a meeting with one of Kirsten's friends tonight. He pretty much promised me a job. He seemed so cool, babe. He said he and Kirsten went way back and any friend of Kirsten's is a friend of his."

"Hmmmm. Interesting. Does Kirsten's husband know you're going to dinner with this guy?"

"Yeah, I told him that Jason invited him and Kirsten to come to dinner with us as well. They're all cool."

"Ummm, is that when he and Kirsten started acting crazy?"

"Well, now that you mentioned it, that is when they turned into a nut job on me."

"Be careful, Daniel. There's more to this story than you think. How many people offer you a job without even knowing what skills you have? He might be trying to use you to get next to Kirsten."

"Oh, I don't mind being used," Daniel said, laughing. "I think you're right though, Mel. When he came to our table at lunch, Kirsten started acting like she was about to die. It was very weird and when I was trying to tell Everett who I was going to dinner with Kirsten kept changing the subject. I bet she was trying to keep me from talking about it."

"Yeah, it sounds more like an ex than just an old friend, Daniel. Well, let me know how dinner goes," Melah said, then she changed the subject and started talking about her day. Meanwhile Kirsten was in the other room getting the third degree from Everett.

"So, Jason just walked up to your table at lunch and offered Daniel a job?"

"Yes, that's pretty much what happened. Well, Daniel became a blabbermouth and told Jason that he was moving to Atlanta and was looking for a job, but yeah, after that, Jason pretty much promised him a job."

"That dude won't stop at anything, huh? Kirsten, I need to ask you a question and I need you to be totally honest with me, okay?"

"Okay," she said, nervously.

"Have you talked to Jason at all, in any form since we've been married?"

"NO! I haven't even seen him, Everett. I wouldn't do that to you!"

"Okay, next question. Do you have any feelings for him whatsoever?"

"Uhhh—"

"Hey, you guys, I just wanted to—" Daniel interrupted, not realizing that Everett had just asked Kirsten a serious question.

"Not now, Daniel. I need to talk to my wife for a minute," Everett responded in a harsh tone.

"Okkkaaaaayyyyyy," Daniel said, going back to his room like a little kid on punishment.

"Kirsten, I need to know," Everett said, sternly.

"Everett, I do not want Jason. I am happily married to you. Very happily married. You are the man for me. You are everything I need and want. You are my best friend and I will never, ever jeopardize what we have for anyone," she said, walking up to him and kissing him on the neck, then the cheek, then on his lips.

Everett felt himself getting weak. Kirsten locked the door and started unbuttoning her blouse. Soon, Everett forgot all about Jason, and by all the noise they were making, they obviously forgot they had company in the house as well. It was a good thing Daniel was taking a shower because that would have surely added to his notion that Kirsten and Everett were indeed bipolar.

Soon, everything was calm again and Kirsten was very happy about that. They all eventually got dressed for their evening out. Daniel grabbed his resume and his biography, then rushed out the door to have dinner with

Jason B. Glaznyte, one of the most prestigious business owners in Atlanta. Kirsten and Everett hugged and kissed some more, then grabbed their keys and left for dinner as well.

CHAPTER

"Ryan's Blues and Jazz, Ryan's Blues and Jazz. Where is this place?" Daniel said, as he turned the corner and saw the sign on top of the building.

"Oh, good! I'm here."

He parked his car and ran inside, hoping to beat Jason there.

"Welcome to Ryan's Blues and Jazz, sir. Will you be dining alone?" the strikingly beautiful waitress asked Daniel.

"No, I'm supposed to be meeting someone here," Daniel said, trying not to show how beautiful he thought she was.

"Are you Daniel Stine?" she asked, sweetly.

Daniel gave her a weird look.

"Ummm, yes, I am, and who are you?"

She laughed, "Right this way, Mr. Stine. Mr. Glaznyte is waiting for you upstairs."

"Awww, man! I was hoping I'd beat him here."

"That would be impossible," she said, laughing,

leading him to the elevators. "Mr. Glaznyte is thirty minutes early for everything."

"He's been here for thirty minutes already?"

"Yes, but no worries. He likes to come and clear his head before meeting with a client."

"Does he have all of his meetings here?" Daniel asked.

"Well, within the last year, he's started having his dinner meetings here. He's a great man to work for if you're lucky to get a job."

"You seem to know him pretty well. He must spend a lot of time here," Daniel said.

She laughed some more.

"He owns the place, Mr. Stine. He's our head boss and he's very good to his employees. Well, we are here," she said, as the elevator stopped on the fourth floor.

"This is a roof top," Daniel said, getting out of the elevator.

"Yes, it's gorgeous up here. Come on, I'll walk you to Mr. Glaznyte's table," she said, touching his back.

Her touch startled Daniel. He gave her a quick glance and she gave him a subtle smile.

"Mr. Glaznyte, Mr. Stine has arrived," she said, as she gently tapped Daniel's shoulder.

Her perfume smelled like something an angel would wear and Daniel was trying hard to stay focused. When she walked off it took everything in him not to glance.

"It's okay, you can look, Daniel. Jill has a special glow about her that makes all men drool," Jason said.

Daniel laughed out loud and Jason laughed along

with him.

"Am I that transparent?" Daniel asked.

"Well, you looked like you were in pain, so I figured I should let you know that you're normal. It's okay to look, but it's the touching that will get you into trouble. Well, sometimes the looking gets you into trouble as well," Jason said, laughing even louder.

"Yes, looking can definitely cause trouble," Daniel said, nodding his head in agreement.

"But, I want you to relax, Daniel. This will be very informal. I just want to talk about what my company does and what you feel you can bring to the table," Jason stated.

"The waitress told me you own this place," Daniel mentioned.

"Oh, did she?" Jason said, in a disapproving tone.

"Was she not supposed to tell me that?"

"No, it's fine. I don't normally advertise it, though. I like to keep myself detached from this place when dealing with business partners because this is where I come to relax. When I'm here, I just want to be Jason, the country boy from Louisiana and I want my clients to be relaxed as well. If they know that I own this place, and something happens that they don't like, they probably won't tell me because they're trying to impress me. I just feel they'll be more honest if they don't know that I'm the owner. Nevertheless, the secret is out, so let's get down to business."

"Does Kirsten know you own it, because if not, I won't mention it," Daniel said, reassuringly.

"Oh, yeah! She knows all about this place, but

enough of that. What do you do now, Daniel?" Jason asked, trying to change the subject.

"I work in the accounting department."

"Oh, very good! I actually have an accounting position coming open in about five to six months. It's a pretty high position, though, so you'd really have to know your stuff to get that job. The person in it now has worked for me since I started my own company twenty years ago. He oversees the accounting for all my businesses. He's sixty-five now, and says it's time for him to go. I love him like a father. I don't know what I'm going to do when he leaves," Jason said, remorsefully.

"I am the best accountant you will ever meet," Daniel said, confidently. If you give me the job, I'll come up once a month at my own expense and train with him until he leaves."

"Hmmm, sounds interesting. So tell me, what do you know about accounting?"

Daniel proceeded to give Jason his spiel about everything he knew about the accounting process. "I even have my CPA license," Daniel told him. "I am the man for this job, Mr. Glaznyte. You can't go wrong with me."

"That's impressive, but please call me Jason. Daniel, according to your resume, you just graduated college about six months ago. There's no way you're ready to oversee seven companies."

"Seven companies? My goodness," Daniel said, rubbing his hands over his face.

"Well, actually, you'll oversee the other seven accountants in each company. Basically they'll do all the work, but you'll check their numbers to make sure everything adds up. Every penny needs to be accounted for. You will be my right hand, but you will also need to have a great working relationship with the other seven accountants as well. They will need to trust you so they can feel comfortable telling you when something is screwed up. If they don't trust you, they won't tell you anything. I will rely on you to keep me, and them, out of jail. My guess is you're probably a bit young to take on that kind of responsibility."

"Jason, you said you started your first company twenty years ago? That would have put you around twenty-five years old? I'm twenty-three, so if you started your own company at twenty-five, then I can oversee the accounting for seven companies at twenty-three, right?"

Jason laughed. "I was actually twenty-four when I started my own company."

"Even better! How about this. Let me meet with your head accountant tomorrow and if he thinks I'm ready to do his job, then will you consider me for the position?"

Jason laughed some more. "I'm impressed by your persistence. I think it's a great idea for you to meet with Mr. Cross tomorrow. He'll be happy to show you the ropes and see what you know. I won't promise you the job, though, but I will get you a job somewhere in my company. Is that fair?"

"Yes sir, that's fair, but I want this job and I'm willing to wait five months to get it. You won't find a better accountant than me."

"Okay, Daniel. Come to my office tomorrow and

I'll let you to sit with Mr. Cross all day. After you see what he does, then let me know if you still want the job," Jason said, laughing.

"Sounds like a plan."

"Can we eat now?" Jason asked, like he was worn out from the conversation.

Daniel laughed. "Yes, sir."

Jason beckoned for the waitress to come over. They ordered their food and drinks and chitchatted about their lives for the rest of the evening, with neither of them mentioning Kirsten. Then they decided that it was time to go and said they would see each other in the morning.

On the way back to Kirsten's house Daniel called Melah and told her about the accounting position.

"Oh, you got that job, baby! You can do accounting standing on one foot, with one hand tied behind your back," Melah said.

"I sure can, Mel. I'm going to meet with the head accountant tomorrow and if I can make a good impression on him, then I know Jason will give me the job."

"You can't help but make a good impression, baby. You're a natural."

"Dang, girl. I love—I mean—well you know what I mean."

"No, I do not, so tell me. You love what, Daniel?"

Daniel yawned. "Well, it's late, Mel. I better not talk and drive. I'll give you a call tomorrow and tell you how it goes, okay?"

"Okay, scaredy cat," Melah said, laughing. "Have a good night."

"Good night, Mel," Daniel responded.

When he got to Kirsten's house he wasn't sure if he should mention what happened at dinner or not, so he pretended he was sleepy and headed straight to his room, hurrying past Kirsten and Everett, who were laying on the couch watching television.

"Hey!" they both yelled at the same time.

"What happened at dinner, man?" Everett asked.

"Yeah, did you get the job?" Kirsten chimed in after Everett.

"Well, I'm going to meet with his head accountant tomorrow and if I can make a good impression on him, I have a feeling that Jason will give me his job."

"Give you Mr. Cross' job?" Kirsten asked surprisingly.

Everett looked over at Kirsten, giving her an unfriendly look for knowing about Jason's employees. Kirsten quickly realized that she was talking too much and decided it was in her best interest to just keep her mouth closed. Daniel wanted to ask Kirsten what she knew about Mr. Cross, but he had a feeling that he should stay clear of the subject as well.

"Yes, Mr. Cross is retiring. Jason said he's sixty-five years old and he's tired of working."

"Jason? Y'all are on a first name basis already?" Everett asked, sounding jealous.

"Stop it, Everett," Kirsten said, in an aggravated tone.

"I'm just playing, man. Kirsten and Jason used to date and he and I had a run-in a while back at the mall. I don't care for him, but if he gives you a job, then I'm sincerely happy for you."

"Ohhhhhh! That explains a lot. I wasn't—"

"I didn't know you two had a run-in. Why didn't you tell me that?" Kirsten asked, cutting Daniel off.

"Yeah! I told him to stay away from you and I meant it."

At this point, Daniel was totally uncomfortable, but he dared not get involved and he definitely wasn't going to walk off and miss anything either.

"Oh!" was all Kirsten said, then Daniel chimed back in, trying to make the moment less awkward.

"I wasn't sure what was wrong with the two of you earlier, but I figured it had to be something like that. I really appreciate your support, though, and Everett, don't be jealous. No one can take your place," Daniel said, laughing.

"Man, shut up with that!" Everett said, laughing. "Just don't invite us to go to dinner with y'all because I might nut up on you, again."

"No worries. I won't even mention his name around you," Daniel said, laughing.

Everett laughed too.

"It's not that serious, man. We're all grown and everyone has a past. It's just that Kirsten's past keeps popping up in her present."

"Everett! Stop it!" Kirsten said, sounding embarrassed.

Everett laughed some more.

Daniel yawned.

"Well, I'm heading to bed," he said. He wasn't sure what turn the conversation was about to take and he had had enough, so pretending to be sleepy is what Daniel did when he wanted to avoid a discussion. He went into the bedroom, while Kirsten and Everett finished watching television.

"Does Jason know you're married?" Everett asked, unexpectedly.

"Yes," Kirsten responded quickly, hoping he wouldn't ask any more questions.

"I'm going to have to kill him to get rid of him, aren't I?"

"Everett, don't say stuff like that."

"You know I'm not serious. Well, I guess I'm not serious," Everett said, smiling. "I don't blame him, but I have a feeling that he's never going to go away and this stunt he pulled with giving Daniel a job is crazy. Kirsten, he is setting himself up to be in your life forever. You know that, right?"

"Yeah, I got that feeling too, but don't worry about him, babe. I love only you," she said, kissing Everett's neck in three different places.

"Oh, I see your game. When you want me to stop asking questions, you try to seduce me. Well in that case, I'm going to start asking you questions every chance I get. That'll teach you to play games with me," he said, laughing.

Kirsten laughed too.

"Let's go to bed," he said, pulling Kirsten off the couch and tapping her on her butt. I have lots of questions to ask you. It will probably take all night for you to answer them all."

"I will only be taking fifteen to twenty minutes of questions, Mr. Larson, then I'm going to sleep," she responded.

"Okay, good enough," he said, grabbing her hand and leading her down the hallway.

CHAPTER

The next morning, Daniel got up excited to spend the day with Mr. Cross.

He arrived promptly at 7:30, and of course Jason was already there, diligently working.

"Jason, do you ever run late for anything?" Daniel asked him.

"Nope! Lateness comes from poor planning. If you allot time for the unexpected, then you'll never be late."

Oh, boy! This is going to be fun! Daniel thought.

"Come right this way, I'll show you where Mr. Cross sits."

Daniel met Mr. Cross who seemed like a really nice, but stern man. They went through everything Mr. Cross could think of. Daniel had always wanted to be an accountant ever since he was little. His dad and uncles all let him balance the books for their companies, so Daniel was very familiar with the process. There was nothing Mr. Cross threw at him that Daniel didn't know, but it seemed as if Mr. Cross was purposefully taking unnecessary steps to make things seem harder than they actually were. Daniel wanted to show him that there was a better way to do it, but he knew that wouldn't have gone over well. It was like Mr. Cross was intentionally trying to discourage Daniel from wanting the job.

There's no way he does all of this work! And when does this man take a break? I can't even get up to get a snack. This is crazy! When I get this job, I will be taking breaks. No wonder he's ready to quit, Daniel thought.

As the day went on, Daniel wondered what time Mr. Cross was going to lunch…11:00 came, no lunch…11:30 came, no lunch…12:00 came, still no lunch. By the time 12:30 rolled around, Daniel was thoroughly aggravated.

"Mr. Cross, I'm starving! Are we going to break for lunch anytime soon?" Daniel asked.

Mr. Cross looked up at the clock. "Ahhhh, hungry are we? Well, in accounting, we eat, sleep, and breathe numbers. It is all we need to survive," he said, in a harsh tone. "But if you can't handle it, then go on and get you something to eat."

You have got to be kidding me! That doesn't even make sense!

"Mr. Cross, with all due respect, that's not logical. Food nourishes the body, so you can think clearer when balancing all of these numbers. You're doing this company a disservice if you try to work all day without eating anything."

Mr. Cross looked at Daniel with one eyebrow raised.

"Goodbye, Mr. Stine. This is obviously not the job for you. I will inform Jason of my observation."

"Whoa! Are you serious? I just asked about eating."

"Yes, I'm very serious, but you, obviously are not."

"Mr. Cross, I didn't mean to offend you, I—"

"Good day, Mr. Stine."

"Mr. Cross, I—"

"Please leave, Mr. Stine," he said, turning his back to Daniel.

"I can't believe this! You're penalizing me because I want to eat? Is lunch not a part of the work day?" Daniel asked harshly, but Mr. Cross kept his back turned, as if he didn't hear him.

Daniel went to Jason's office to let him know what happened, but Jason wasn't there. The secretary offered to leave a message, but Daniel insisted on waiting until Jason came back.

"Mr. Stine, Mr. Glaznyte will be out of the office for the rest of the day. I can leave him a note to call you in the morning if you'd like," the receptionist said, as nicely as she knew how.

"He's not coming back?"

"I'm afraid not, sir. I just don't want you to sit here all day waiting."

"Okay, thank you. I'll come back in the morning," Daniel said, walking towards the door. Then he made an abrupt stop and headed back down the hallway to Mr. Cross' office. When he got there Mr. Cross had a big bottle of hot sauce on his desk and was eating a pork chop sandwich.

"Are you serious, Mr. Cross?" Daniel shouted out without even realizing it. "A pork chop sandwich!"

Mr. Cross had just taken a big bite of his sandwich, and had a piece of bread hanging out of his mouth when he looked up and saw Daniel.

"There's no getting rid of you, I see," he said, with his mouth still full of food.

"No, there's not, and I'm trying to figure out why you would want to."

Mr. Cross gulped his sandwich down, took a deep breath, then he burst into tears. Daniel didn't know what to think. He came in and closed the door behind him.

"Mr. Cross, what is going on?"

Mr. Cross wouldn't answer; he just continued to cry like he had lost his best friend.

"I'm dying, Daniel," he finally said, as he sobbed uncontrollably. "I have Hemochromatosis; it is hereditary and it is my family's killer. My father, my grandfather, even my great grandfather had it. My brother died last year and now it's come to get me."

"But Mr. Cross, just because you have Hemochromatosis, that doesn't mean you're going to die. If it's treated early, you can still live a long, healthy life."

"No, no, Daniel. Every man in my family has died from something that began as Hemochromatosis, and then it turned into something fatal like liver disease or heart disease. No one has survived it!"

"But if this is hereditary, I don't understand why your doctors didn't start treating you for it earlier."

"They tried, but I wasn't really having any symptoms at the time, so I figured I was fine. I guess I didn't want to accept it, so I ignored it until it became unbearable. I didn't even tell my family, until it was too late."

"Mr. Cross, your family needs to know so they can get checked."

"Yeah! I know that now. All of my kids have gotten checkups. Some have traces of it in their blood, and some do not, but they're all keeping an eye on it."

"It's good that they're keeping an eye on it. I'm very sorry all of this has happened; is that the reason you're retiring?"

"Yes, and I just told Jason two days ago and he's already replacing me. I've given him twenty years of my life and the minute I tell him I'm leaving, he sends in some young buck with a fancy degree to give me the boot. I'll bet he's been waiting for me to kick over and die."

"No, that's not true. I may not know Jason that well, but he told me himself that you were like a father to him and he didn't know what he would do without you. He told me that I wasn't experienced enough to even take over your position. I had to pretty much beg to even get a chance to meet you. He said only if I impress you, will I be considered for this job. That doesn't sound like a man who's waiting to get rid of you. He honestly thought you were tired and just wanted to retire."

"He said all that about me?" Mr. Cross asked, wiping tears from his eyes.

"Yeah, actually he did. You're not just an

employee to him, Mr. Cross, you're his family."

Mr. Cross smiled, then said, "Go on and get you some lunch, Daniel. When you get back, I'll let you balance the books."

"Huh? You're gonna let me come back to sit with you?"

"Yeah, I didn't give you a fair chance earlier. I intentionally tried to make everything seem difficult so you wouldn't want the job. If you promise not to tell Jason, then I'll teach you everything I know and I'll make sure I tell him that I was thoroughly impressed with you."

"My lips are sealed, and don't give up on your health, Mr. Cross. You can beat this thing."

"Nah, it is fatal now. The doctor has given me six months to live, but there's a lot that I can do in six months, isn't there?"

"Yes, sir! There sure is."

"Well then I'm going to go do it. Who knows, I might leave this job sooner than six months and go see the world. That would be wonderful, wouldn't it?" Mr. Cross said, with a big smile.

"Yeah, it would, Mr. Cross. Go do it!"

"Oh, hush up! You're just trying to take my job," he said, laughing. Daniel laughed too.

"Go on, get you some lunch. Go nourish your soul; we have a lot to do today."

"Okay, I'm leaving, I'm leaving," Daniel said, heading towards the door.

"Daniel," Mr. Cross called out.

"Yes, sir?"

"Thank you! You're the only person at work who knows about my illness. Thank you for listening."

Daniel smiled. "You're welcome," he said, as he walked away.

Daniel went to lunch and when he came back, he and Mr. Cross worked diligently on the company's records. Daniel saw several things he would do differently, but he dared not mention anything to Mr. Cross. When the day was over, Mr. Cross gave Daniel a handshake and thanked him again for being there during his outburst. He promised that he would put in a good word for Daniel and he welcomed him to the team.

Daniel jumped in his car and headed to Kirsten's and Everett's house. He couldn't wait to call to Melah. She was his calmness whenever his world was chaotic. He knew he had fallen in love with her, but it was happening way too fast for his liking. He wanted to push her away so he could think, but he missed her like crazy when she wasn't around.

When he got to the house, Kirsten and Everett were both already home and looked like they were up to no good.

"Ummm, did I interrupt something?" he asked.

"Yeah, you interrupted what married people do when they don't have kids in the house," Everett said.

Kirsten punched him in the arm. "Everett, stop it!"

Just then Daniel received a phone call.

"Hello. Hey, Jason!" he said. "I'm sorry I didn't get a chance to say bye, but your secretary said you would be gone for the rest of the day."

"No problem, Daniel. I got a call from Mr. Cross a few minutes ago."

"Ummm, you did?"

"Yeah! It seems you've made quite an impression on him. He told me that I would be crazy not to hire you as his replacement."

Daniel started laughing, "Wow! He said that?"

As Daniel continued to laugh, he was given dirty looks from Kirsten and Everett. He wasn't sure if the looks were because he was hee heeing and haw hawing with Jason or if it was because they wanted to get back to doing whatever they were doing before he came home. Either way, he was ready to get away from those two nutty fruitcakes and get back to Melah.

"Now, Daniel, I'm not completely offering you the job yet, but if you commit to coming up once a month to train with Mr. Cross like you mentioned, then we'll put you on probation and after your six months are up, we'll make our final decision. Either way, I'll still have a job for you somewhere in my company, and of course we'll give you a day's pay for each day you're here in training, as well as mileage for traveling. Does that sound like a fair deal?"

"Absolutely!" Daniel said, excitedly.

"Okay, get with my receptionist and she'll get all the new employee paperwork to you and will also come up with a schedule for when you can start your training. I'll plan to see you in about a month, alright?"

"That's it? I got the job?"

"Yes, tentatively."

"So, I'm going to be on your payroll?"

"Yes, Daniel, temporarily until your probation period is over, but if all goes well with Mr. Cross, I'll put you in his position as a permanent employee."

"So, you mean—"

"Daniel, you're hired, okay? You got the job, so don't screw up within the next six months," Jason said, laughing. "And tell Kirsten I said hello."

"Thank you so much, Jason, thank you so much! Okay, I'll tell her," Daniel said before they both hung up.

He was so excited and without thinking, he turned to Kirsten to give her the *hello* from Jason, but the looks on her and Everett's faces brought him back to his senses. He wiped the big grin off of his face and hesitantly said, "I got the job."

Kirsten and Everett wanted to be happy for Daniel; honestly and truly, they did. However, they knew their lives were somehow about to change for the worse. The one person they never wanted to see again had conned his way back into their lives and it seemed as if he was going to be around for a very long time.

Daniel knew they wanted to say something, but he didn't give them a chance to get it out. He hurried to his room, packed his things and told them goodbye before they went into their crazy mode again.

"You're not going to eat dinner?" Kirsten asked.

"No, I'm going to hit the road so I can take Melah out to dinner tonight."

"Awww, that's so sweet. Please bring her next time you come."

"Ummm, okay, but we'll probably get a hotel next

time."

"A hotel? No, you are wel—"

"Nah, let them get a hotel. Ain't nobody coming in my house and doing the nasty on my guest beds," Everett said.

"Everett! Stop! Daniel, is it Everett? I know he's been acting crazy the whole time you've been here. He's normally not like this."

"Me? Kirsten you're the one doing all that crazy sneezing and coughing and choking because you didn't want me to know Daniel was going to dinner with your ex-boyfriend."

"Yeah, well you're the one—"

"Thank you guys for the hospitality. I'm going to hit the road now," Daniel said, interrupting, as he rushed out the door.

"I'm sorry, Daniel. Please give us another chance when you come back to Atlanta. We're not normally this crazy. I promise."

"Yes, we are," Everett said.

Daniel laughed. "I think I believe Everett, but nevertheless, thank you for letting me stay with you guys."

"Daniel, we're sorry. Call me and let me know you made it home safely, okay?"

"Okay, I will," he said, hopping into his car and backing out of the driveway like he was desperate to get away from them.

"Things will be different next time," Kirsten shouted, trying to sound reassuring.

Daniel threw up his hands and waved goodbye

while Everett flipped through the channels like nothing strange had happened.

"Everett, that is so rude! You didn't even say bye to him."

"Listen, baby," he said, pulling Kirsten closer to him. "The worst thing you can do is make people feel so welcomed that they don't want to leave. If they get too comfortable, they are going to want to stay longer and bring people with them. If he's moving to Atlanta, he might even try to move in until he can get on his feet. There's not enough room in this house for two grown men, and since my name is on the mortgage, I get to decide which grown man gets to stay."

"What's with the big ego, Everett?"

"Hey, there's nothing small about me, baby."

Kirsten gave Everett a sideways look.

"Now can we please get back to what we were doing before the intruder came knocking at our door?" Everett asked.

"Yes! I'd love to," she said, as she gave Everett a sweet kiss on the lips.

CHAPTER

On Daniel's way home, he called Melah to see if she wanted to go to dinner that evening. He figured he'd just leave a message since she was probably still in class, but instead of getting her voicemail, she actually answered the phone."

"Hey! Why aren't you in class?" he asked.

Melah grunted, "I feel so bad, babe. I've been in bed all day."

"Aww, I'm sorry you're sick. I wanted to take you to dinner, but I'll just bring something over for us to eat."

"Oh, you're on your way back home? That's great! I haven't eaten all day. I probably need to get out of the house; it may make me feel better, so let's just see how I feel when you get here."

"Okay, get some rest. I hope you feel better."

"Thanks, baby. I'll see you later."

"Okay. Bye, Mel."

"Bye," Melah responded then laid back down on the

couch, covered herself up in a blanket, and slept for two more hours.

"KNOCK! KNOCK! KNOCK!"

"Ahhhh, who's there?" Melah asked, groaning, and pulling herself off of the couch to answer the door. It was her friend, Anna.

"Girl, you look tore up from the floor up! What is wrong with you?" Anna asked.

"I think I have some type of virus," Melah responded.

"Well, that's what happens when you go kissing on white men."

"That's not funny, Anna."

"I'm just kidding, but I could never date a white man. Something about it just isn't right. We're all different for a reason. Blacks need to date blacks, whites need to date whites, Hispanics need to date Hispanics, and Asians ne—"

"Enough already!" Melah said, sounding aggravated.

"I'm just saying, Melah. We're not supposed to be intermingled. Besides, it's nasty! I don't see how you sleep with him."

"Very pleasurably, thank you very much. Now can you please go get me some ginger ale and crackers because that's all I can keep down today?"

"Yeah, a virus is going around on campus. I hope you don't pass it to me. Here!" Anna said, handing Melah a pack of crackers and a cup of ginger ale.

Just then she heard another knock on the door.

"Aaaahhh, now who could that be?" Melah moaned.

"Yo white man," Anna said, looking out of the peep hole.

"Oh, no! Has it been two hours already? I was supposed to be dressed by the time he got here."

"Hmmm, you're sounding like a slave already," Anna said.

"That's not funny or appropriate, Anna. Daniel doesn't treat me like his piece of property. Seriously, don't be disrespectful, and can you please open the door and let him in?"

Anna opened the door and stood behind it.

"Mel, you're not even dressed yet! How are we going to dinner?" Daniel asked, as he stepped into Melah's apartment. He was trying not to sound agitated at seeing Melah still in her pajamas and slippers.

"Daniel, I told you, I've been sick all day."

"Yeah, I know, baby, but I thought you were feeling well enough to go to dinner."

Anna closed the door and gave Melah a *you sound like his property to me* look and Melah gave her a *you better not say one more word* look in return.

"Oh, hey, Anna. I didn't know you were here," Daniel said.

"I'm not! I was just leaving. Bye, Melah," Anna said, hurrying out of the house.

"What's with her?" Daniel asked Melah.

"Crazy! There's no other explanation."

"Okay," Daniel said, laughing.

"Just give me a few minutes to shower and change

into something beautiful for you," she said, flashing a smile his way.

"You're already beautiful; you're my beautiful oreo cookie."

Mel gave him a frown. "Your what? Oreos are brown on the outside and white on the inside. What are you trying to say? I'm one hundred percent black on the inside and out, Mr. Stine."

"Okay, Malcom X, I wasn't trying to start a revolution. I like oreo cookies. I want to eat the whole bag," he said, pulling Melah closer and nibbling on her arm.

"Stop, Cookie Monster! I stink. I haven't taken a bath, I haven't brushed my teeth, I haven't combed my hair, no deodorant, no soap, no lotion, no perfume. To sum it all up, anything that will help me smell good today, I haven't done it."

Daniel threw his hands up in the air like he wanted nothing to do with Melah's stinkiness.

"Well, please go do it! Hurry!" he said, with a frown on his face.

She laughed and went to take a shower, while Daniel laid on the couch and watched television.

As soon as he got comfortable, his phone started ringing; it was his cousin, Jake.

"Hello," he answered, wondering whose number it was.

"What's up man, this is Jake."

"Hey, man! I haven't talked to you in a while. What have you been up to?"

"Just working, man! Being a grown up is not as much fun as I thought it would be," Jake said, laughing. "I was just calling to see when the promotion party was."

"How do you know about the promotion?" Daniel asked, as if he was surprised.

"Dan, you told me when you first got the job that they said you were going to get a promotion at your six-month mark. It's been six months, hasn't it? It's time to drink some beer, man."

"So, you've been counting down until I reached six months?"

"Yeah, of course I counted down. I capitalize on all opportunities to party," Jake said, laughing. "That's what family does. We mooch off of other family members."

"Ha, ha, ha," Daniel said, laughing. "Okay, moocher. You know I don't drink."

"But I do, and right now you're holding up the party progress."

"I didn't get the promotion, man," Daniel responded, unhappily.

"What do you mean, you didn't get the promotion? I thought they told you it was yours!"

"Yeah, they did, but the minute Melah came into the office, they started acting weird. The next thing I knew, they gave the job to Todd."

"Todd? The nerd with the Clark Kent glasses? And who's Melah? The black chick you were tutoring in college? Why would she have anything to do with your job?"

"Well, we're dating now and she stopped by to see

if I wanted to do lunch."

"Dan, Dan, Dan! What were you thinking? I thought that was just a business deal between you two. What happened to you tutoring her in math and her feeding you home cooked meals? I guess she became the home cooked meal, huh? I can't believe this," Jake said, shaking his head in disappointment. "Man, you know you can't be dating black women. Did you not learn anything from the Player Nation Stud Club of Swag, I spearheaded?"

Daniel laughed. "Man, you didn't spearhead anything and you don't have any player swag. Besides, Mel is a great woman and nobody tells me who I can date."

"Okay, what does your dad have to say about this?" You know how Uncle Dan is. I don't know why you would do this, man."

"Do what? My dad will be fine."

"Does Aunt Sarah know?"

"Yeah, she knows and she's fine with it."

"So y'all are just keeping it from Uncle Dan?'

"I'm not keeping it from anybody. I'm not ashamed of her."

"Okay, Mr. Not Ashamed! And where has not being ashamed gotten you? It's gotten you no-mo-money, that's what! I'm sorry, man. When a chick starts messing with the money, she's gotta go, exit stage left," Jake said, laughing, but Daniel wasn't finding anything Jake was saying funny. "Don't get me wrong," Jake continued. "I think all white men fantasize about being with a black woman, and I'll bet that all black men fantasize about being with a white woman, but it's just a fantasy, man! I guess you didn't get the memo on that. I do think Melah is gorgeous, though, except for her hair! Why are black women going back to them twisty things and afros? I don't like—"

"It's called going natural, man. Their hair is naturally curly, so to keep it straight, they have to put unhealthy chemicals in it. They're tired of doing all of that, so they're embracing the natural texture of their hair again. That's how it was in the 70's, so I think it's cool."

"Ummm, okay, whatever! Anyway, as I was saying before you interrupted with all that natural 70's hair gibberish, I think Melah is a pretty girl, but it's going to be more trouble than it's worth. That is a line you just don't cross, man, and then you let her come to your job? Tisk, tisk, tisk. Dude, you've obviously forgotten where you live."

"I hate ignorant people!" Daniel said.

"I'm not ignorant, I just—"

"You are ignorant; you and ninety percent of the rest of the people here. I don't understand why anyone in this universe should care about who I date!"

"Dan, I'm your friend and your cousin, and I'm here to tell you that if you start flaunting that black girl around your office, you're gonna find yourself without a job."

Daniel sat there very patiently listening to Jake, but nothing was going over well with him.

"I'm not ashamed of her, man!" Daniel said, raising his voice and forgetting that Melah was in the bathroom taking a shower. "I care about her! She's allowed to stop by my office and ask me out to lunch. It's that kind of ignorant thinking that keeps the world at odds with each other. People should be with who makes them happy, not with who makes others feel most comfortable. I don't even know why I'm having this conversation with you."

"Me either," Jake said, sarcastically. "I just called for some beer, man. Personally, I don't care who you date," he said, laughing. "But seriously, you just graduated college and were lucky enough to land a great job, where you were being considered for a promotion. Now that's not even a consideration anymore. Don't mess up your career over some black chick. Yes, have some fun with her, but don't get serious about her. She's never going to fit into your world, Dan. Be realistic, you guys are going to always have problems," Jake responded, as if he was really concerned. "I'm just—"

"I gotta go, man. I'll talk to you later."

"Yeah, sure. I know you don't want to hear it, but just think about your future and the things you could be giving up. Ask yourself if you really think it's worth it. That's all I'm saying, Dan."

"Later, man," Daniel said, sounding ill-tempered.

"Later," Jake said, right before hanging up.

That conversation lasted way too long for my liking, Daniel thought. He wanted to blow off everything Jake said, but he couldn't help but wonder how many more promotions he was going to have to give up in his lifetime in order to keep his relationship with Melah. Daniel had to be honest with himself; some of the stuff Jake said actually made sense. He was very hopeful that things would be different after he moves to Atlanta.

About an hour and a half had passed since Daniel arrived at Melah's, and she was finally dressed and ready to go.

"This makes no doggone sense, Mel," Daniel said, fussing. "Women act like they're getting dressed for the red carpet in Hollywood or something. Why y'all gotta take so long?"

"Are you in a bad mood, Daniel? Because this is the second time you've fussed at me about something since you've been here. If you're tired, we can postpone our night out until later," Melah said, calmly.

"Nah, I'm sorry. Jake called while you were in the shower and he got on my nerves pretty bad. Please forgive me."

"Who is Jake? The crazy boy from college who used to walk around with straws up his nose and in his ears in hopes some girl would find him amusing enough to give him her phone number?"

Daniel laughed. "Yep! That's him. He's actually my cousin. Jake thought he was a Mac Daddy in college, didn't he?"

"He sure did," Melah said. "He thought every woman on campus wanted him. I was like, 'Dude, you hang with five good looking guys, of which you're the least attractive. Technically, that makes you the runt of the litter.'"

"Oooooh! That's cold, babe. So, you thought the guys in our group were good looking, huh? I can only assume that I was the best looking one out of them all."

"Nope, Kyle Pirus was the best looking, but you gave him a run for his money, babe."

"Wow! Really, Kyle Pirus? He was a nerd. He should have been proud that we even let him in our group. He was not the best looking, Mel," Daniel debated, as Melah grabbed her sweater and headed for the door.

"Kyle Pirus had big rabbit teeth and a big nose. How in the world did you think he was the best looking? He couldn't even bench press a hundred pounds."

Daniel went on and on about why Kyle Pirus wasn't qualified to be number one on Melah's eye candy list. Melah snickered at how Daniel's jealousy was turning him into a down right hater. During the entire drive to the restaurant, Daniel talked about everything Kyle did wrong from the first day they started college.

It's a shame how people will turn on you so quickly, Melah thought, as she laughed at Daniel. She decided she should try and calm the situation.

"Babe, I was just joking. You know you were the best looking man on campus. Kyle Pirus could never compete with you. You had looks, brain, wits, and charm," Melah said, winking at Daniel, in hopes that it would get him to shut up about Kyle.

"Well, thank you, baby. I'm glad you were just joking because I knew there was no way Kyle could be better than me," he said, going right back into his spiel about why he was definitely the better choice.

Since she knew she was the reason Daniel was going on and on about Kyle, she decided to just sit patiently and try to stroke his ego as much as possible. She considered that to be a justified punishment for her talking too much.

NEVER tell a man that one of his friends look better than him. Lesson learned! Gee Whiz!

She was hoping the heavens would shine down on her and make Daniel shut up, but there seemed to be no mercy. Melah had taken all she could take and when they finally arrived at the restaurant, she jumped out of the car before Daniel could even put the car in park.

"What is wrong with you, Mel? I hadn't even parked the car yet."

"I'm sorry, babe. I thought we were parked."

"Mel, the car was still moving."

"Oh, was it? My bad! Oh, look. There's no waiting line. That means we can go ahead and be seated," Mel said, trying to distract Daniel.

"Oh, good, because I'm starving."

"Yeah, me too," Melah said, as she grabbed Daniel's hand and they walked through the door, forgetting all about Kyle Pirus.

As they waited for their food, Daniel talked about everything that happened while he was in Atlanta and Melah talked about how excited she was to be done with college.

"Babe, you just don't know how long I've been waiting for this day to come. Do you know I'm the first person in my family to go to college?"

Daniel gave her a funny look.

"Really? Going to college was a must in my

family," he said, sounding like he couldn't understand how there could be an option not to go. "Even Jake's parents made him go and Jake was nowhere near college material," he said, laughing.

"Hush! You're white! All white people go to college, Daniel. Having the opportunity to go to college is a really big deal in black families."

"Oh, here we go! I get so tired of everybody trying to emphasize how different blacks and whites are. My family isn't rich, Mel, but they still sent me to college. If you want your kids to go to college, then find a way to make it happen. It's just that simple. It has nothing to do with the color of your skin."

"It's really not just that simple, Daniel. For a very long time, blacks were just trying to survive, trying to make sure food was on the table, make sure their kids had clothes on their backs and a descent education. Once they got them out of high school, many parents felt that their job was done. They weren't taught that they should continue to help their children by sending them to college, so they could get a good job. If their kids made it through high school, then that was an accomplishment. Going to college certainly wasn't the norm in the black community."

"But how many years ago was that, Mel? People need to stop living in the past. Stop letting the past cripple them. Sometimes it seems like blacks would rather stay where they are and blame society for why they don't have what someone else has instead of getting off of their butts and making it happen."

"Wait a minute, Daniel! You don't know—"

"I know that Kirsten's dad started his own business and he became very successful, so don't tell me that the white man keeps the black man down. If the black man is down, it's because he's keeping himself down!"

"Daniel, that is not—"

"If you go to an interview looking like a thug, then, no, sorry! You're not getting that job, but if you dress nice, shave, do your homework on the company, practice speaking and answering questions, then you'll have as good a chance as anyone else. I'm just saying, Mel. If someone wants to be treated equal, then they need to act, dress, and talk like they're equal."

"Really, Daniel? So, you really think blacks aren't trying to—" was all she could get out before the waitress walked up with their food.

"Here's your dinner. We have the fresh lobster tails for you, sir, and the chicken parmesan for you ma'am," she said, placing their food in front of them. "Can I get you any—"

"BLAAAAAAAAHHHHHHHH," was all the waitress heard before Melah vomited all over her and the delicious chicken parmesan she had just placed on the table.

"Ewwwww! That's gross!" Daniel said, not knowing what to do next. Melah wanted to knock him upside the head, but she couldn't stop vomiting everywhere. The waitress ran in the kitchen for some napkins and Daniel just sat there screaming, "I thought you hadn't eaten anything. How are you throwing all of that up?"

"GET THAT CHICKEN PARM AWAY FROM ME!" Melah screamed.

Daniel frantically moved the chicken parmesan from in front of Melah and replaced it with his lobster and she proceeded to vomit all over that as well. Just then the waitress, who was still covered in vomit, came back with some help. Everyone was trying to clean up the mess Melah made. The manager was holding a trash bag in front of Melah just in case she started spraying everyone again and Daniel was staring at his lobster that was now covered in vomit. He was starving and all he could think about was the thirty more minutes he was going to have to wait for them to bring out another lobster. He looked over at Melah, who looked like she had just been hit by a train.

"You okay, babe?" He asked, hesitantly.

She gave him a *do I look okay?* glance, but she managed to nod her head and apologize for the mess. The manager reassured her that it was no problem and asked the waitress to fix them another plate.

"Oh, no! None for me, thanks," Melah said, waving her hand in the air. Daniel got up to help Melah out of her chair, so the waitress could finish cleaning off the table.

"Would you like us to fix you another plate, sir?" the waitress asked Daniel.

"Yes, I'll take mine and hers to go, thank you."

Melah gave him a dirty look.

"What, Mel? I'm hungry!"

"Well, please just drop me off at my place and you can go home and eat. I can't stand the smell of anything right now."

"What is wrong with you? Why are you so sick?" Daniel asked.

"A virus is going around campus. A lot of people are sick this week."

"Well, I hope you feel better soon, because we can't be messing up good food like that, babe," Daniel said with a crooked grin on his face.

Melah responded by smacking him on the back of his head. They rounded up their things, went up front to wait for their replacement meals, then headed back to Melah's apartment.

CHAPTER

On the way home, Daniel debated on whether to drop Melah off so he could go home and eat his food in peace, or go back to her place to make sure she was okay.

I'm starving! If I don't get something to eat, I'm going to start eating my own flesh, he thought.

He looked over at Melah and she seemed to be back to her normal chipper self; Daniel was very happy about that.

"What? Why are you staring at me?" Melah asked.

"I'm just glad you're feeling better," Daniel responded.

"Me too. It's just a virus. It'll pass within 24 hours."

"Well, I'll stay with you tonight just to make sure you don't need anything."

"That's really sweet of you, but you need to eat your food and that stuff isn't welcomed in my home," Melah said, looking at Daniel with a stern look on her face.

Daniel smiled and said, "Oh, that's okay. I will leave it in the car until you're asleep. Then I'll bring it in the house and eat it."

"Men are so hardheaded!" Melah said, shaking her head at Daniel, then falling asleep for the rest of the ride home.

"Oh, my goodness, I'm so tired, baby," Melah grumbled when they got to the apartment. She was walking slow like she just ran a marathon or did a strenuous workout of some sort.

"Mel, you haven't done anything all day, how are you tired?" Daniel asked.

Mel cut her eyes over at him.

"Good night, Mr. Stine. You better be glad I'm not evil or I would cut off your baby toe while you're sleeping. You think it's not important, but try to balance your body without it," she said, laughing as she walked down the hallway.

Daniel laughed too.

"So not only have I discovered that my wonderful, sweet girlfriend eavesdrops on my conversations, she also threatens to cut off body parts. You're making a great impression, babe. Keep up the good work," he yelled, as Melah slammed the bedroom door behind her, paying no attention to what Daniel was saying.

As soon as Melah's door shut, Daniel ran back to the car to get his food. When he came back in, and made himself comfortable on the couch. He took his pants off, threw them on the floor, grabbed one of Melah's blankets, and turned on the television.

"I smell food, Daniel," Melah yelled from the back room, but Daniel ignored her while he attentively chowed down on his lobster tail and watched movies for the rest of the night.

The next morning, Melah woke up in a great mood. She got dressed for school. Since finals were over, she knew the day would be a walk in the park.

In a few weeks I will be a graduate. It seems like forever that I've been in school. There's nothing that will ruin my mood, she thought, as she laughed and skipped down the hallway singing. Unfortunately, her happiness was soon cut off when she saw Daniel laid out on the couch and his pants just thrown on the floor.

Men! I swear they are just like little kids. They always want a clean house, but they are the main ones leaving their mess all over the floor.

Melah snatched Daniel's pants to lay them across the couch, but when she picked them up, a piece of paper fell out of his pocket.

Okay, so now I have to pick up his trash too.

Melah grabbed the paper, and as she was placing it back in Daniel's pocket, she saw a girl's name on it with a phone number. At the end of the phone number was a smiley face. Melah wasn't the jealous type, but the fact that Daniel had another girl's phone number in his pocket really bothered her. Matter of fact, it enraged her.

"WHO'S MANDY?" she screamed, throwing Daniel's pants in his face.

"Babe, I'm asleep. Why did you throw these pants at me?" Daniel asked, still half asleep.

"WHO'S MANDY, DANIEL?"

"Mandy? How do you know Mandy?" he mumbled, rolling over, trying to go back to sleep, but Melah kept screaming.

"NO, THE QUESTION IS, HOW DO YOU KNOW MANDY? THIS IS AN ATLANTA NUMBER, DANIEL! SO, YOU WENT TO ATLANTA AND PICKED UP A GIRLFRIEND?"

"Mel, why are you screaming?" he asked, rolling back over and looking up at Melah, who was hovering over him, holding the paper in the air so he could see it.

All of a sudden, Daniel's eyes got really big as he realized that this was indeed a crisis, which he should give some attention to.

He sat up and said, "Aww, Dang it! I didn't know she put that in my pocket," but the look on Melah's face told him he'd better come up with something better than that.

He took a deep breath and tried to explain.

"She was flirting with me, but I told her that I had a girlfriend and I wasn't interested. She offered her number, but I didn't take it. Well, I guess I did take it, but I didn't know I took it," he said, stumbling over his words.

Melah stood there, with an angry, yet dumbfounded look on her face, and it wasn't helping that Daniel was not sounding the least bit convincing.

"Look, Mel! I didn't know she put the paper in my pocket. You're the only woman I want, so if it makes you feel better, you can tear the number up and put it in the trash. I don't need it and I won't ever call it, okay?"

Melah smiled, "Okay, but I'll just take this number with me and throw it in the trash at school," she said, giving Daniel a sarcastic look and walking out the door.

Daniel took a deep breath, laid down on the couch, and went back to sleep.

About a month later, it was time for Melah to graduate. Her parents lived about fifteen minutes away, and her entire family was coming to help celebrate. By this time, Melah and Daniel had been dating for five and a half months. Melah decided that this would be a good opportunity to introduce Daniel to her family. She was very nervous about what they would say, but Daniel didn't seem to have a care in the world.

"Melah, why are you so worried about me meeting your family? Do you not know that chocolate and vanilla marbled cakes are the most requested cakes in the bakery? That alone should tell you that swirling us together makes a delicious treat," he said, giving her a kiss on the forehead. Melah didn't respond. Actually, she looked sick to her stomach.

"What's wrong, Mel?"

"Oh, nothing. I'm just nervous. That's all."

"Well, you look like you're about to throw up."

"No, I'm fine, babe. I just need some Pepto Bismol," she said, grabbing a big bottle from her purse and guzzling it down like it was a shot of liquor.

Daniel gave her a frown.

"I'm just ready for this day to be over. I'm so tired and stressed," she said, taking another swig.

"Mel, do you always carry Pepto Bismol in your

purse? And you should be enjoying this day. All your family is in town and you're finally walking across the stage to get your diploma. That's a big deal!"

"Yeah, I know it is," she responded, ignoring his question about the Pepto Bismol. "And I am very happy. I'm just stressed, that's all."

"Okay, well let's go. We've got to get you to the school early so you can get in line and do whatever you need to do."

"No, baby, we've got to go to my mom's house first. I want you to meet my family before we go to the ceremony. Everyone is waiting for us."

"Oh!" said Daniel. "Well, let's go then."

"I just told them this morning that you were white, so it won't be a total shock for them. Well, actually, I only told my mom and she was okay with it. I'm not sure about the rest of my family, though. My parents aren't together anymore. My dad has remarried and my mom just started dating this much younger guy, and ALL of the males in my family are very upset, so do you know what that means?"

"No, what?"

"They won't even notice that you're white," Melah bellowed, letting out a huge laugh.

"Yeah, right! In your dreams," he responded, opening the car door for Melah and heading to her mom's house.

"So, will your dad's wife be at your mom's house too?" Daniel asked, sounding like he was ready to watch some drama unfold.

"Yes, of course she'll be there. My family is very

civilized, so you can put your bucket of popcorn away. There will be no drama movie playing today."

"Aww, bummer! I love to see families go at it. I have two uncles that fuss every time they get together. Every time, Mel! It's the funniest thing ever. For some reason, they're always competing with each other. Have you ever seen, *The Johnson's Family Vacation* movie?"

"Yeah! Several times. I love that movie."

"Well, my uncles are like the two brothers in that movie."

"Really?" Mel asked, laughing.

"Yes, really. You'll see when you meet them."

"You're taking me to meet your family?"

"Ummm, yeah! You're taking me to meet yours, right? So, I'll take you to meet mine. You'll love everybody. My family is cool."

"I won't hold my breath," Mel mumbled.

"They are. You'll see," he said.

Melah smiled and they chit chatted another ten minutes or so before pulling into Melah's mom's driveway.

Melah's uncles and brothers were all standing around outside when they pulled up.

"Uncle Nate! Uncle Charles," Melah said, running up and giving her uncles a hug. She hadn't seen them since she was in high school.

"Hey, everybody!" Daniel said, giving a quick head nod.

"Who is this white boy you bringing to meet us, Mel?" her brother asked, giving Daniel a repulsive stare.

"Hush, Corey! Everybody, this is my boyfriend,

Daniel."

"Mmm!" one of her uncles said.

"Boyfriend?" her brother asked.

"Yes, my boyfriend and where is momma?"

"She's in the house listening to daddy cry about her new boy toy. I had to leave out of there before I pulled his man card. Mel, it was ridiculous," her brother said.

"Oh, he calls you Mel just like I do," Daniel said, leaning over and whispering to Melah.

"Why you all over my sister, man? I hope you ain't sleeping with this dude, Mel. That's nasty!"

Melah hit her brother upside the head and opened the door to go in the house, but Daniel couldn't resist the urge to taunt him.

"Yes, she likes cream in her coffee," Daniel whispered as he passed by her brother.

"Boy, I'll beat—"

"Hey! Leave that boy alone," said one of Melah's uncles. "She can date who she pleases, even if he's not our preferred color of black."

Melah looked back, "Uncle Nate, please don't do that."

"Do what? I was trying to save whitey over here from getting his butt whooped by your brother."

"Yeah, he's trying to save him," her brother chimed in. "And you better tell him to keep his mouth closed."

Daniel laughed. "Come on, man. Stop giving me a hard time. I'm just trying to meet the family, that's all."

"Yeah! Whatever, man. Don't come back over here talking about cream in her coffee or else you're gonna—"

"Daniel, did you say that?"

"Nah, baby. You see what had happened was—"

"Mel, I don't like this dude, and now it ain't even because he's white. I just don't like him," her brother snarled.

Daniel started laughing again; that was until Melah elbowed him in his side.

"You're not making a good impression, Daniel. So stop it!"

"That's right, Daniel. You're not making a good impression," her brother mimicked.

Melah heard her parents talking in the kitchen, so they closed the front door where her brother and uncles were and went inside.

"Sharron, you can't convince me that this lil boy can provide for you like a real man. What can he bring to the table?" Melah's dad was asking her mom.

Melah felt that this would be a good time to rescue her mom, and she did just that.

"Hey, momma and daddy. I'm here!" she said, giving them both big hugs.

"Thank you! You came just in time," her mom whispered.

"You're welcome," Melah whispered back.

"Oh, you must be Daniel. We've heard so much about you," her mom said, giving Daniel a hug.

"Ummm, no we haven't!" her dad exclaimed.

"Daddy, this is my boyfriend, Daniel Stine."

"Uhhh, I didn't send you to college to major in

white men!" her dad snapped.

Daniel let out a huge laugh.

"Well, at least he has a sense of humor," her dad grunted. "And speaking of relationships that should not be taking place, I was just talking to your mother about this thirty-two year old little boy she's bringing around my kids. He can't possibly know how to be a good parent."

Everyone gave him a blank stare.

"Daddy, me and Corey are both grown and out of the house. Momma's boyfriend is not going to have to be a parent to us."

At this point, Daniel was doing everything he could to keep from laughing at Melah's dad, who was looking like he was about to cry.

"Besides dad," Melah continued. "You got married right after you and momma got divorced, so I don't understand why you're acting this way. Momma has found someone who makes her happy and I think we should support her."

"Well, my wife is my age, so I'm not—"

"No she isn't," Melah's mom interrupted. "She is seven years younger than you and you were probably cheating on me with her the whole time we were married."

"Now, Sharron, you know that ain't true! You were the one who wanted the divorce, not me! I gave you twenty-five years of my life, and as soon as the kids graduated high school, you said we had nothing in common anymore. Well, we had two kids in common and that should have been enough! Now you're running off with someone who is fifteen years younger than you. He could be your child! It's disgraceful to—"

"And a delightful fifteen years younger he is," Melah's mom said, with a big grin on her face.

"Ewww, ma!" Melah said, frowning.

Just as Melah's dad was about to go into an uproar, everyone came in from outside. Evidently they were waiting on breakfast to arrive because all of Melah's aunts came in with big bags of food and started setting the table like they were in a catering business, barely even noticing Melah or Daniel. Then one aunt blurted out, "Melah, you're getting fat."

"Aunt Sue, you haven't even said hi to me yet."

"Sorry honey, I just caught a glimpse of your butt sticking out around the corner and I had to speak on the matter."

Everyone laughed.

Daniel had noticed Melah's weight gain as well, along with several other weird habits, like drinking Pepto Bismol straight from the bottle, but he dared not say anything.

Melah's aunt apologized and gave her a hug. "And who is this?" Melah's aunt asked, pointing to Daniel. Just then, Melah's grandma came in from the back room, barely moving about on her cane.

"Hey, Grandma!" Melah said, racing over to give her a hug.

"Hey, suga! How is grandma's baby doing?"

"I'm good, grandma."

Melah's aunt moved closer to Daniel.

"So, who's this strapping young, white stud you got

here, Melah?" her aunt asked, looking Daniel up and down.

Daniel tried to smile, but Melah's aunt was really invading his space and rubbing on his arms, which made him pretty uncomfortable.

"This stud is my boyfriend, Auntie, so please stop rubbing on him," Melah chimed in, gently lifting her aunt's arm off of Daniel.

"I bet them fast-tail skanks be all over him," her grandma interjected.

When Daniel heard those words, the expression on his face was priceless.

"I told you there was such a thing," Melah mouthed to Daniel, but he just shook his head in disbelief.

"Well, you better claim him before I do," her aunt said, laughing. "I'm just kidding. I don't date white men and he's way too young for me," she added.

Melah's dad couldn't resist joining in.

"Oh! It's fine! Dating younger men obviously runs in your family, because your sister over here has found her a little boy to play with."

"Oh, give it a rest," argued another one of Melah's aunts. "Y'all have been divorced for four or five years now, and you're remarried, so let this woman have some fun," she said, as she passed by Melah with a sausage, egg, and cheese biscuit in her hand.

Melah immediately put her hand over her nose and darted down the hallway. There was so much commotion going on that no one noticed her abrupt exit, except Daniel.

Once the food was placed on the table, all the family quickly gobbled down their meals, then went outside to see who was riding with who.

"Melah, come on, we're all leaving," her mom yelled down the hall.

Melah finally came out of the bathroom and was greeted with a very strange look from both Daniel and her mother.

"Girl, what took you so long? I hope you weren't in there stinking up my bathroom. Did you at least turn on the vents?" her mother asked.

Melah laughed, trying to play it off.

"Yes, momma. I turned on the vents. It will be all cleared up by the time we come back to the house."

"I sure hope so. The last thing I need is to entertain company with a funky bathroom," her mom said, laughing, as they locked the house and left to go to Melah's graduation.

CHAPTER

"Melah, I'm going to ride with you and Daniel," her mom yelled, as she jumped in Daniel's car.

"Sharron, you could have ridden with me," Melah's dad shouted.

"Where is your wife?" Melah's Aunt Sue yelled out.

"Don't start with me, Sue. I'm picking my wife up on the way to the ceremony; we can all ride together."

"What do I look like riding somewhere with you and your wife, Bill?" Melah's mom asked. "Besides, I don't want to hear any more of your mouth about my love life."

"Well, you obviously need to hear it, so you can understand that what you're doing is wrong, but suit yourself. I'm leaving!" Melah's dad answered, arrogantly, then drove off.

The rest of the family carpooled to the graduation ceremony and quickly found an area that would seat everyone. Melah's dad and stepmom eventually made their way to the ceremony, and down to where everyone was sitting. Her dad made a point to sit by her mom. His wife, Patricia, rolled her eyes, placed herself in between them, and said "Bill, leave Sharron alone! You had your chance and you blew it, so she can date whomever she wants."

"Thank you, Patricia," Melah's mom responded, then she and Patricia gave each other a quick glance and both let out a big laugh.

Daniel leaned over and whispered to Melah's mom, "Ms. Sharron, do y'all really get along that good?"

Patricia over heard him and interjected, "Child please, there's no need for us to bicker. We both know what we're dealing with. She was just wise enough to get out while she still had her sanity," and they all let out a boisterous laugh.

"What are y'all laughing about?" Melah's dad asked, with a frown on his face.

"Nothing," Patricia and Sharron both said at the same time, as the announcer stepped up to the podium to begin the ceremony.

When he called Melah's name, her family was overjoyed. They were yelling and screaming as loudly as they could, despite the fact that the announcer repeatedly asked everyone to hold their applause until the end. It didn't matter, though. There was no way they were going to let this moment pass quietly. What made it even worse was that her brother and cousins were all acting like they were in a fraternity, yelling step chants and stomping all over the bleachers. Daniel wanted to join in, but he knew

Melah's brother hated him, and the last thing he wanted was to set himself up for "white boy" jokes, so he sat there quietly, but seemingly enjoying it all. Melah, on the other hand, was thoroughly embarrassed and this was the one time she wanted to disown her entire family.

After the ceremony was over, everyone went back to Melah's mom's house and they danced the night away. Daniel watched Melah to see if she was going to make any more abrupt exits to the bathroom, but she seemed to be her old self again, which made Daniel very happy. For the last month or so, Melah didn't seem to be herself at all. Daniel knew he needed to bring the subject up, but he figured he would mention it when Melah wasn't so stressed and didn't have so much going on. He sat on the porch watching her dance all over the back yard. Everyone was having fun. Melah and her cousins had a dance off; they asked Daniel if he wanted to join them. Melah's brother even asked him if he wanted something to drink. For a brief moment, they all seemed to forget about Daniel's skin color. They also seemed to have forgotten about Ms. Sharron's new man, Jonathan, who was bold enough to make his appearance at the after party. Thank goodness, by that time, Melah's dad was long gone.

Soon, Melah had danced herself tired and she was ready to go home.

"You ready to go, baby?" she asked Daniel, while giving him a kiss on the cheek.

"Hey! Hey! Cut that out!" Melah's brother yelled from across the yard.

"Corey, leave them kids alone. He makes her

happy and that's all that matters to me," her mom said. Corey rolled his eyes and Melah and Daniel packed their things up to leave, making their rounds to say goodbye to everyone before they left. Everyone waved goodbye, except Melah's brother, Corey.

"Bye, Corey," Melah said, running over and giving him a hug and kiss. "Just be happy for me. If he turns out to be a jerk, I'll let you beat him, okay?"

"I hear you, Mel," Daniel interrupted.

Melah smiled, "I'm just kidding, baby," she said, giving him a wink.

"I'm not," Corey said, giving Melah a half grin. "Mel, it ain't right to date him," Corey explained as Melah thanked everyone for coming. She looked back at Corey.

"It's right for me, Corey," she replied, as she and Daniel jumped in the car and headed back to Melah's house. Daniel decided to make a quick stop at a convenient store on the way. He parked the car and jumped out.

"I'll be right back," he said to Melah.

"Okay," she responded.

While Daniel was inside, Melah's leg began to cramp up, so she got out of the car to stretch. As she was standing there, two guys walked up to her.

"Hey! Don't I know you from somewhere?" one of the guys asked.

"No, I don't think so," Melah replied.

"I think I do. What's your name?" he asked.

"Melah," she responded, bashfully.

"Oh, that's a pretty name. I really think we've seen each other before. Can I call—"

"Mel, are you ready to go?" Daniel asked sternly, as he walked up to the car.

"Oh, she's a sellout, man," the other guy yelled.

"I'm not a sellout. You don't know any—"

"Get in the car, Mel," Daniel demanded.

Melah turned to get in the car, then the first guy asked, "Is this white boy beating on you?"

"NO! He ain't be—"

"MELAH! LET'S GO, NOW! Excuse us fellas. I don't mean to be rude, but we have somewhere we've got to be," Daniel said, trying to sound cordial.

Melah gave him a weird look and jumped in the car.

"Daniel, why are you acting funny? Those guys knew me from somewhere."

Daniel looked over at Melah. The fire in his eyes told her that he was beyond furious.

"Why are you looking at me like that? What's wrong with you?" she asked.

"Melah, we are in a black neighborhood!"

"So! What is that supposed to mean, Daniel?"

"In case you haven't noticed, I'm a white man in a black neighborhood with a black woman."

"What's your point, Daniel?"

"Dangit, Mel! Can't you understand that black guys don't like seeing white men with their women! You should know that just by how your brother acted. If those guys would have tried to jump me then what do you think would have happened?"

"You would have kicked their butts, that's what, because you got skills," she said, laughing.

"WRONG! I would have gotten killed, because when fights break out in black neighborhoods, all the neighbors come out to see what's going on. As soon as the rest of the neighborhood found out that a white man was with a black woman, they would have all beat me to a pulp. That's what would have happened!"

Melah wanted to laugh because she knew Daniel was right about the whole neighborhood coming out to see what was going on, but she tried to keep a straight face.

"Daniel, what do you know about black neighborhoods?"

"I lived in a black neighborhood for four years and it was the longest four years of my life. That's how I know about black neighborhoods. So, while you're over here grinning in their faces and acting like you're hanging out with old buddies, they could be plotting to kill me. Those guys don't know you and I really don't understand why you even got out of the car in the first place. You act like you can't comprehend the risk we take when we go places. Everyone hasn't warmed up to the idea of interracial couples, Mel! Some people actually hate the idea and will go to great lengths to express their dislike. You've got to be mindful of who and what we are and where we live! Don't put me in a bad situation like that anymore," Daniel said, harshly.

"Just take me home," Melah responded, with a bitter attitude.

"Fine!" Daniel responded.

Melah gave him the silent treatment all the way to her house. When he walked her to her door, she tried to slam it in his face, but he put his foot in the door, and blocked it with his hands.

"Here, take this," he said, shoving a small box in her hand that he got from the convenient store.

Melah frowned. "What's this?"

"It's a pregnancy test. I'm not leaving until you take it."

Melah shoved the box back into Daniel's hands like it was contagious. "I'm not taking that!" she said defiantly.

"Oh, you're taking it and I will wait here for the results."

"Who do you think you are? You're not my father! You have been bossing me around since we left the party. I'm not your slave!"

"Slave? Really, Mel? So you're going that route now?"

"Well, you're acting like you own me. Nobody owns me, Daniel."

Daniel looked at Melah with a nonchalant look on his face.

"You can try to pick a fight with me if you want, but I'm not leaving here until I know the results of that test."

"What makes you think that I'm pregnant?"

"I know you're pregnant, and you know you're pregnant, so take the test, Mel!"

"Daniel, I just graduated college. I have a job interview with a major corporation next week. I am not going to ruin it by becoming another statistic of being a single black mother, struggling and trying to survive. I am not going to be that girl! I don't have time for a baby; it's going to ruin everything! I have dreams and goals. I'm not taking that stupid test, Daniel!" she said, breaking down in tears. "I'm not taking it, okay?"

Daniel had never seen Melah so emotional before. He felt bad that he was forcing her to take the pregnancy test.

"You won't have to do this alone, Mel. I will not allow you to be a statistic."

"I don't want you to marry me out of obligation, Daniel. You will hate me and we'll end up divorced. I can't do this! I can't deal with the thought of having a baby," she said, still crying.

"Melah, there is a baby growing inside of you whether you like it or not, and ignoring it is not going to make it go away. You're throwing up every time you get a whiff of food, you're tired all the time, you're gaining weight, and you don't even want me to touch you anymore. Do you really think I haven't noticed all of these things? You need to go to the doctor, Mel."

Melah didn't say a word. She snatched the box out of Daniel's hands and went into the bathroom. She took the test, laid it on the bathroom sink, and immediately went and got into her bed, without waiting for the results. Daniel looked at her as she walked down the hall, sobbing hysterically, but he didn't say anything. He went into the bathroom to see what the results were. Since he didn't know the first thing about pregnancy tests, he grabbed the instructions and started reading them.

"If there's only one line, then she's not pregnant. If

there's two lines, then she's pregnant," he read out loud, then looked at the test. Sure enough, there were two lines in the little window. He walked into Melah's room and kneeled down beside her bed. He gave her a kiss on the lips. "It's going to be alright, Mel. I love you and I am not going to leave you," was all he said.

He got in the bed and put his arms around her. He didn't try to talk anymore, he just held her while she cried for what seemed to be all night. This was the first time Daniel was able to get the words "I love you" out without breaking into hives. Melah definitely noticed it and it made her feel good, but unfortunately, she was way too distraught to bask in Daniel's "I love yous"; she was way too distraught to bask in anything but tears.

The next day Daniel woke up to Melah's gagging over a trash can.

"Mel, are you okay?"

"No, Daniel. I wake up every morning sick to my stomach and my breasts feel like they weigh a ton of bricks," Melah responded, miserably.

"How long has this been going on?" Daniel asked.

"For almost two months, I guess."

"Two months, Mel? You've hidden this from me for two months? I don't even know what to say right now."

"If I told you, or even admitted it to myself, that meant I would have to do something about it and I just had too much going on. I couldn't add anything else to my plate. I am sorry I kept it from you. Really I am."

"We're going to the doctor today, Mel. Do you need me to call and make the appointment?" he asked, in an uncompromising tone.

"No, I'll do it," Melah responded, disappointedly.

She called and made an appointment as she promised and that afternoon they both went to the doctor.

"Well, congratulations. Yes, you are indeed pregnant!" the doctor said, excitedly. "Looks like you're right at eight weeks. I can prescribe you some prenatal vitamins, or you can buy them over the counter. Make sure you take them every day. The baby is going to demand a lot from your body, so you need to replenish it with nutrients, okay?"

Melah didn't even respond. She just sat there like she was having an out of body experience. Then she burst into tears like this was the first time she had heard the news. Daniel looked over at her with a shocked look on his face. He was not sure what to make of her outburst, but he vowed that he would be supportive no matter what.

On their way home Daniel asked, "Mel, why are you crying? You already knew that you were pregnant."

Melah didn't respond. Matter of fact, she had nothing to say for the remainder of the day. Daniel didn't know how to respond to her constant tears throughout the day, but he was determined to not leave her side.

The next day Melah's eyes were swollen from all of her crying, but she eventually decided to break the silence with Daniel.

"I'm going to have an abortion," she said, looking him in his eyes, then walking away.

Daniel's head dropped.

"Why, Mel? We can make this work. I told you

I'm not going to leave you."

Melah turned around and came back in the living room where Daniel was.

"Daniel, I want to be something other than a mother. I want to be a business woman. I want to be able to afford my own house and a nice car. I have an interview for my first real job next week! If I get the job, I don't want to have to say, 'Oh, by the way, I'm pregnant and in about seven months, I'm going to need to take six weeks off.' I want something better for my life."

"Mel, you act like having a baby is a curse."

"Daniel, you missed out on a promotion because your girlfriend is black. If they find out that I'm pregnant, you're never going to get any promotions and you may not even have a job."

"I have another job, Mel. That's why I'm moving to Atlanta."

"And where am I moving, Daniel? Me and this baby? We will be here and you will be there. That's my whole point. I don't want to be a single mother!"

"Melah, wherever I am, that's where you and the baby will be. I'm asking you not to abort this baby. It's not right in the sight of God."

"DON'T DO THAT, DANIEL!" Melah screamed. "I can't take that right now," she said trying to calm her tone. "Besides, sex before marriage isn't right in the sight of God either, but you weren't complaining about that now, were you?" she asked, sarcastically.

"Melah, I may not be where I need to be spiritually, but I am still very spiritual. Just because I don't always do what's right, doesn't mean I don't want to do better. I want to get my life right with God. Trust me, I think about it all the time."

"Well, Daniel, I'm not religious, you know that. I've just never been taught all that church stuff."

"It's not church stuff, Mel. It's an adjustment to your lifestyle."

"Don't preach to me Daniel! You're the father of this child, remember?"

Daniel kneeled down and put his face on Melah's stomach.

"Please don't take this baby from me, Mel. Give me a chance to be a father."

Melah's eyes filled with tears.

"Stop it, Daniel! You shouldn't get attached to this baby."

"It's my baby! Don't tell me not to get attached," Daniel said, sounding upset.

Melah took a deep breath.

"Please just give me some time alone to think, okay? We'll talk it over later."

"Okay. I'll give you some time. Just don't shut me out, Mel," he said as he got off of his knees and headed to the door. "I love you and I'm going to be here," he said, kissing her forehead.

There's the L word again, Melah thought. She was quite surprised that Daniel said it twice and it came out so naturally, like he had been practicing it. At the moment, Melah wasn't sure how she felt about Daniel, seeing how he was the cause for her getting pregnant.

I can't believe he didn't wear any protection that night. I wish I wouldn't have been so caught up in the moment. I wish I would have noticed. I wish I—"

"Earth to Mel," Daniel said, interrupting her thoughts.

Melah gave Daniel a slight grin. "I'm sorry. I was just thinking about the night I got pregnant."

"Huh? You know what night you got pregnant?"

"Yes, it was the night you forgot to use a condom. What other night could it have been?"

"Oh, yeah! I remember that. What a great night that was," Daniel said, chuckling.

Melah gave him a blank stare and a deep sigh.

"There's nothing about this that's amusing, Daniel."

"I know, baby, and I'm really sorry about that night. You can blame everything on me."

"Oh, I already do, but thanks for your permission."

Daniel laughed. "I just hope you won't make any decisions without me. That's all I'm asking of you, Mel. Can you promise me that?" Daniel asked.

"Yeah, I can do that," Melah agreed, as she told him goodnight and closed the door.

CHAPTER

Daniel gave Melah a few days to think things over, but bright and early on the next Saturday morning, he received a phone call from her.

"Hey, baby. It's great hearing from you. Why are you up so early on a Saturday?" he asked.

"I couldn't sleep," she said, sounding depressed.

"What's wrong, Mel? You don't sound—"

"I went ahead and called the abortion clinic," Melah said, abruptly.

"You did what?" Daniel said, angrily.

"Don't get all worked up. I'm only doing a consultation with them. I haven't made any permanent decisions."

"I thought we were going to make these decisions together, Mel."

"Daniel, you're way more religious than I am. I know you don't believe in abortions, so any input you give is going to be biased and it's going to make me feel horrible about myself. I need to talk to a neutral party who can give me facts not based on emotion or religion. I just want to weigh all my options, that's all."

Daniel took a deep breath. "We are unequally yoked, Mel."

"What? What does that mean?"

"It means, spiritually, we don't even believe the same things."

"Do we have to?"

"Well, yeah! If we believed the same things, then we wouldn't be having this conversation about abortions right now."

"So, do all Christians think the same way, Daniel? Does anyone have their own opinion?"

"Of course we have our own opinions, but we're all supposed to believe what the Bible says."

"I can't believe how you've turned holier than thou on me, as if you're not the one who got me pregnant in the first place."

"Mel, I'm not trying to act holier than thou, but there are some things I do believe in and abor—"

"Like not fornicating? Is that something you believe in, Daniel?" Melah asked, sarcastically. "No, I guess not, because if you did we wouldn't be having this conversation, either, now would we? Anyway, I have an appointment this afternoon. If you want to go with me, you can, but since you've decided to be 'Christian Craig' all of a sudden, then you probably wouldn't be caught dead in a place like that. I guess that's only where the sinners go."

"Come on, Mel. I didn't mean it like that. If you're

adamant about going, then of course I'll go with you. I just wish you would reconsider. That's all."

"Whatever, Daniel! Please be at my house by 1:00 if you want to go," Melah responded, sounding agitated.

"I'll be there," Daniel said, and they both hung up the phone.

When Daniel arrived, he looked like he had been crying. He felt very conflicted about what was taking place. All of his life, he had thoroughly been against abortion, but here he was, going to the clinic with his pregnant girlfriend. The thought of Melah having an abortion made Daniel feel ill, but he knew he needed to be there for her. Daniel had to admit that having a baby would definitely put a damper on his career as well as Melah's, but he didn't care about any of that right now. The last thing in the world he wanted was for Melah to have an abortion.

Thoughts were racing through his head and he couldn't bring himself to get out of the car.

I understand the point Melah is trying to make about the negative side of bringing a baby into our lives right now, but I don't understand why she would get rid of the baby now that it's here. I don't understand that at all!

The more Daniel thought about Melah having an abortion, the angrier he became, so he decided to not think about it at all. He got out of his car and knocked on Melah's door.

"Come in," she said, somberly, opening the door and walking back into her bedroom.

He grabbed her arm and gave her a hug. "I'm sorry,

Mel. I hate that I put you in this situation. Please forgive me."

Melah's eyes filled with water along with Daniel's, but she didn't want to have a breakdown in front of him, so she quickly wiped her face and gave him a cold, "It's fine! Are you ready to go?"

"Yeah, I guess," he responded, as they got into his car and headed to the abortion clinic.

The ride to the clinic was quiet and dejected. They both attempted to make small talk, but neither of them were in much of a mood to talk. They felt so detached from each other. Daniel often wondered where his sweet Melah had disappeared to. Now, all he had was someone who seemed to hate the sight of him.

They finally arrived at the abortion clinic. There was a small group of protesters across the street, walking in circles with their pro-life signs and pictures of aborted babies. When they saw them, Melah's and Daniel's hands started shaking. Melah tried to act confident, but Daniel could see through her façade.

"We don't have to do this," he said.

"It's just a consultation, Daniel. Relax!"

Daniel rubbed his hands across his arms like he was cold and opened the clinic's door for Melah.

"Hi, please sign in here, fill out this paperwork, and you'll be called back shortly," said the girl at the front desk, as if Melah and Daniel were just another number.

Melah filled out her information and returned it to the girl. Then she looked around to see where Daniel had gone. As she glanced over the room, she felt sick. There were several young girls there with their mothers, or some other relative. Some of the girls looked to be as young as 12 years old. The silence that filled the room was eerie; even the people who came together weren't talking to each other. She spotted Daniel in the back of the room sitting across from two middle-age women who were defying the odds and chatting up a storm. She hurried back to where they were in hopes that it would take her mind off of her decision.

As much as she wanted Daniel to think she knew what she was doing, fear was all over her face.

He rubbed his hand over hers as she sat beside him. She wanted to look at him, but she couldn't. She knew she was hurting him.

There's just no way he could possibly understand the predicament this puts me in. He doesn't know how this makes me—"

"The last thing we need is another mixed baby in this world," one of the ladies whispered to the other lady sitting beside her, interrupting Melah's deep thoughts.

They both glanced over at Daniel and Melah, and Daniel raised one of his eyebrows.

"I'm sorry, did you say something to us?" he asked the lady.

"No, I was just talking to my friend here," she responded innocently, like she wasn't looking for any trouble.

Melah sat there with her eyes stretched as far as they could go and her mouth wide open.

"Did she just say what I thought she said?" Melah

asked Daniel.

"Yep, but it just goes to show that there are ignorant people everywhere, Mel. We will be the bigger people here and not stoop to their level."

Melah was still sitting there with her mouth open, when all of a sudden, Daniel kissed her.

"Daniel, we're in public," Melah said, timidly. She and Daniel hadn't kissed since she he made her take the pregnancy test; she forgot how wonderful his lips felt. At that moment, she also forgot all about how angry she was with him for getting her pregnant. She smiled and he smiled back, and for a split second it felt like old times. It seemed as if they were the only two people in the clinic, that was until one of the ladies let out an abrupt, "Ewww!"

Both Daniel and Melah looked over at them.

"Ewwww, what?" Melah snapped, sitting straight up in her chair. "What's so disgusting about a man who loves me enough to come to an abortion clinic with me, even though it's tearing him up inside? What is so disgusting about two people who just want to be together, but can't live in peace because the world can't get past the fact that they are two different skin colors? It is ridiculous that everywhere we go, someone wants to point out our differences and treat us bad. They want to tell us that we don't belong together, that we're not meant to be together. This man makes me happy and he is very good to me, yet, people like you are still determined to not see us together, because he's white and I'm black. We are one nation, under God, with liberty and justice for all, so why do you insist on keeping us divided?" Melah asked.

"Melah Thompson," the assistant called out as the door to the back room swung open. "Melah Thompson," she called out again.

Melah was at the point of bursting into tears, so the assistant's timing was perfect. When Melah stood up, Daniel held his fist up in the air and said, "Power to the people, Mrs. Al Sharpton has spoken! Power to the people!"

Melah couldn't help but let out a loud laugh and so did several of the other people in the clinic.

"Stop calling me that!" she said to Daniel, while still laughing. She looked around at all the smiles on everyone's face. She was glad that she and Daniel could add a little bit of amusement to such a daunting situation. She missed how much fun she and Daniel had before she found out she was pregnant. Daniel missed it too, but right now, they seemed closer than they had been in weeks, maybe even months.

Daniel and Melah followed the assistant to the back room.

"Melah, you can hang your jacket here if you'd like. The counselor will be in shortly. I'm going to get you set up for your ultrasound," the assistant said.

"Ultrasound?" Melah roared. "They didn't tell me I had to do an ultrasound."

"Yes, we need to see how far along you are, then we can carefully go over all of your options with you."

"I really don't want to do an ultrasound," Melah said.

"Well, dear, even if you don't do the ultrasound

Why Keep Us Divided?

today, we're gonna have to do one before we can perform any procedures on you. We won't be able to help you weigh any options unless we've taken a look at the fetus first," she said, trying to sound supportive. "Ms. Thompson, I know this is very difficult for you, but we want you to make an informed decision and an ultrasound is just standard procedure, alright?"

"Okay," Melah said, reluctantly, and the assistant walked out to get the ultrasound equipment.

"Mel, how much is all this gonna cost?" Daniel asked.

"Don't worry about it Daniel. I made this decision on my own and I will pay for it on my own."

"Mel, I wish you—"

"Okay, Ms. Thompson, are you ready to see how far along you are?" the assistant asked as she rolled the ultrasound machine into the room.

"No, not really."

"Well, it will be quick and then we can start discussing your options, okay?"

"Okay," Mel said, mournfully.

The assistant set everything up and it was time to see the baby. Daniel leaned forward so he wouldn't miss anything.

"Okay, so here's your amniotic sac right here," the assistant said. "And the white spot there is your baby."

"Where? Where is the baby?" Daniel asked, excitedly while Melah turned her head so she couldn't see. "What's that flickering?" Daniel asked.

"Oh, that's the baby's heartbeat."

"His heartbeat?" Daniel asked as if the moment had become truly surreal. He leaned back in his chair and stared at the screen with tears in his eyes. Neither he nor the nurse seemed to notice the tears already running down Melah's face.

"Well, it looks like you're right at nine we—"

"I don't want to do this! Please let me up! Daniel, please get me out of this place," Melah said, as she jumped off the table.

"Wait, Ms. Thompson. The counselor will talk you through everything. Please don't leave," the assistant begged. "At least let the counselor come in and talk with you."

"No! I'm done!" Melah said, heading to the bathroom to change back into her clothes.

"Ms. Thompson, wait. We will—"

"Let her go!" Daniel said, placing his hand in front of the assistant to stop her from chasing after Melah. The assistant sat back down, then she said she was going to go get the counselor to come in and talk to Melah before she left.

"No! We're not talking to anyone," Daniel said with a stern voice. "If we need you, we'll call you, okay?" he said as he grabbed Melah's jacket and purse off the hook. Melah threw on her clothes and she and Daniel quickly headed out the door.

The ride home was just as somber as the ride to the clinic, except the fact that Melah couldn't go through with the appointment made Daniel extremely happy.

When they got to Melah's apartment, neither of

them mentioned the abortion clinic. They sat on the couch and watched movies like old times. Melah laid her head on Daniel's shoulders and he placed his arms around her, both choosing to forget about what just happened.

"Mel, in about three weeks it's going to be time for me to go back to Atlanta to train with Mr. Cross, ya know?"

"Oh really? Well, I forgot to tell you that my supervisor has scheduled me for a conference in Atlanta three weeks from now as well. I'll check the dates, but it's all expenses paid, so if you don't want to stay with Kirsten and Everett, you're welcome to stay in the hotel with me," she said, flashing a big, pretty smile.

"No, I definitely don't want to stay with Kirsten and Everett," he stated, and Melah laughed.

"Well, it's settled; we'll stay together then," she said.

They both figured it would do them some good to get away for a few days, especially since Melah's morning, noon, and night sickness seemed to be finally wearing off.

"I'd love to stay with you."

"Good! I'm very happy you're going," she said, snuggling up under his arm.

"You are? I thought you hated me!"

Melah kissed his cheek. "No, I could never hate you. I know I've been in such a bad mood lately."

"Yeah, you have. You were killing me, Mel," Daniel responded with a half grin.

"Well, believe it or not, your love for me did not go unnoticed. I really appreciate you staying by my side and I forgive you for getting me knocked up," she said, giggling.

Daniel hadn't seen Melah giggle in a while.

Abruptly, she stopped right in the middle of her laughter.

"Thank you," she said, with tears in her eyes.

Daniel could tell the subject had changed and he wanted to ask, "For what?" but he already knew she was thanking him for going to the abortion clinic with her.

"Anytime you need me, I'll be here for you, Mel. Whether I agree with you or not."

"Yeah, I know," she responded, as she turned and continued to watch the movie. Then all of a sudden, she started taking off her clothes. Daniel looked around the room as if they were in high school, skipping class, and was almost caught by a teacher. It had been a while since he'd seen Melah naked; he almost felt uneasy about the whole thing and started to ask her what she was doing, but then he thought, *What? Are you crazy? You know exactly what she is doing and she should not be stopped!*

Melah didn't seem to have any hesitations, as she stripped down to nothing, still watching the movie, and not saying a word to Daniel. He looked down at Melah's small budging belly and he wondered if sex would hurt the baby, but he quickly pushed those thoughts aside as Melah laid her body on his.

"I've missed you so much," Melah whispered.

Well, I sure couldn't tell, he thought, but he dared not ruin the mood by saying it out loud.

"I missed you too, Mel." he said, as he gently caressed her back. "Don't ever go away from me again," he requested, as he turned the television off and made adoring love to Melah like it was their very first time.

CHAPTER

Three weeks soon passed, and Melah and Daniel packed their bags and headed to Atlanta. When they checked into the hotel room, Melah flopped down on the bed.

"I'm so tired, honey. This baby is kicking my butt," she said laughing.

Daniel smiled. This was the first time Melah joked about being pregnant.

"You look so beautiful. I love seeing you pregnant."

"Yuck! Why?"

"Why?" Daniel asked with a frown. "I think all pregnant women are gorgeous, but the pregnant woman in front of me is the most beautiful of them all."

Melah let out a huge holler!

"Yeah, right! You're just trying to get laid and I'm the only woman around."

"Well, yeah! That would be nice too," Daniel said, laughing. "But seriously, Mel. Pregnant women have a special glow about them."

"Nah, that's just the fat radiating off of us. There's no glow."

Daniel threw his hands up in the air.

"I can't even give you a compliment. If I would've said you're fat, you would have tried to kick me out of this room."

"Yep! That is true!" Melah said, growling, then letting out a loud laugh.

"So, are you dropping me off for my training or am I dropping you off?" Daniel asked.

"Your choice, but I'd hate to run into that Mandy girl because—"

"You still remember Mandy? Please forget about her."

"Of course I still remember Mandy and I'm going to beat her with my belly if she tucks any more notes in your pocket," Melah replied, rubbing her stomach, which was now starting to look like a soccer ball.

"Mel, you're really starting to show."

"Yeah, I know. I'm three months now. I guess we should go ahead and start telling our families, huh?"

Daniel's eyes got big.

"You're gonna keep the baby?" he asked, as he sat on the bed beside her.

"Well, what choice do I have? I obviously flunked the abortion test," she answered, with a slight grin.

Daniel returned the grin, except his seemed to cover

his entire face.

"You didn't flunk, Mel; it was a lot to take in. It was overwhelming for me as well, but I'm very happy that you're keeping the baby," he said, as he touched Melah's stomach.

"Yeah, I was thinking about it all last week. Ya know, sometimes you just can't plan these things. I believe God's will has been done," Melah said, looking up to the ceiling.

Daniel looked up to the ceiling too, thinking there was a bug or something up there.

Melah laughed. "Why are you looking at the ceiling, silly?"

"Oh, I thought something was up there," he said, laughing. "Melah, when did you start believing in God?"

"Daniel, I'm appalled! I've always believed in God. I'm just not very religious, that's all, but I think I'm ready to learn a little more about Him."

"Oh, I can teach—"

Melah put her hand in front of Daniel's mouth.

"Oh, no! You can't teach me anything about God. You were right there with me, sinning. I need to talk to someone who's practicing what they preach."

"That hurts, Mel," Daniel responded. "Okay, maybe I'm not the best candidate to tell you about God. I know I don't live a Godly life, but, I'm going to get it right. We can start going to church. We'll become a family."

"Whoa, Einstein! Slow your roll. Don't try to rush my spirituality or my relationship commitment. Allow me to get there at my own pace, please. Geez! I'm just in the baby-acceptance stage. I'm not ready to take any more plunges just yet, but maybe going to church every now and then won't be so bad."

"Okay," Daniel said, smiling. "I'd like that."

"Well good. That settles it then; we'll find a church to attend services once a year," Melah said, laughing. "I'm just kidding. We will go to church more than once a year, unless they start getting on my nerves, then it'll be once every two to three years," she said, laughing some more.

Daniel smiled. "Okay, Mel. Now let's get some rest. We both have big days planned tomorrow," he said, turning out the lights.

"Okay. Goodnight, babe."

"Goodnight, Mel."

The next morning they both got up, got dressed and hurried downstairs to eat breakfast at the hotel.

"I love free food," Melah said.

"Hmmm. At this point, you love any kind of food," Daniel replied.

Melah rolled her eyes.

"Whatevvvvv," she said. "So, you're dropping me off, right?"

"Yeah, and I guess we better hurry up before we're both late."

"You're right. Let's go," she said, grabbing two bananas, an apple, a muffin, and a packet of hot chocolate.

"Melah, you just ate a huge breakfast," he said, looking like he was embarrassed.

"Stay in your lane, Daddy Yo! You were the one who did this to me, so just be glad my food expenses aren't coming out of your pocket."

"Yet!" Daniel chimed in.

Melah twisted her mouth. "Yes, not yet, so be grateful."

Daniel laughed as they walked to the car to leave for work. When Daniel started the car, the radio came on.

"OH THIS IS MY JAM!" Melah screamed, as she turned up the volume.

Daniel gave her a weird look.

"Please don't act like you've never heard this before," she said, as she started singing along with Luther Ingram.

♪ ♪ ♪ If loving you is wrong, I don't want to be right. If being right means being without you, I'd rather live a wrong-doing life. Your momma and daddy say it's a shame. It's a down right disgrace— ♪ ♪ ♪

♪ ♪ ♪ But as long as I got you by my side, I don't care what your people say— ♪ ♪ ♪ Daniel said, jumping in and interrupting Melah's solo.

"Uh! Excuse you, Mr. Intruder! This is my song!" she said to Daniel, with an evil glare.

"Oh, I thought you were singing to me, because you want me so bad," Daniel said, laughing.

Melah let out a deep breath.

"Are we almost there?"

"Nope, about five more minutes. Plenty of time to finish singing our song."

Melah laughed and decided it wouldn't hurt to let Daniel sing along with her, so that's what they did until they reached the building where she was going for her conference.

"Mel, do you have money for lunch? I'm honestly not sure if I'll be able to come back to take you anywhere," Daniel said, as Melah got out of the car.

Melah gave him a dirty look.

"Oh, now you don't want to feed me?" she asked.

Daniel laughed.

"Of course I want to feed you, but I just don't know if I'll be able to leave at the same time you're leaving for lunch. Here's thirty dollars. Do you think you can eat for two with this?"

Melah snatched the money really quickly.

"I sure will give it my best shot, Mr. Stine," she said, as she got out of the car, closed the door, and walked off. "Later gator," she shouted, waving to Daniel as he watched her walk.

"Later, Mel," he replied, with a smirk on his face.

When Daniel arrived at Mr. Cross' office, he wasn't there, so Daniel decided to grab some of the accounting books and read over the company's policies and procedures while he waited.

"I just can't seem to get rid of you, huh?" Mr. Cross said, sternly as he walked into the office.

"I didn't know you still wanted to."

"Of course I still want to get rid of you. You're making me look bad, coming in here with your fancy degree, and your shirt and tie and all. No young kid should know this much about accounting!"

Daniel threw up his hands.

"Mr. Cross, I thought we were past all of that. I thought we bonded last time I was here."

"Yeah, yeah! Sit down and let's get to work. Nobody has time for all that mushy stuff."

"Okay, well I guess there's no need for me to ask you how you've been doing, huh?"

"Nope, there sure isn't," Mr. Cross said, as he shuffled through some papers.

It was almost as if Mr. Cross had forgotten all about what happened last time Daniel was there.

Oh, no he didn't! I consoled this grown man while he was crying like a baby and now he's acting like he barely even knows me. I feel used. I'm not his sidekick. He's gonna respect me. I'm worth more than that! Daniel thought, wanting to burst out into laughter.

Mr. Cross looked over at Daniel, who had a huge smile on his face.

"What are you smiling about?" Mr. Cross asked, sounding aggravated.

Daniel let out a small laugh.

"Nothing, I was just thinking about something that was fun—"

"Mr. Stine, are you here to work or to keep yourself entertained?"

"I'm here to work, Mr. Cross. I'm ready whenever you are," Daniel responded, trying not to get Mr. Cross upset.

They went over all the accounting numbers from the different companies and soon it was time for lunch. Just like last time, Mr. Cross acted like he didn't know what time it was, but this time, Daniel was ready for him. He took out a sandwich that he got from the cafeteria on his way into the building and started eating it while still working on the accounting books. Mr. Cross looked over at him, but he didn't say a word. Mr. Cross' stomach started growling and it was obvious that he desperately needed to eat something as well.

"Do you need to take a break for lunch, Mr. Cross? I know you normally don't go to lunch, but—"

"You think you're smart don't you?"

"No, I just don't understand why you dislike me so much. Your stomach is turning flips over there, but you'd rather starve just to make me suffer. I'm already eating my sandwich, so you're really the only one who's suffering. I think we can make a powerful team, Mr. Cross if you allow me to be on your team."

"I run solo," he responded, getting up from his chair and walking off. "Just meet me back in here in an hour."

"Okay, enjoy your lunch," Daniel said, but Mr. Cross just made a grunting noise.

Daniel decided to step outside and give Melah a call.

"Hey, babe. Are you still on your lunch break?" he asked.

"Yeah, but I only have about three minutes left. How's your training going?"

"It's going. I can't figure this guy out. I thought he liked me, now he acts like he hates me again. Kinda like you, Mel, except, I know I didn't get him pregnant," Daniel said, laughing.

"And I bet that's why he doesn't like you, because you think you're so funny."

Daniel laughed some more.

"So how's your conference?" he asked

"It's fine, but Mr. Jack, my head boss is here. I had no idea he was coming. He keeps talking to me, but it's weird, Daniel. I can't explain it, but he doesn't understand personal boundaries."

"What do you mean?"

"Well, every time he talks to me, he touches me. It's really weird and creepy."

"Oh, I see. I'll be over there in a few minutes."

"Stop it, Daniel. Don't you dare come over here."

"Well, he better get off of you then. He's throwing out bait, Mel. He's trying to see if you're gonna bite. I guarantee he's going to ask if you want to go to dinner with him tonight or he's going to try to find out what hotel room you're staying in."

"Oh my gosh! He already has. He said he tried to get in the same hotel that I was in, but they were all booked, then he asked if I was busy later this afternoon. I told him yes, I was going to be very busy. He creeps me out, Daniel. How did he even know what hotel I was in?"

"Mel, if he's your head boss, he can find out what hotel you're staying in. I don't like the fact that he's being inappropriate with you. I have a big problem with that."

"Yeah, so do I. Well, I have to go, babe. We'll talk later."

"Okay and just try to keep your distance from this guy before I have to punch him in the throat. You know I took karate lessons. I'd hate to go to jail, Mel."

Melah laughed.

"Bye, silly!"

"Bye, babe!"

Melah hung up the phone and headed back into the conference.

"Hey, Melah, you can come sit at the VIP table with me," her boss said as she was walking into the room.

"Where did you come from? I didn't even see you standing there, but no thanks, I'm not VIP status."

"Sure you are. Besides, you can be my date for the day," he said laughing.

Melah gave him faint smile.

"Neither my boyfriend nor your wife would like that."

"Oh, you have a boyfriend, huh? Well in that case, you can be my work partner," he said, chuckling.

"But you're my boss. I don't think I can be any kind of partner to you," she said, with a serious face.

"Very well then!" he said, raising his hands in the air as if he understood that she was totally off limits. "You're still free to enjoy the VIP perks. Our meals are better and we get lots of extra snacks and goodies. One of the guys didn't show up, so please take his seat."

Melah really didn't want to sit with him, but since she had made it very clear that there wasn't going to be anything between them, she figured it wouldn't hurt to enjoy the life of VIP, and especially all the free food that came along with it.

For the remainder of the day, Mr. Jack seemed to be on his best behavior and Melah was starting to feel a little more comfortable around him. He introduced her to several other "big wigs" and Melah enjoyed all the networking she was doing. She rubbed her belly and let out a sigh.

I just wish I could get my career established before I start having kids. I had really hoped to—

Just then, she looked down and noticed she had a text from Daniel. "Tell him I will punch him in the face if he puts even one greasy paw on you," was all the text said.

She couldn't help but laugh, and she didn't bother to respond. She knew Daniel only sent the text to make himself feel like he was in charge and she dared not ruin it by telling him he wasn't.

The rest of the day went fairly smoothly for both Melah and Daniel. Well, as smooth as can be expected given the fact that they both seemed to be dealing with coo-coo birds at work. The good thing was they were planning to try to have dinner with Kirsten and Everett that night. Melah was very excited to finally meet them, but first she needed a snack and a nap, and as soon as they got back to the hotel room, she had both.

"Goodnight, Mel. I'm going to call Kirsten. I'll wake you up in about an hour," Daniel whispered, opening the door to leave.

"Okay," she grumbled, as he closed the door behind him.

CHAPTER

"Buzzzzz, Buzzzzzzz, Buzzzzzz," Kirsten heard just as she was stepping into her house. She looked down at her phone vibrating and saw that it was Daniel calling.

"Hey, Daniel," she said.

"Hey, what are you guys doing tonight?"

"Nothing really. Everett wants me to cook this new recipe he saw online; it's some Indian Cuisine. I just bought all of the ingredients. I sure hope it turns out okay because I don't know what I'm doing. I wanted to ask him, 'Do I look like I know anything about Indian food?' but I decided to give it a try. He can eat it at his own risk," Kirsten said, laughing.

Daniel laughed too, and said, "I'm sure it will turn out fine. Mel and I are in town and we wanted to take you guys out to dinner tonight, but since you're cooking—"

"Well, why don't you come over here and we can all die from my cooking?"

"Ummm, how about I ask Melah if she will help you and maybe between the two of you, we can come up with a meal that's edible."

"That will be great. I'll definitely take all the help I can get, but you may want to make sure she wants to help first."

"Oh, she loves to cook. She won't mind. Ya know, that's really how she and I started dating, but I'll tell you that story later," Daniel said, laughing.

"Okay, maybe during dinner you guys can share your love story."

"Haha, yeah. Maybe," Daniel said.

"So, I'll see you guys around 6:00 pm?" Kirsten asked.

"Sounds good," Daniel responded right before saying goodbye.

Since his conversation with Kirsten only lasted a few minutes, Daniel decided to go hang out in the hotel lobby so he wouldn't disturb Melah's nap.

"Oh, a Western movie is on! Whoop! Whoop!" Daniel said, sitting down and making himself comfortable. The guy at the front desk came over and started making small talk, seemingly desperate to talk to anyone who would listen.

Dude, I'm trying to watch the movie. Beat it! Daniel thought, as he tried to ignore the guy, but he continued to stand there talking about everything he could think of. Just as Daniel was about to come up with a reason to leave, the guy brought out pictures of his wife and daughter.

"Here's a picture of my little Rachel. She's three and boy I tell ya, she's my everything," he said to Daniel.

Daniel looked down at the photo.

"She's beautiful, man. I know you must be very proud of her," he responded, thinking about the baby Melah was carrying. "So, what was it like when your wife was pregnant? Was it hard to deal with?" Daniel asked.

"Oh, no! Pregnancy was wonderful. Well, initially, it was a little rough because she was sick a lot, but after that, it was smooth sailing. Around five months, we started seeing the baby kick, and that was awesome, but seeing your baby being born is by far the most amazing and surreal thing a man could ever experience. There's nothing like it! I don't understand how a man can intentionally miss the birth of a person he helped create. I wouldn't have missed that for anything in the world."

"Really?" Daniel asked. "I've honestly never even thought about it like that."

"I'm telling you, there's nothing in this world like it. Think about it; it's a real live person living inside of another real live person. It's amazing, man! Then when the baby comes out, you see those little hands and feet and that little sweet face looking up at you! Nothing like it! I take it you don't have any kids, huh? Well, when you get some, make sure you're there for their birth," he said, not waiting for Daniel to answer whether or not he had any kids.

"Okay, I'll make sure I'm there," Daniel responded, with a nervous grin.

"I'm telling you, you won't regret it," the man said, excitedly. "Well, I've done enough chitchatting. I've got to get back to the front desk. It was great talking to you!"

he said, shaking Daniel's hand and walking off.

"Yeah, same here," Daniel responded.

Daniel tried to go back to watching the movie, but his mind kept drifting to what his and Melah's baby was going to look like.

"I wonder if it will have my pointed nose," Daniel said, laughing out loud. He could feel himself getting anxious, and he tried to change his thoughts, but he just couldn't think of anything else.

"Melah should be up now, I'm going back to the room," Daniel said as he headed towards the elevator.

"Have a good day," the guy at the front desk said as Daniel passed by.

"Thanks, you too," Daniel responded, hopping on the elevator.

When Daniel opened the door to the room, Melah was sitting up in the bed watching television.

"Daniel, I'm starving!" she said.

"You're starving? But we have another hour before we're supposed to be at Kirsten's and she wants you to help her cook this Indian meal."

Melah let out a loud scream of laughter.

"Do you really think I'm about to wait an hour to go to their house and then take my butt in the kitchen and cook for another one to two hours? I will eat up all the furniture by the time the food is done. Besides, I don't even know how to cook Indian food. Why would you volunteer me to help her?"

"I didn't really volunteer you to—"

"Liar! You did volunteer, but we will be picking up

Chinese food on our way over there and that's what we will have for dinner."

Daniel laughed.

"That sounds great to me. Let me call Kirsten and tell her."

"Do you think she's going to be upset?" Melah asked, as if she was all of a sudden concerned about someone other than herself.

Daniel gave her a cold stare.

"Why are you looking at me like that?" she asked, as she laughed, then left to take a shower.

Daniel called to break the news to Kirsten. "Hey, Kirsten," he said. "This is Daniel."

"Hey, Daniel. Everett, this is Daniel on the phone," she yelled to Everett.

"What's up Dan, my man?" Everett yelled back.

"So, ummm, Melah wants to know if you guys just want us to pick up Chinese food on the way over. That way you guys won't have to try to cook something new and be disappointed if it doesn't turn out right. I know you really wanted to—"

"Oh, thank goodness! Yes! Please get some Chinese food. We'll pay you back when you get here," Kirsten blurted out. Then she yelled, "Everett, we're just gonna have Chinese food, okay, babe?"

Everett came running into the kitchen.

"Chinese food? What happened to my special Indian Cuisine meal you promised to fix for me?" he asked, in a whiny tone.

"Tell him to man-up and stop all that crying,"

Daniel said laughing.

Kirsten laughed too.

"So y'all are laughing at me, now?" Everett asked.

Kirsten put the phone on speaker so Everett could hear the conversation. Then she said, "Daniel told me to tell you to man-up and stop crying."

Everett responded, "Says the man who doesn't even watch sports."

"Well, we'll be there in about an hour, so you can put on all the sports you want while I eat my Shrimp Fried Rice."

"Daniel, leave my husband alone. He's sad about his meal. I'll make it up to you baby," Kirsten said, turning to Everett and giving him a kiss.

"Daniel, get off the phone with my wife, so she can make this meal up to me before y'all get here," Everett said.

"Is that all you guys do in your spare time?" Daniel asked, shaking his head.

"Man, I waited eight months to be with my wife, so you better believe that's all we do," Everett said.

"EVERETT!" Kirsten yelled.

"Wow! Y'all waited eight months before y'all had sex? That's pretty impressive. How were you able to do that? I think me and Melah waited two days," Daniel said, laughing.

"DANIEL, I KNOW YOU DIDN'T JUST TELL THEM THAT!" Melah screamed as she came out of the bathroom.

Daniel's eyes got big.

"Yeah, keep talking trash, bruh," Everett said, laughing.

Kirsten was laughing so hard, she had pretty much walked off and left the phone on the counter.

"Okay, we'll see y'all in about an hour," Daniel said, hurrying off the phone.

"That's what you get," Everett retorted, as he hung up.

He and Kirsten laughed some more and hoped that Daniel didn't get into too much trouble, but when Daniel and Melah arrived an hour later, everything seemed to be fine. Melah gave Kirsten and Everett a hug like she had known them all her life.

Kirsten was very grateful that they rescued her from having to cook. She grabbed the bags, then she and Melah began to set the table, while Everett and Daniel continued to talk trash to each other.

"I swear those two act like brothers," Kirsten said.

Melah smiled, "Yeah, they do."

"So how long have you guys been dating?" Kirsten asked Melah.

"Seven months."

"Oh wow!" Kirsten responded, as if that was a long time. "By the time Everett and I hit our seven-month mark, we were both ready to pull our hair out," she said, laughing.

Melah gave her a weird look.

"Why?"

Kirsten hesitated. She didn't want to bring the subject up again about she and Everett waiting until marriage to have sex, and she definitely didn't want to get

Daniel into any more trouble for telling that he and Melah only waited two days.

"Why?" Melah asked again.

"Because we didn't have sex until after we got married. It was rough, let me tell ya!"

Melah looked down at the floor.

"I wish we would have waited, then I wouldn't be in the predicament I'm in right now," she said.

Kirsten gave her a funny look.

"What do you me—"

"Hey, ladies! Are y'all gonna feed us or what?" Everett said, as he and Daniel came into the kitchen, interrupting the conversation.

"Yes! Let's eat. I'm starving," Melah responded, and they all sat and gobbled down their food like they hadn't eaten in weeks.

After dinner they sat around and talked. Daniel and Kirsten talked about what it was like when they were growing up and how Daniel's dad moved into an all-black neighborhood by mistake.

"Daniel, you never told me that story before," said Melah.

"Yes, I did! I told you I lived in a black neighborhood for four years."

"Yeah, but you didn't say it was a mistake!"

"Oh! Well, it was. When my dad was growing up, it was an all-white neighborhood and there was a house he always loved and said he was going to buy one day when he could afford it. Well, when he graduated high school, he went into the military, but when he moved back home, he saw the house was for sale. He was so excited and without even thinking, he put a down payment on it and within three weeks they were closing. He had no idea that all the white people had moved out. When we moved in, I was just starting Kindergarten and my sister, Roslyn was just starting high school. My mom already knew Kirsten's mom from their younger days, so of course they loved the thought of being neighbors, but as soon my dad started noticing that all his neighbors were black, he flipped out. Oh, y'all should have seen the look on his face; it was priceless. He immediately tried to put the house back on the market, but he wasn't going to get out of it what he paid. Roslyn and Kirsten had become good friends, so she and my mom ganged up on my dad and he decided to just stay there until Roslyn graduated high school, but as soon as she graduated, we were gone. My mom was so angry with him."

"Wow," Kirsten said. "I had no idea that's why you guys moved right after Roslyn and I graduated."

"Yeah, and I survived, but all the guys in the neighborhood hated me. It was the longest four years of my life."

Kirsten laughed.

"Melah, don't believe a word he says. All the guys in the neighborhood liked Daniel; I never once heard them call him a racial slur. It was only when he started talking trash that they wanted to beat him up, and Daniel talked trash all the time."

"Hmmm, I see some things never change," Everett interjected.

Melah and Kirsten laughed.

"I had to talk trash or else I was going to get my butt kicked and I'm too pretty to die," Daniel said.

"Oh gosh!" Melah responded.

"And my baby is going to be pretty just like his daddy," Daniel said, reaching over to rub Melah's belly, then he quickly snatched it back, hoping no one had noticed.

Kirsten and Everett looked at each other.

"Ummm, is there something y'all wish to sh—"

"So, Daniel, the only reason your dad wanted to leave the neighborhood was because he found out that there were all blacks living there?" Melah asked, cutting Kirsten off. "Was the neighborhood bad or anything? Surely there had to be another reason he left."

"Nope! That was pretty much it," Daniel replied.

"But, Daniel, I'm black," Melah said, sounding upset.

"Yeah, Mel! I noticed that."

"If your dad didn't want to live in a good, safe neighborhood just because he found out that all black people lived there, then there is no way he's going to accept me or our child."

"I KNEW IT!" Kirsten screamed, but Melah and Daniel both ignored her.

"Congratulations, you guys! How far along are you, Melah?" Kirsten asked, trying to find out all she could about the baby.

"Daniel, he's going to flip out again when he finds out about me," Melah said, totally ignoring Kirsten's question.

"No, he's not, babe. My dad is cool. That was a long time ago," Daniel said, trying to comfort Melah, but she, Kirsten, and Everett all gave him a blank stare and Melah twisted her lips.

"Nah, man! Your pops is not going to be okay. I'm just saying," Everett chimed in.

Daniel made it obvious that he did not want Everett's opinion, so Everett decided to be quiet.

Kirsten wanted so badly to ask about the baby again, but she knew it was no use. She really hated that Daniel even brought the story up, because it had really changed the entire atmosphere, and Melah looked like she was about to go into emotional breakdown mode.

"Well guys, I think we'll probably head back to the hotel. It was great seeing you," Daniel said, as he got up from the table. "If possible, we'll try to get together again before we leave."

Melah tried not to show how upset she was, but she wasn't very good at camouflaging her feelings.

"It's going to be okay," Kirsten whispered to her. "Call me if you need to talk. I really want to hear all about your bundle of joy too."

"Okay, thank you," Melah responded, as she hugged Kirsten goodbye and said good night to Everett.

As Daniel and Melah were leaving, Everett whispered, "Sorry man, you should have waited until y'all got married."

Daniel looked back at Everett, "Shut up! Your jokes aren't funny, man."

Kirsten elbowed Everett in his side.

"Ow! What did you do that for? Daniel knows I'm just trying to lighten the tension up a little bit."

Daniel looked back at Everett and said, "Keep your day job man. Comedy is not your thing. Bye, Kirsten. Thank you guys for inviting us over."

"Yes! Thank you guys for the invite," Melah yelled from the car.

"How could she even hear us?" Everett asked.

"Oh, I hear everything," Melah responded with an evil grin.

"She really does man, but it's mainly because she's eavesdropping all the time," Daniel responded.

"You better hush, man, you're already in trouble," Everett said.

"I can't be in trouble for something my daddy did eighteen years ago. I was in Kindergarten."

"Yes, you can," Melah responded.

Kirsten and Everett laughed and waved goodbye as Daniel and Melah drove off and headed back to the hotel.

Daniel was hoping he could have a peaceful ride back to the hotel, but he wouldn't be so lucky.

"Daniel, why would you even date a black girl, knowing how your dad feels about blacks?" Melah asked.

"Mel, my dad is cool. He's going to like you. You'll see. He's not racist. It's just how those times were back then. He's never really said anything too harsh about blacks."

Melah gave him a crazy look.

"Too harsh?" she asked.

"Mel, that happened a long time ago. He'll be totally fine with us dating and he'll be very happy about the baby. If you don't believe me, I'll take you to meet them next weekend. You'll see that he's not racist. Now, your brother, on the other hand, he's the racist."

"My brother is not—well, maybe he is a little, but a brother is different than a dad."

"My dad will love you and I can't wait for him to meet you."

"Really? Aww, that's sweet, baby. I can't wait to meet him too—I guess," Melah said, nervously.

Daniel was very happy that Melah had calmed down, because the only thing he wanted to do when they got back to the hotel room was go to bed, and as soon as they got to the room, that's exactly what he did.

"Goodnight, Mel," he said, as he turned off the lights.

"Goodnight, John Boy," Melah responded, giggling, then rolling over and giving him a kiss. She kissed him again, and again, and again.

"Melah, is there something you want from me?" he asked, suspiciously.

"Yes!" she said, smiling.

"But, I don't want to hurt the baby, Mel."

"Really, Daniel? This baby is closed off in a dungeon. There is no way you're gonna hurt him."

"Him? Do you know what we're having?"

"No, silly and you are really ruining the mood. Goodnight," she said, turning her back towards Daniel.

"Wait, Mel. I want to, but I just need to know how

it affects the baby, that's all. I'm ready now."

"The mood has passed. You ruined it," she said, closing her eyes.

"Are you sure? Maybe we can start over."

"Nope! It's ruined."

"Darn it! Well, let's definitely revisit this in the morning, okay?"

"Yeah, yeah!" Melah responded, as Daniel gave her a kiss goodnight, then immediately went into a deep sleep.

Melah turned back over and looked at him snoring. "Men!" she said, then dozed off into a deep sleep as well.

CHAPTER

The next morning when Daniel got to work, Jason called him into his office.

"Hey, Daniel! Come in and have a seat."

"Hey, Jason."

"How's it going? Is Mr. Cross treating you well?"

"Yes, Mr. Cross is great!"

Lord, please forgive me for the lie I just told, Daniel thought.

"Well, good! Mr. Cross always speaks very highly of you."

Daniel gave him a frown.

I don't know why Mr. Cross is being so fake; he knows he hates my guts! I wonder if he has a split personality. One minute he's trying to starve me to death, the next he's crying on my shoulder, then he's telling me how I think I'm better than him because I have a degree. The man is looney—

"Daniel, are you okay? You seem to be in a daze." Jason said, taking Daniel out of his deep thoughts.

Daniel laughed. "Oh, I'm sorry. I guess I drifted off."

"Well, I know I'm boring, but at least pretend for me, man," Jason said, laughing. "Anyway, the reason I called you in here was to see if you wanted to go out with me and few guys tonight. We'll meet at my restaurant around 6:30."

"Yes! Definitely count me in," Daniel said, excitedly.

"Do you still remember how to get there?"

"Yeah, I think the address is still in my GPS."

"Okay, great. I'll see you later on tonight then."

"Sounds good. Thanks for the invite," Daniel replied, as he walked out of Jason's office.

"Oh, Daniel. I'll be out of the office for the rest of the day, so if you need anything, you'll have to call my cell phone."

"Okay. Thank you, Mr. Glaz—I mean, thank you, Jason."

"There you go! You're getting the hang of it," Jason responded.

Daniel laughed as he continued down the hallway to see what personality Mr. Cross was going to showcase for him today.

"Ya know, tardiness is a sign of weak mindedness," Mr. Cross said as Daniel walked in his office.

"Oh, get off your high horse," Daniel replied, without even thinking.

"Excuse me?" Mr. Cross said.

"I'm sorry. I didn't mean to say that. It just kinda slipped out," Daniel said, trying to explain himself. "Sorry I'm late. I was in Jason's office. He stopped me in the hallway and asked how things were going."

"Oh!" Mr. Cross said, changing his entire tone. "Did he ask you anything about me?" Mr. Cross asked, fearfully.

"Ummm, yeah! He wanted me to help plan your going away party this week. Man, I sure hate you're leaving us so soon, Mr. Cross. I thought I had a few more months to train with you."

"Going away party? I'm not having a going away party! I don't leave for another four or five months," Mr. Cross mentioned, nervously.

"Ooops!" was all Daniel said as he grabbed a notepad and a pen.

"Are they firing me?" Mr. Cross asked, then all of a sudden his face turned red, then blue, then purple. Next thing Daniel knew, Mr. Cross was lying on the floor unconscious.

"Mr. Cross! Mr. Cross!" Daniel yelled. "Oh, No!"

Daniel screamed for someone to call 911, but no one seemed to hear him. He ran to the phone and dialed it himself, while continuing to scream down the hallway for someone to come help. He was trying to talk to the 911 dispatcher, yell for help, and keep Mr. Cross alert all at the same time.

"SIR!" the dispatcher shouted. "Don't worry about anyone else but me. I need you to calm down, please!" she

Why Keep Us Divided?

said to Daniel, but all he could think about was how he didn't want to be accused of murdering Mr. Cross.

The ambulance finally made it to the building, then all of a sudden everyone started running outside to see what was going on.

"I've been yelling for you guys for the past fifteen minutes. Where were you?"

"We were all in training downstairs. Why weren't you in there?" they asked.

"Because Mr. Cross passed out!" he said, irritably.

Just as all of this was going on, Kirsten called.

"Hey, Kirsten. I'm so glad you called. Can you please come get my car and take it to Melah? Mr. Cross is heading to the hospital and I need to go with him."

"Daniel, I'm not—"

"Not now, Kirsten. I have to go. Melah needs to get the car. Please!"

"Ummm, okay. I'll see what I can do."

"Please, Kirsten," he said frantically, as he hopped into the ambulance and headed to the hospital with Mr. Cross.

"Uggggghhhh! Come on, Mandy. I need you to help me get Daniel's car and take it to his girlfriend," Kirsten said, in an aggravated tone.

"Oh, you mean my Daniel?"

"Nevermind, I'll call Everett," Kirsten responded, walking back into her office to give Everett a call, but his phone just rang and rang and rang.

"Dang it! He's probably out mowing lawns!" Kirsten said, throwing the phone in the chair.

"Well, I'm still available," Mandy said as she stood in the door, watching Kirsten stressing over going to Jason's workplace.

"I don't want to go over there! Why do I have to be the one to go over there?" she asked right before receiving a text from Daniel.

"Oh, Kirsten, can you please go in Mr. Cross' office and get my wallet off of the desk? The keys should be there too. No worries, Jason is out of the office for the rest of the day. Thank you so much. I know this is awkward for you, but I wouldn't ask if I didn't need you," he said.

"Yeah, yeah! Whatever! Let's go, Mandy," she said, and she and Mandy hurried out the door.

"Mandy, you can drive my car and I'll drive Daniel's car."

"Oh, that's too bad. I was looking forw—"

"I'm not in the mood, Mandy," Kirsten said, shaking uncontrollably.

Mandy gave her a scary glare. "Mrs. Larson, why are you shaking so bad? We're just going to get a car. I'm not riding anywhere with you until you calm down."

"Okay, I'm calm," Kirsten said, grabbing a paper bag and breathing inside of it.

"Ummm, call me when you've pulled it together," Mandy said, walking back to her desk.

"No, I'm fine! I just needed to take a few deep breaths. I'm fine! Really! Let's go."

"Okay, but I'm driving," Mandy demanded.

"Great! Thank you, Mandy. I really appreciate it."

Why Keep Us Divided?

"No problem. I knew one day you would need me," Mandy said, smiling.

Kirsten didn't bother to dispute it, because she did in fact need Mandy. They hopped in the car and drove over to Jason's company. When they got there, Kirsten got out of the car and looked up at the building. It brought back so many memories of her and Jason's relationship. She just stood there in a daze.

"Mrs. Larson, are you going to get the car?" Mandy asked.

"Oh, yes! Sorry, Mandy. This is just a really nice building."

"Yeah, much prettier than the piece of junk we work in," Mandy said, laughing.

"Mandy, I have to go inside to get Daniel's wallet and keys, then we can take the car to his girlfriend," Kirsten said, not returning the laughter.

"Okay," Mandy responded.

As Kirsten hurried into the building, Jason pulled up into the parking lot. He came back to talk to all of his people about Mr. Cross' condition. They were all waiting patiently for him in the training room. The first thing he noticed was Kirsten's car. He parked beside it and continued to stare. Mandy anxiously rolled down the window.

"Hi," she said.

"Oh, hey," he responded. "I thought you were an old friend of mine. She has a car just like yours."

"Is her name Kirsten?"

Jason squinted his eyes, "Yeah, is she here?" he asked, surprisingly.

"Yeah, she went inside to get Daniel's wallet. We have to take his car to—"

"Ok, thanks. I gotta go," Jason said, running towards the building.

Meanwhile Kirsten was inside looking for Mr. Cross' office since no one was around to ask.

"Oh, here it is," she said, walking through the doorway. "Now, where is Daniel's wallet?" Kirsten said, looking frantically around the desk. "Oh, it's way over here by the window, geez!" Kirsten said, running over to grab Daniel's things, then heading back towards the door.

"God knows I miss you so much, Kirsten!" Jason said, as he stepped in the door, grabbed Kirsten and pinned her up against the wall. Kirsten was so shocked that her mouth flung open, but as she felt Jason's tongue down her throat, his hands all over her body, and one hand up her skirt, she quickly came to her senses and pushed him off of her. She slapped him as hard as she could.

"DON'T YOU EVER TOUCH ME!" she screamed and ran out of the building.

"Kirsten, I know you still love me, I can feel it," he said, as he watched her leave.

Kirsten ran to Daniel's car and drove off as fast as she could. Mandy didn't know what to think so she pulled off as fast as she could too. Kirsten was driving so frantically, that Mandy thought she was going to crash, but thank goodness, they both made it safely to the building where Melah was working. Kirsten got out of the car and asked Mandy if she would run the keys in to Melah.

"I'm just shaking too bad to go in there," Kirsten explained, hysterically. "I have to calm myself down."

"You sure do! But, yes, I'll take his girlfriend the keys," Mandy responded. "Mrs. Larson, are you gonna be okay?"

"Yeah, I'll be fine. Thanks, Mandy. I really owe you."

"Do you need a cigarette or something to help you calm down? Maybe some Jack Daniel's or Crown Royal? Vodka? Tequila? Something? You are stressed, Mrs. Larson."

Kirsten tried to give Mandy a smile, but there was nothing that could make her smile.

"No, Mandy. I don't need anything. When you go inside, just ask for her; her name is Melah Thompson. Someone should be able to help you."

"Okay, got it!"

Kirsten sat in the car wondering how she got herself into this situation. She wondered why it took her so long to push Jason off of her. She also wondered if deep down inside she actually enjoyed it. She wondered if she was just fooling herself by thinking she was in love with Everett and if she was not really over Jason like she kept proclaiming. She wondered a lot of things, but what she wondered most was if she should tell Everett what happened.

"There's no way he's going to understand that I didn't mean for any of this to happen. God, I just wish you would remove Jason from my life all together. I don't want to have to keep dealing with him! I'm so tired of him coming up in my marriage. God, please help me come to grips with what's really going on here, because I'm going to lose the best thing that has ever happened to me if I don't get rid of Jason."

While Kirsten sat there with tears rolling down her face, Mandy was about to encounter a surprise of her own.

"Melah Thompson, Melah Thompson, can you please come to the front desk," the receptionist called over the intercom per Mandy's request.

Mandy stood there, patiently waiting to get a good look at Melah, the girl Daniel would refuse to give her the time of day for.

"Hi, I'm Melah Thompson," Melah said to the lady at the front desk.

"Yes, this young lady is here to see you."

Melah gave Mandy a strange look.

"Who are you?" she asked, cordially.

"I'm Mandy, Daniel asked me to bring you his car," Mandy said, holding out Daniel's keys.

"Excuse me? Daniel asked you to do what?"

"To bring you his keys."

"How did you get his keys, Mandy?" Melah asked, angrily.

"Duh, I just told you that Daniel asked me to bring them to you."

"Uh! Is there a problem here?" the lady behind the desk asked.

"Nah, there's no problem," Mandy responded.

"Oh, there is a problem! I don't know who you think you are but you better stay away from my man," Melah said, pointing her finger in Mandy's face. "I saw the phone number you left in his pants pocket and I am nothing to play with. You do not want to mess with me. You—"

"You better get your hands out of—"

"Mandy, what are you doing?" Kirsten said, running in to diffuse the situation. She snatched Daniel's keys out of Mandy's hands and handed them to Melah, along with Daniel's wallet that she still had in her purse.

"Melah, Daniel asked me to go pick up the car and bring it to you because Mr. Cross had to go to the hospital. He rode went with him and didn't want you to be without a vehicle. Mandy only went with me to drive my car back," Kirsten said rolling her eyes at Mandy.

Mandy didn't bother to respond. She just turned and walked back to the car like she hadn't done anything wrong.

"I can't believe her," Kirsten said to Melah.

"Kirsten, you better keep that girl away from me before she comes up missing."

"I'm so sorry, Melah. I should have known better. Daniel does not want her, trust me!"

"He better not, because he was almost about to walk home," Melah said laughing.

"No! Please don't make him walk home. He's innocent," she said, giving Melah a hug.

"Okay, let me get back to this conference. I'll talk to you later, girl."

"Okay, bye," Kirsten said to Melah, then she turned to the receptionist. "Please forgive me. I did not know that was going to happen."

"It's okay, I'm just glad it got resolved, but between me and you, I don't blame Melah for letting her have it; I would have done the same thing."

Kirsten and the receptionist both laughed.

"Me too," Kirsten said, as she walked out the door.

CHAPTER

"Mandy! What in the world is wrong with you? Why would you go in there and pretend that Daniel asked you to bring Melah his keys? Just when I think you're changing, you revert right back to the woman I don't like and will never trust!" Kirsten said to Mandy, as she got in the car.

Mandy just sat there, silent, as if Kirsten wasn't talking to her.

"MANDY!" Kirsten yelled!

"Huh? Did you say something?" Mandy asked, taking out her earbuds.

"Oh, nevermind! Let's just go back to work," Kirsten said, furiously.

Mandy remained quiet; she dared not look in Kirsten's direction. She was hoping that her aloof attitude would keep her from having to hear Kirsten's mouth all the way back to the office. Mandy knew what she did was wrong, but the truth was, she got a kick out of making other women think their man wanted her, even if she knew they didn't. It somehow made her feel empowered. It made her feel beautiful and loved, which were two things Mandy never felt growing up. She enjoyed being the center of a man's attention, even if he was taken. It didn't matter who she hurt along the way or whose relationship she destroyed. "It's not my fault if a woman is not secure in her relationship," was Mandy's mentality, so day by day, month by month, and year by year, Mandy sought to be loved by any means she could, even if she knew it wasn't real love. It provided superficial happiness and to her that was enough.

Kirsten looked over at Mandy, who was beep-bopping to some song she was listening to on her iPod. Kirsten felt disgusted; she couldn't wait to get Mandy out of her car.

I can't believe I actually thought that things could change between me and Mandy. If nothing else, I thought we could at least develop a better working relationship, but now, I'm so done with her!

Kirsten wasn't sure how she was going to do it, but from that day forward, she vowed to have nothing else to do with Mandy, professionally or personally and speaking of wanting nothing to do with someone, Melah was ready to put her boss in that same category as well.

"Hey, where did you go?" Mr. Jack asked Melah when she returned to the conference. "Good thing we cut for a break because you would've missed something important," he said, sternly.

Melah tried hard not to roll her eyes or smack her lips. As politely as she could, she replied, "I just had to go up front for a minute, that's all."

"Why do you sound so dry, Melah? You must not have gotten any sleep last night, eh," he said, with one eyebrow raised and sniggering.

"No, I slept just fine. I'll see you in the conference, sir," she responded, professionally.

"I didn't offend you, did I?" he asked, with a slight grin on his face. "I wasn't sure if you met someone while you were here and he kept you up all night," he added, not concealing his grin at all this time. "So, are you sitting at my table when the break is over?"

"No, sir! I'm going back to my original seat, but thank you for the offer."

"Hmmm, don't want to sit by the boss, huh? That's a big strike, Melah," he said with a serious face, then let out a laugh. "I'm just messing with you. Go on in, I'll see you around," he said, patting Melah on the shoulder.

She quickly moved out of the way of his reach and hurried into the conference.

THAT MAN IS SO CREEPY! she screamed, with her inside voice. She could feel his eyes still on her as she walked away.

Greasy, dirty, old paws touching me! YUCK!!!! I can't stand him!

Melah made her way to her seat which was far away from Mr. Jack, but it didn't matter, because on every break, he somehow found his way to her. By the end of the day she was thoroughly stressed out and was unsure if she should inform her immediate supervisor of what was going on. She knew she was being harassed and she was not very happy about it, but she had just started working for this company and everyone loved Mr. Jack. She didn't want to cause any trouble for him or for herself.

It's fine. He never comes to our department, so after this conference is over, I'll be rid of him for good, she thought.

When the day ended, Melah scurried out of the conference, so Mr. Jack wouldn't try to talk to her. She raced to Daniel's car and sped off.

THANK GOODNESS! I'm finally outta there!

She grabbed the phone and called Daniel to see if he was still at the hospital.

"Hello," he whispered.

"Hey," she said, whispering too.

Daniel laughed. "Mel, you don't have to whisper."

She laughed. "So you're still at the hospital, huh?"

"Yeah, but Jason is here and so is Mr. Cross' family, so I can leave now. Thank goodness!"

"Why did you say it like that?"

"I'll tell you later, just hurry. I'm ready to leave."

"Okay, I'll be there as quickly as the GPS can get me there. You know I'm not from here."

"Yes, I know, just do the best you can, but hurry," he said laughing.

"Okay, I will. So, how's Mr. Cross?"

"He's fine. They're not sure what happened to him. They're going to keep him overnight to run some tests, but they say he looks fine."

"Good! I'm glad he's doing okay. Well, I'll see you shortly," Melah said. "Oh! And please remind me to tell you what that little skank did today," she added, angrily.

"Oh, no! I was hoping I'd never have to hear that word again."

"Well, I was hoping I'd never have to run into anymore skanks again, but apparently they all have a thing for you."

"Mel, what are you talking about?"

"Mandy! I'm talking about Mandy, the fast-tail skank!"

"Mandy?" I thought we squashed the Mandy subject. I told you, I didn't know she put her phone number in my pocket, Mel."

"No! She came to the conference and gave me your keys and when I—"

"Oh, My God!"

"Wait! There's more! When I asked her how she got them, she got smart with me and said you gave them to her."

"NO! I did not! I did not give her my keys. Kirsten was the one—"

"Well, it was a good thing Kirsten came running through the door with your wallet and calmed the situation down. She told me that she asked Mandy to ride with her so Mandy could drive her car back. She assured me that you made no contact with Mandy, but that is not the picture Mandy was painting."

"I can't believe she did that! I would never give her

access to my car or give her access to you, for that matter."

"Well, she almost got her face broken," Melah replied.

Daniel laughed.

"I'm glad you did not break anyone's face, Mel."

"Well, I almost did. Anyway, I'll be there in a few, okay?"

"Okay. Bye, baby."

When Melah pulled up to the hospital, Daniel was anxiously waiting for her outside.

"Hey!" she said, excitedly, jumping out of the driver's seat and giving him a kiss on the cheek.

"Hey! How was work, other than the stunt Mandy pulled?"

"Horrible!" she blurted, without even thinking. She paused. Melah knew that if she told Daniel the things Mr. Jack said, it was not going to go over well.

"What do you mean, horrible?"

"Oh, nothing! It was just boring, that's all," she responded, trying to sound convincing.

"So, was the creep bothering you again?" he asked.

"Well, yeah! He just kept talking to me. I don't think I like him, Daniel."

"Oh! I know I don't like him," Daniel replied. "Mel, you need to watch out for that dude! He likes you and if you're not careful, it's going to turn into sexual harassment."

It already has, she thought.

"I can handle it. Don't worry about him," Melah said, trying to reassure Daniel that everything was fine.

"Mark my words, Mel. This guy is going to be trouble."

"No, he's not! After this conference is over, I'll rarely see him anymore. He works in our building downtown and they never interact with us," Melah said.

"Okay, if you say so, but I don't trust him," Daniel responded. "Anyway, I need to stop by the store for a minute before we head back to the hotel."

"Uh, oh! The last time you needed to stop by a store, you came back with a pregnancy test," said Melah.

Daniel laughed.

"No, I'm pretty sure I don't need another one of those, but I do need some shaving cream."

"Okay, that's good, because if I take a pregnancy test, it's going to come up positive, ya know?"

"Yeah, I know, Mel. For the next six months it's going to be positive."

"Wow, Daniel. We only have six months before we become parents. That's kinda scary."

"Yeah, it definitely is," he said, soberly.

When they got to the store, Melah hopped out of the car too.

"Mel, I'm going straight to the razors and shaving cream, then I'm leaving. I don't want to be in here forever."

"Okay, that's fine," she said, but as soon as they got inside the store, Melah immediately became distracted by some baby items hanging on racks at the front of the store. Daniel just shook his head and kept walking. By the time he made it back up front to pay for his items, Melah had filled up a shopping cart with all kinds of baby stuff.

"Melah, c'mon. You're barely three months pregnant. Do you really need to buy all of this stuff right now?" he asked.

"Look as these cute booties and bibs, babe. Look! This one says, 'Daddy's little helper.' I've got to get it. They're all so—"

"Melah, are you expecting?" Mr. Jack asked surprisingly, as he walked up to Melah and Daniel.

They both stood there looking dumbfounded, but Daniel automatically knew who he was.

"Ummm," was all Melah managed to get out of her mouth as Mr. Jack waited like he felt entitled to an answer.

Melah let out a loud fake laugh. "Me? Pregnant? Oh gosh, that's funny. I was just looking at all of these baby clothes someone left in this shopping cart! If they didn't want them, they should have at least had the decency to put the clothes back on the rack," she said, shaking her head.

She looked over at Daniel as he gave her a *you Big Fat Liar* stare. She ignored him and looked back at Mr. Jack.

"I used to work at a Department store and I'm telling you, this was by far my worst pet peeve," she continued, taking the clothes out of the cart and hanging them back on the rack.

"Oh!" Mr. Jack said, sounding relieved. "Yeah, that's a lot of clothes they had there. Sir, can you tell me where the shoestrings are located?" he asked, looking over at Daniel.

"Unno, I don't work here!" Daniel said, as if he was offended.

"Oh, I'm sorry. I thought you were helping this young lady put these clothes back on the rack, plus you have on khaki pants, so I just assumed you—oh, nevermind. So, Melah, you're not planning to hang all of these clothes back up are you?" Mr. Jack asked.

"No, she is not, "Daniel chimed in, "Because I'm not standing here waiting while she does. Maybe the person who put them there will come back for them," he said, looking at Melah with a blank stare.

"Ummm, and who are you again?" Mr. Jack asked Daniel, as if he was irritated by his constant interruptions.

"I'm the good Samaritan's boyfriend," he said, pointing to Melah, as she was still pretending to hang up clothes.

Mr. Jack looked at Melah for some type of confirmation as to whether Daniel was telling the truth.

Daniel gave him a *mean-mugging gansta* look, so Melah decided she should speak up before things got out of hand.

"Yes, this is my boyfriend, Daniel Stine."

"Oh! I didn't know your boyfriend was up here with you."

"Yes, I am here," Daniel chimed in, hostilely.

"Well, good! Melah shouldn't be up here in the big city by herself. There are crazy people in this world, ya know. I'm Luis Jack," he said, reaching out and shaking Daniel's hand. "I'm over the company Melah works for and I'm protective of them just like a father," he said grinning. "It was great meeting you, Daniel, but I'll let you two love birds go now. Melah, since this was our last day at the conference, I guess I'll see you when we get back to the office," he said, waving good-bye and walking away.

Neither, Melah nor Daniel gave him much of a reply. Melah seemed very disappointed that Mr. Jack was planning to see her back at the office and Daniel was sure Mr. Jack was going to be nothing but trouble.

"I told you that dude is not going away," Daniel fussed.

"No, it doesn't look like he is, does it?"

"Nope," Daniel said, hurrying Melah to the checkout counter so he could buy his items and leave.

"Stop rushing me! I want to go back and get some of those things in the shopping cart."

Daniel pointed his finger at Melah like she was his child.

"No, Mel! I have a business dinner with Jason and some other guys tonight and I don't want to be late. We've already spent more time in here than we needed to," he said.

"A business meeting? That sounds like a bunch of men trying to find a reason to get drunk, party, and talk about women."

"Yes, it is, now can we please leave?" Daniel asked, touching Melah on her back.

"Don't push me," Melah responded.

"I just touched your back, Mel. I didn't push you."

"Well, you wanted to," she said.

Daniel didn't bother to respond because he knew

Melah was trying to pick a fight, so he wouldn't go out to dinner, but he wasn't falling for it. During the entire ride back to the hotel, Melah found reasons to complain about something. At first she was too hot, so Daniel turned the air conditioner on, then she was too cold, so he turned it off. Then she needed fresh air, so he let the window down.

You can do whatever you want but I am hanging out with the guys tonight. We are going to do guy things and talk about guy stuff and there's nothing you can do to stop me, he thought.

"I'm hungry! Can we stop and get me something to eat?" Melah asked.

"Mel, there's a restaurant in the hotel. Why can't you eat there?"

"Ewwww, they may not have what I want."

"What do you want?"

"A barbecue, bacon cheeseburger with American and pepper jack cheese, onion straws, lettuce, tomatoes, pickles, ketchup, mustard, blue cheese dressing, a side order of curly fries, with a baked potato, a fruit cup and a Pepsi with Mountain Dew and Sierra Mist mixed together."

"Oh, my gosh! That's insane! But, I saw their menu, and you can get all of that from the hotel restaurant. Just tell them you want to add all of that to your burger."

"But I'm hungry now, Daniel."

"We'll be at the hotel in less than five minutes."

Melah gave him an evil eye glance and sat quietly until they arrived at the hotel.

"Do you want me to order your burger for you?" Daniel asked as they pulled into the parking lot and headed inside the hotel.

"No! I'm not hungry," Melah said, heading straight for the elevator.

He smiled, "Come on, Mel. Every man needs to go out with his boys every now and then," he said, getting on the elevator behind her.

"You don't even know them. How are they your boys?"

"Well, you know what I mean," he said, as the elevator stopped on the second floor.

When Daniel opened the room door, he hurried into the shower. In record time, he had showered, gotten completely dressed, and was rushing back out of the hotel room like he had just been freed from prison.

"Just make sure you come back the same way you left" Melah yelled as Daniel blew her a kiss goodbye.

"Yes, mommy. I love you," he said, closing the door behind him and heading down stairs.

CHAPTER

As Melah sat on the bed, moping, her phone rang; it was Kirsten.

"Hello," Melah said, skeptically, not recognizing the phone number.

"Hey, Melah. This is Kirsten. Daniel told me to call and give you my number just in case you needed anything."

"Oh, did he now? He must feel sorry for me. Can you believe he left me to go have dinner at some jazz restaurant with a bunch of hard legs? I'm almost offended."

Kirsten laughed.

"Yes, and he told me you'd be pouting about it, so that's why I'm calling to cheer you up. Besides, men need that bonding time with other guys or "hard legs" as you call them. They need to know that a relationship hasn't changed them and taken away their manhood," Kirsten said, giggling.

"Their manhood? Really? It ain't that serious."

"Oh, it is to them and it's very important that we understand their need for that. You shouldn't give him a hard time for going out with his friends. Just trust him to make good decisions while he's out there."

"I do trust him. I don't think he would ever cheat on me, I just want him here with me."

"Clinginess is the best way to lose your man, dear. Give him all the freedom he needs. If you start questioning everything and getting angry about everything, it's only going to make him feel trapped and suffocated and although we can't imagine anyone needing a break from us, because we're so awesomely wonderful, they do need breaks. They are wild beasts and they need to run in the thicket of the woods, so they can feel free," Kirsten said, laughing.

"Okay, fine. I'll let him go run in peace."

"Good, now do you want to come hang out with me? Everett went straight to his mom's house after he was done with the yards, and when he goes over there, she gives him enough work to do for a whole year. I'll probably see him next week sometime."

Melah laughed.

"That's hilarious. Girl, Daniel is a momma's boy too. When he talks to his mom, he turns into a little 5-year old, but yeah, I'd love to come over, but I don't have a ride, remember."

"Oh, yeah, well do you want me to come there and

we'll go to dinner or something?"

"Okay, that sounds great. See you in a few."

"Okay, bye."

"Bye."

Melah tried her best not to eat up everything in sight while waiting for Kirsten to come.

As Kirsten was getting dressed, her mind kept drifting back to what happened between her and Jason. As bad as she wanted to get it out of her head, she couldn't help but think about it. She felt like it was all her fault and she feared that if she told Everett, he would blame her and say she should have never gone over there.

God, I love Everett so much. Please give me a sign if I should tell him what happened or not. Everett is the best thing that ever happened to me. I don't want to lose him. If I don't tell him and he finds out that Jason kissed me, I don't know what he will do. I don't even want to think about what he would do. God, please help me!

Just then the phone rang; it was Everett. Kirsten sat there staring at the phone like she had just seen a ghost. Her hands started shaking just like they were earlier that day.

"Uh, hello," she answered.

"Hey! I just saw that you tried to call me several times today. I got your messages. I'm really sorry I didn't answer. It was such a crazy, busy day!"

"Oh, that's okay. It worked out fine."

"So, Daniel needed you to come and get his car, huh? What happened to the man that passed out? Is he okay?"

"Yeah, I guess he's okay, because Daniel and some of his co-workers are all at dinner now. I'm gonna go have dinner with Melah. She's sitting in the hotel pouting. She said, 'Can you believe he left me to go have dinner at some jazz restaurant with a bunch of hard legs,'" Kirsten said, laughing. "You should have heard her, babe. She was pathetic."

"A jazz restaurant?"

"Yeah, you know that Blues and Jazz restaurant out by Lawrenceville."

"Oh, ok! So you went to get Daniel's car?"

"Yeah, Mandy and I went to pick it up, then we took it to Melah."

"Oh, how long did you have to stay there?"

"Not long. We just dropped it off with Melah and went back to the office."

"No, I mean, how long were you at Daniel's job?"

"Oh, not long at all."

"Oh, okay. So, you were able to just go get the car and leave?"

"Well, I—"

"So, are you going to answer my question before I ask or do you just want me to ask?" Everett said.

"What do you mean?" Kirsten asked, as her heart started beating profusely. She tried to tell herself to stay calm, but she didn't know what Everett was about to ask her and she didn't know how she was going to respond. She just had to trust God that everything would be okay.

"Did you see Jason while you were there?"

"Uh, Ummm, yeah! Briefly."

"Did he try to talk to you?"

"Everett, I don't want Ja—"

"Just answer the question, Kirsten."

"Yes, briefly."

"Is there anything else I need to know?"

"Ahhh, well, not—"

"Kirsten, why are you fumbling over your words? Would you like to go ahead and tell me what happened between you and Jason today?"

Kirsten put her hand over her head. It seemed like her heart was literally beating on the outside of her body.

"Everett, I love you more—"

"Just answer the question, please."

"Yeah. Something did happen, Everett."

"Okay, I'm listening," he said, calmly.

Kirsten took a deep breath and told Everett everything that happened between her and Jason, not leaving out one detail. After she was done, Everett sat on the phone totally quiet for at least three minutes.

"Everett?" Kirsten called out. "Please say something."

"Kirsten, let me ask you a question and I need you to be honest, okay?"

"Okay."

"Do you still love Jason?"

"No, I do not. That's the honest truth."

"Next question. When he kissed you, did you kiss him back in any shape or form?"

"NOOOOOOOO! I swear I did not kiss him back. I immediately pushed him off of me and I ran out of the building."

"So, how do you feel? Did it spark any unresolved issues or feelings?"

"No! I'm over Jason. I'm with the man I want and I would never do anything to jeopardize what we have," Kirsten explained desperately.

"But you weren't going to even tell me. I had to coax it out of you, Kirsten."

"That doesn't mean I wasn't going to tell you, Everett. I just didn't know how to tell you and I didn't want you doing anything crazy, so I needed to think through everything, that's all."

"There is a chance that you were going to keep this from me, and that bothers me, Kirsten, but we'll deal with that later. Go ahead and have dinner with Melah. I'll see you when you get home, okay?"

"Ummm, Everett, are you okay?"

"Yeah, I'm good. I have to go, but I'll see you later, okay?"

"Uh, okay."

"I love you," Everett said, hanging up the phone, not giving Kirsten the opportunity to respond.

Kirsten couldn't tell if Everett was really okay or not, but either way, she figured he'd be ready to rehash the entire thing when he got home. She was relieved that it was out in the open, though and for now, she was going to put it out of her head and try to enjoy her night out with Melah. She hurried and finished getting dressed, then headed out the door.

When she arrived at the hotel, she called Melah and

told her she was downstairs. Melah came out dragging her feet like she was 12 months pregnant.

"Girl, I can't believe you're pregnant. Are you excited?" Kirsten asked Melah, as she flopped down in the seat.

"Not really, but I can't go through with the abortion, so I might as well be excited."

"Abortion? Why would you want to have an abortion?" Kirsten asked as she drove off.

"Let me guess, you're religious too?" Melah asked, sarcastically.

Kirsten smiled.

"Yes, I'm spiritual, but I'm not judgmental. So what happened with the abortion?"

"I just couldn't go through with it, that's all. I felt sick to my stomach in that place; all those little girls in there with their moms. It was horrible, Kirsten. They shouldn't even be having sex. I felt so sorry for them. Then here I am, just getting ready to graduate college and I've gotten myself pregnant too."

"Kirsten, I'm just another statistic," Melah continued, with tears in her eyes. "Just one more black single mother trying to survive and take care of her kids," she said, trying to hold back her tears. "I'm the first one in my family to graduate college; the first one, Kirsten! No one else even thought about going to college, but not only did I go, I graduated. My family is so proud of me," she said, wiping her face with the sleeve of her shirt.

"Everybody came to my graduation. Everybody, Kirsten! It was a big deal and there I was, afraid to even eat anything because I knew I was going to throw it all up and then they would know that I was pregnant. I starved myself the entire day, because I was so afraid of them finding out."

"They're going to be so disappointed in me. I'm so disappointed in myself, and I hate myself for not going through with the abortion, but when I saw the baby on the ultrasound, I just couldn't do it. As much as I wanted to, I wouldn't have been able to live with myself," Melah said, putting her face in her hands.

"But Daniel is a great man, Melah. He's not going to leave you to raise this baby alone," Kirsten said, reassuringly.

"There's no guarantee of that!" Melah snapped. "Yes, Daniel is great, now, but what happens when his family turns their backs on him for getting a black girl pregnant? You heard what he said about his dad; he didn't even want to stay in the same neighborhood as blacks. His dad is going to flip out when he finds out about me and this baby. They are not going to want to have a mixed grandbaby. Our lives are going to be miserable if we have this child," Melah said, still sobbing. She kept trying to wipe her tears, but they were flooding down her face.

"Kirsten, I feel so trapped," she continued. "Daniel is so happy and I am so sad. I just don't see how anything good can come from me having his baby."

Kirsten's mouth fell open.

"Melah, so many good things can come from having this baby. For one, you will end up with a wonderful husband and father to your child."

"Just stop, Kirsten! You don't know that! Yeah, he said he would stick around, but how do I know he's telling the truth? How do I know he won't dump me for some white chick that his family will approve of? A family's opinion carries a lot of weight and as soon as they tell him to dump me, he will. I know how this works. I'm not stupid! If I have this baby, I have no control over anything! I just don't want to be a statistic. I don't want to sacrifice everything for him only for him to turn his back on me. I will be so humiliated and everyone will say they told me so."

Melah let out a loud cry and said, "I lay in my bed at night and I pray that God will let me have a miscarriage. I pray that he will somehow get me out of having this baby and I hate myself for feeling that way. I have become this horrible, evil person. I'm not religious, Kirsten, but I don't know how God will forgive me for wanting to have a miscarriage solely because I don't want to tell my family that I'm pregnant. Only an evil person would pray for that," Melah said, crying so hard that she looked like she was about to vomit.

Kirsten pulled into a parking lot, reached in her back seat and gave Melah a bottle of water and a roll of paper towels she found under the seat.

Kirsten said looking deep into Melah's eyes and said softly, "Melah, you have every right to feel the way you feel."

Melah gave her a strange look.

"But you have to forgive yourself for getting pregnant; you have to forgive yourself for falling in love with a man whose family may not accept you, and forgive yourself for having evil thoughts against your unborn child. You are human and everything you feel is human. It may not be right, but it is human and sometimes we have evil and cruel thoughts. Sometimes we only see the negative side of our situations and sometimes we choose to only see the bad in others. You're human, Melah. You're not perfect; no one is. Not even your family, and it's unfair for you to put that burden on yourself."

Melah was crying so hard that Kirsten thought she was going to have a panic attack.

"Melah, you've got to calm down," Kirsten said, fearfully. "Here, lean your seat back and just relax for a minute."

Melah leaned back and seemed to be calming down a little.

"I'm sorry, Kirsten. I just don't know what to do. I feel so helpless."

"Well, you're gonna have to go to the hospital if you keep doing this to yourself. You are a good woman, Melah. You're not evil and you're going to make a wonderful mother. Daniel loves you, and if your families don't approve, they can all go suck on frog eggs. Stop beating yourself up over this! You have a beautiful life growing on the inside of you and that's something to be happy about. When that baby gets here, I promise you, everyone is going to spoil it rotten. Everything is going to be fine, Melah. Here," Kirsten said, reaching on her dash board and grabbing an index card. "I know you're not religious, but this is one of my favorite scriptures. I recite it every day on my way to work. It says, 'Do not be afraid, because I am with you. Do not be discouraged, for I am your God. I will strengthen you and help you. I will uphold you with my righteous right hand.' This scripture has helped me through a lot of rough times," *and it is going to help me through a lot more if Jason keeps coming around, because Everett is going to kill him,* she thought.

"Thank you," Melah said, trying to regain her composure.

"I'm not trying to push religion on you, Melah, but it really does help to know that you have someone who is bigger than you to help you with your problems. It takes some of the stress off of you so you don't feel like you have to try to fix everything. Just pray about it and let God work it out."

"Kirsten, I don't really know God like that. I just don't know if He wants to help me."

"Just because you don't know the Bible from front to back or go to church every week, or at all, doesn't mean that God doesn't still love you. He does love you and He doesn't think that you're evil. He'll help you through this, Melah, okay?"

"Okay! Thank you. I'm glad we had this talk because I swear I was about to lose it."

"Yeah, you were, Mel," Kirsten said, smiling. "Does Daniel know how you feel?"

"Oh, no! I could never tell him that I want to have a miscarriage. He would leave me for sure."

"Yeah, you're probably right about that," Kirsten said, laughing. "Hey, there's this comedy show downtown that also has dinner. Would you like to go there? You could probably use a good laugh."

"Boy, could I? Yes, let's go there," Melah said, so Kirsten turned the car around and headed downtown, while Melah tried to reapply her make up that had been wiped all over the sleeve of her shirt. "Good thing my shirt is black," Melah said, laughing. "I wonder what Daniel is doing. He's probably getting drunk for the first time in his life," she mentioned.

"It doesn't matter. We are going to have fun without them. You don't think about Daniel and I won't think about Everett, okay?"

"Okay, that's a deal," Melah agreed and they both laughed.

CHAPTER

"There are so many blues and jazz restaurants near Lawrenceville! How am I ever going to find this dude?" Everett said, in a frustrated tone, adamantly searching the internet, trying to pinpoint where Jason was having dinner.

Everett had a bone to pick with Jason and he was planning to do it face-to-face; man-to-man. He wasn't a violent man by any means. Actually, he was a man who truly loved God and had always prided himself on doing the right thing. He wasn't sure how what he was about to do would affect his relationship with God, or what his pastor or the people at church would say. At the moment, Everett wasn't sure about a lot of things, but what he was certain of was if Jason Glaznyte was bold enough to put his lips on Kirsten, he'd better be bold enough to suffer the consequences for his actions.

While Everett diligently searched for the restaurant,

Jason and the rest of the guys had all made there and just placed their food orders.

"Hey, gentlemen," Jason said, capturing everyone's attention. "Now that we've gotten our orders out of the way, I just wanted to say I'm glad you were able to come out tonight. I believe people have better working relationships if they view each other as friends instead of co-workers. So, on that note, how about we go around the table and introduce ourselves? We'll start with the newest member of the team, Daniel Stine. Just tell us your name and a little bit about yourself," Jason requested of everyone.

"Hey, everyone! As he just said, I'm Daniel Stine and I'm kinda an intern for now, but if all goes well, I'll be taking Mr. Cross' place when he retires."

"Oh, okay! I'm Richard Nims and I'm over the Accounting Department at the Oxcon location. We'll have a lot of dealings with each other."

"And I'm Marcus Capes," another man chimed in. "I oversee the Human Resources Department."

"I'm Arthur Wade," another guy said, "But everyone calls me Rat Lover."

Daniel gave him a weird look.

"Okaaaaayyy! I'm sure there's a story behind that and I would love to hear it," Daniel expressed.

Rat Lover laughed.

"Yeah, there is, but don't judge me for it. Anyway, I'm over the Shipping Department."

"So, you really want me to call you Rat Lover?" Daniel asked.

"Well, you don't have to, but you'll be the only one calling me Arthur," he replied.

Jason interrupted.

"Daniel, it took me a while to get used to it too, but whenever I had shipping questions, no one seemed to know who Arthur Wade was. It was easier to conform and just ask for Rat Lover," he said, laughing loudly.

"Okay, Rat Lover it is," Daniel said, throwing his hands in the air. "And what about you?" Daniel asked the guy sitting next to him.

"I'm Kayin Campbell. I'm over the Security Department."

As the next guy introduced himself, Everett had finally stumbled upon something interesting.

"Ryan's Blues and Jazz! Hmmm, I remember Kirsten saying that Jason had a son name Ryan. I wonder if this is it. I wonder if Jason owns this place and it's named after his son," he said, as he picked up the phone to call the number to the restaurant.

"Ryan's Blues and Jazz, Jill speaking," the lady answered.

"Yes, I'm trying to see if Mr. Jason Glaznyte is the owner of this restaurant?"

"Yes, sir. He certainly is. Would you like to make a reservation?"

"No, he's supposed to be having dinner with a lot of guys tonight. I'm just trying to see if I'm too late to join them?"

"Oh, no, sir!" she said. "The waitress just took their orders, so if you're on your way now, you should be fine.

Should I let him know you're running a little late?"

"No! No! No! That won't be necessary. I just wanted to make sure I didn't miss him, that's all."

"Well you're in luck because they're still here," she said, giggling. "Just ask for Jill when you get here and I'll take you up to their table."

"That will be awesome! Thanks, Jill," Everett said, hanging up the phone and heading towards Lawrenceville.

As the waitresses brought bread and salad to the table, the guys gazed in amazement at how beautiful all the women were that worked there.

"Boss man, you have a nice variety to stare at here," Rat Lover said, smiling at one of the waitresses.

Jason laughed.

"Well, I don't do the hiring, so I can't take any of the credit," he said.

Marcus turned and looked at Rat Lover.

"I bet you didn't even notice the beautiful black ones, did you?" he asked.

"What does that mean?" Daniel asked.

"Rat Lover only likes white women."

"Why is that?" Jason asked Rat Lover.

"Because, black women need to step their game up and learn how to treat a man. They're always nagging me about something and they're never satisfied. White women let me do whatever I want and they don't complain about anything."

All the men just shook their heads.

"I know for a fact that isn't true," Daniel said. "I've dated plenty of white women and they all complained.

Now, I'm dating a black woman and she complains as well. That's just women for ya, but the key is to make them feel secure. If she's not secure, then watch out, because she's going to bring out the crazy," he said, smiling like he was an expert on women.

"Shut up! What do you know about women? You're barely even legal," Rat Lover replied.

Daniel shrugged his shoulders and let out a small laugh.

"Nah, he's right," Marcus added. "A woman gets crazy for three reasons: She feels like you're just using her for your own convenience, she feels like you're lying to her, or she feels like you're cheating on her. Either way, these three things will get you introduced to the crazy. If she's secure, she may still get mad about stuff, but she won't be slashing your tires and throwing dishes at you."

"Yep! All women are crazy. Every last one of them," Kayin agreed. "It just depends on if you provoke them enough to bring it out. It's definitely in there, though, so don't be fooled."

Everyone laughed and nodded their heads in agreement.

"Do you know what my problem is with dating?" Richard said. "People are so broken from their previous relationships. They bring so much baggage to a relationship that when they have something good right in front of them, they don't even know how to relax and love the person or let the person love them. They automatically assume they're going to get used or dogged, so they never invest themselves completely. It's like the relationship doesn't even have a chance from the beginning and this is from both sides; males and females. It's like everyone's attitude is 'Dog them before they dog me.' Now that I'm divorced and back on the dating scene, I don't want to spend any more time trying to tear down walls to get to the real person. I want to be with someone who wants to be with me. I just don't have time for the drama anymore."

As all the guys agreed with Richard, Marcus contested, "And this is why I have a problem with Rat Lover wanting to put white women on a pedestal. I told him a long time ago, 'a rat is still a rat, no matter what color it is,' but his response was, 'Well, white rats are better,'" Marcus said, shaking his head.

Everyone laughed.

"Oh, my, gosh! Y'all are crazy," Jason said. "Do you know I've never even kissed a woman who was outside of my race? Never!"

"Me either," Daniel agreed. "Not until Melah came along," he said, then he looked back at Marcus. "So, is that where the name Rat Lover comes from?" Daniel asked.

"Yep!" Marcus said.

"So are you saying that white women are rats?" Richard asked, like he was offended.

"No, no! I'm not saying that at all. The name Rat Lover really has nothing to do with race. My point is he could be living with a rat, but as long as she's a white rat, then he's happy."

"Hmmm," Richard said, still sounding like he was somewhat offended. "I don't think I like—"

"Richard, white women are not rats, okay? Please

don't go slashing my tires or throwing dishes at me," Marcus said, cutting Richard off.

"Well, I'm just trying to get clarification on the rat issue," Richard said, laughing.

"Y'all, don't pay any attention to Marcus," Rat Lover interrupted. "He and I grew up together, so he thinks he knows me, but he doesn't. I don't put white women on pedestals; they were just always nicer to me and always complimenting me on something. Black girls just wanted to know what I could do for them; they always had their hands out, wanting something."

"Wanting what, man? You don't have anything!" Marcus argued.

"Shut up, man," Rat Lover said, throwing something at Marcus.

"I've never dated a black woman," Richard said, "But they've always been very nice to me. One girl used to bring food in just for me, and she never asked for anything in return, so Rat Lover, I don't agree that all black women want something. Some of them are very giving. Right now, I'm dating an awesome white lady, who's also very giving, so in the end, it's not about race, it's about what's on the inside of a woman that matters."

"I'll be honest," Daniel chimed in. "I've never been happier with any woman than I am right now. I agree with Kayin; it would be easier if I didn't date outside of my race, but Melah is the only woman I want to spend my life with. She makes me feel like I can do anything that I put my mind to and we, as men, need someone strong standing beside us, encouraging and believing in us."

"I don't believe she's the only woman you want to spend your life with," Kayin said, confidently and everyone gave him a strange look.

"It is a known fact that men are not meant to be with just one woman," he continued. "Our natural instincts tell us that we should never settle down. No man wants to be with just one woman forever. Not one! You're lying if you say you do! Look at all these beautiful women in here. You mean to tell me that you don't wish you could have at least one of them? The only reason we're faithful is because we don't want to lose the woman we're with. If she didn't mind us having other women, we would be more than happy to have several by our sides. We're dogs by nature! Stop fighting it and just embrace it!"

"Now that's what I'm talking about!" Rat Lover said, excitedly, like Kayin had just given him the cure to world hunger.

"But Kayin, you're happily married, so what are you talking about, dude?" Marcus inquired.

"You're darn right I'm happily married and I plan to stay that way. I'm faithful too! My wife is wonderful and I am not losing her for nobody, BUT that doesn't change what I said. However, if you find a woman that makes you happy and you don't want to lose her, then you'll just have to suppress your beast nature to roam around looking for other prey. I've been married for fifteen years and I've never strayed. I'm not saying I've never wanted to, because I have, but I'm not jeopardizing my marriage for it."

"Okay, so, technically, you've been neutered?" Rat

Lover asked.

All the guys let out a boisterous laugh that filled the entire room.

"Yep! I sure have, and I'm quite content that I no longer feel the need to go pee on everything."

"Whatever, man!" Rat Lover replied.

"So, white women are okay with you sleeping around?" Kayin asked Rat Lover.

"Are you crazy? No, they're not okay with it."

"Have you ever actually dated a white woman before?" Richard asked Rat Lover.

"Yeah, of course I have. Well….not like dated them, because they didn't want their parents and friends to find out, but I've talked to a lot of white women and I know they're better, just by how they talk to me," Rat Lover explained.

"WHAT?" one of the guys yelled out!

All the other men at the table went into an uproar. Marcus just covered his face in disappointment.

"You're sitting here, talking all of that trash and you've never even dated a white woman?" Daniel asked.

"Rat Lover! What about all the women you've told me about?" Marcus asked. "You mean to tell me you made all of them up?"

"Nah, I did talk to them. We were good friends."

"Oh, good grief!" one of the other guys said.

"Just friends?" another guy squawked. Everyone else just shook their heads in awe over Rat Lover's lies.

"Do black women even want you?" Kayin asked. "You know there are some men that black women are very happy to give away. I've heard them talking at work, saying, 'Girl, she can have him, and she better not bring him back, because we do not give refunds.'"

"Whatever, man. You don't know nothing; black women love me. I can pull any chick I want."

"Ahhhhhh," "Blah, Blah, Blah," "Whatever," "Get real," "Liar," and "We don't wanna hear it," were all the things the guys were shouting to Rat Lover, and some of the guys threw napkins at him.

Just then the waitresses started bringing out everyone's food. The guys ate and chit chatted some more about the women in their lives, then all of a sudden, Everett walked in with Jill.

"Hi, Mr. Glaznyte, Mr. Larson is—" was all Jill could get out before Everett punched Jason in the face. Jason's chair fell over, landing him on the floor. Everett jumped on top of Jason and started hitting him as hard as he could, yelling, "YOU STAY AWAY FROM MY WIFE OR I WILL KILL YOU! I SWEAR, I WILL KILL YOU!"

Everything was happening so fast that it took the guys a minute to even process what was going on.

"WHOA!" One guy screamed and Kayin and Daniel immediately jumped in and pulled Everett off of Jason, but it seemed as if Everett had turned into a mad man, because he was literally kicking and punching anything that got in his way, while still screaming threats at Jason. It took several other men to get him away from Jason. Finally, they were able to pin him in the corner and Daniel was trying to calm him down.

"What are you doing man? You can go to jail or get

killed coming in here like that," Daniel whispered.

"When Kirsten went to get your keys, he pinned her up against the wall." Everett explained. "He kissed her, he was rubbing all over her, and even tried to put his hand up her skirt. She ended up pushing him off of her, slapping him, and running out of the building," Everett said, huffing and puffing, staring at Jason, who was still lying on the floor.

"Oh! Well in that case, you can go kill him," Daniel said, moving out of Everett's way.

Everett jumped up and quickly headed back towards Jason.

"NOOOOO!" Kayin yelled, jumping in front of him! "I can't let you do that, man! I don't know what's going on, but I can't let you kill nobody!" he said, giving Daniel an evil look for letting Everett go.

Daniel shrugged his shoulders and said, "Well, sounds like he's getting what he deserves."

"You better hush, man! You're just the intern remember? Jason is still your boss!" Kayin said, looking back at Jason, hoping he couldn't hear their conversation, but Jason seemed to be out cold. Several of the guys were gathered around him, trying to get him to respond and trying to get all the blood off of his face. Meanwhile, Jill had called the cops and they were just arriving outside.

"We've got to get him to the hospital. I don't know if he's even alive," Jill said, hysterically, to the cops as they came rushing in. She took them upstairs, and as soon as they got off the elevator she screamed, "And this is the man, right here! He's the one who attacked, Mr.

Glaznyte," she said pointing to Everett.

"Mr. Glaznyte, the ambulance is on their way. We'll get you some help," one cop said to Jason as he lay on the floor, seemingly lifeless.

The cops asked everyone a few questions about what happened; most people described it as a violent attack on Jason. Daniel told them it was just a small brawl between old acquaintances that got out of hand, but the cops didn't seem moved by Daniel's attempt to downplay the story. Shortly after that, they arrested Everett and hauled him off in the cop car.

The ambulance eventually came and rushed Jason to the hospital. Some of the guys jumped in a car and followed the ambulance. Daniel left to go find Melah and Kirsten, and the other guys just stood around, in a daze, not having a clue as to what just happened to what was supposed to be a perfect night out with the fellas.

CHAPTER

Kirsten and Melah had just finished the comedy show and were heading home when Daniel called Kirsten to tell her what happened between Everett and Jason. She started screaming, "NO! NOOOOOOOOO" and dropped the phone. She was so upset that she had to pull the car over to the side of the road.

"What's wrong?" Melah asked, but all Kirsten kept saying was, "I knew this would happen, I knew this would happen. I knew I shouldn't have told him. I knew I shouldn't have told him," then Melah heard Daniel yelling, "Kirsten, Kirsten!"

Melah grabbed the phone.

"Daniel, what happened?" she asked, frantically. He told her everything.

"Oh, My Goodness! What jail are they taking him to?"

"It happened in Lawrenceville, so it was their police who came and arrested him. Can you drive Kirsten here, so we can try to post bail for Everett?"

"Yeah, sure. Just give me a minute to pull up the police station in the GPS. It shouldn't take us that long."

"Okay, see y'all in a few," Daniel said, hanging up, going to try to find the police station himself.

By the time he got there, he saw a news crew outside giving a report.

"Oh, no! I hope they haven't found out about Everett and Jason," he said, jumping out of the car and walking over to see what they were reporting.

"Everett Larson, a local minister at Faith Christian Worship Center, has just been arrested for assault and battery against a prominent business owner, Jason Glaznyte. Witnesses say Mr. Larson came out of nowhere and started punching the victim and screaming threats that he was going to kill him. The victim is currently in the hospital with a concussion, but he is expected to survive. We've tried to reach someone from the alleged aggressor's church, but there was no response. We will bring you updates to this story as we receive more information from law enforcement. This is Shayla Twin, WXYZ, News Center 2, reporting live at the Lawrenceville Police Station in Lawrenceville, Georgia."

"No! No! No! No!" Daniel said, putting his hand over his head and walking inside to wait for Kirsten and Melah to arrive.

Meanwhile, Everett's pastor's phone was ringing off the hook with people asking him if he had seen the news; he had truly had enough.

"Yes, yes, yes! I saw the news!" he said to one of

the church gossipers. "And I'm as shocked as anyone else, but I know Minister Larson and he is not violent. If he assaulted someone, there must have been a good reason. I'm heading to the police station now to find out what happened."

"Pastor, they said he was acting like a mad man, making threats to one of the biggest business owners in Atlanta. Just when you think you know someone, you find out they have another side to them. I really thought he was a Christ—"

"Wait a minute! He IS a Christian, not WAS. Let's not jump to conclusions here! Like I said, if he assaulted someone, maybe he had a good reason, so before we go casting stones and spreading gossip, let's just see what happened. I'll be turning my phone off now, so if anyone calls you, and I'm sure they will, just let them know that we will not accuse Minister Larson of anything until we find out from him what happened, okay? Can you pass that on for me, please?"

"I sure will, Pastor, because you know I just want the best for Minister Larson. I can't think of any justified reason why he would go around attacking people, though. He just always seems so—" the lady was saying, then all of a sudden she heard the dial tone. "Pastor! Pastor! Pastor, are you there? Hmmm, I think the pastor hung up on me," she said to her husband.

"Probably because you're gossiping like you always do," he responded, unsympathetically, as he watched television.

"I don't gossip. I discuss the matters of the church,

so the other members and I can pray for them."

"So, do y'all ever get around to the "praying" part or does it just stop at the discussions?" her husband asked.

She didn't respond. She just rolled her eyes and went into the other room to make a few more phone calls.

When Kirsten and Melah arrived at the police station, Kirsten went up to the window to ask about Everett's bail.

"No bail is being set for this case ma'am."

"What do you mean, 'no bail is being set?'" Kirsten demanded.

"This is an assault and battery charge. We are unsure if the assailant will go back and cause more harm to the victim if released. Therefore, no bail will be granted," the lady said, coldly.

"EVERETT WOULD NEVER HARM A FLEA!" Kirsten shouted, but the lady just looked at her like she was crazy, because according to witnesses, Everett did in fact harm more than a flea. He harmed a person, who was currently lying in the hospital, unconscious.

Kirsten just burst into tears.

Just then, her pastor came through the door, asking what happened. She told him everything.

"Oh, I see," was all he said.

"Pastor, you know this is not like Everett. I don't know why he would do something like this."

The pastor put his arm around her like she was his daughter.

"Sweetheart, when another man hurts someone we love, we kinda lose common sense. A man should never touch another man's wife; he's asking to die," the pastor said, compellingly. "Now, I don't condone what he did, but if I could be honest for a minute and put myself in his position, I can't say I wouldn't have done the same thing. We are men, Kirsten; our natural instinct is to protect and defend what's ours. Consider yourself blessed to have a man who would risk dying for you. That's what Christ would do for the church. That's the kind of love the Bible says a man should have for his wife. Others may condemn Everett, but sometimes you've got to take drastic measures to get your point across. I bet this Jason guy won't be putting his hands on you anymore," the pastor said, smiling and reassuring Kirsten that everything was going to be okay.

Daniel grabbed Melah's hand.

"I would die for you too," he whispered, trying to capitalize on the moment and score some points with Melah.

Melah laughed.

"Sure you would," she said, giving him a pat on the back.

"What? I would!" he said, winking his eye. Melah smiled and winked back.

"Would y'all like to join us in prayer?" the pastor asked Daniel and Melah.

"Definitely," Daniel said, hopping up, grabbing Melah's hand, and pulling her out of her chair.

"Ummm, yeah. I guess," Melah whispered, bashfully.

The pastor began this energetic prayer and Melah

tried hard to keep her eyes closed, but she had never heard someone pray so fervently before. Chill bumps were going up and down her body. She didn't know what was going on. She looked over at Kirsten who was crying and praying very loudly and at Daniel, who seemed to be consumed in the moment as well. Then she looked back at the lady behind the window, but she had left.

When they first walked in the police station, it seemed to be super busy, but at that moment, it was totally quiet. This kind of frightened Melah, but then again, it all seemed bizarre to her. She never claimed to know much about God, but as they stood in the foyer, she knew she could feel His presence.

When the pastor finished his prayer, he looked at Kirsten and said, "The Bible says 'All things work together for the good of them who love the Lord.' Do you love the Lord?" he asked her.

"Yes," she said, still crying.

"Well, no matter how bad this situation looks right now, God has promised that something good will come out of it, okay?"

"Okay," Melah said, wiping away tears.

Everyone looked over at her and gave her a strange look.

"Oh, I'm sorry," Melah said. "You were talking to Kirsten."

Everyone laughed.

"The Bible applies to anyone who wants to believe, my dear," the pastor said to Melah. "I'm Everett and Kirsten's pastor. I hope you two will visit the church some time," he said, giving both of them a card, then walking off to talk to the lady who had finally come back to the window.

Within a few minutes he returned and said, "Kirsten, there's really nothing we can do tonight, so go home and get some rest, but first thing in the morning, I'll see what I can do to try to get Everett out of here, okay?"

"Okay, thank you," she responded and they all headed for the door.

Just as they were about to walk out, Kirsten looked back at the lady and said, "Can you please tell my husband that I was here?"

"Yeah, I'll let him know," the lady said, with a sympathetic look on her face, which was much different than the look she had given Kirsten earlier.

By the next morning, Jason had regained consciousness and was back to his normal self, minus a swollen face, a black eye, a busted lip and a bruised shoulder blade.

Daniel went to the hospital to visit him and Mr. Cross, who was still getting tests done from the day before.

"Hey, Jason," Daniel said, as he walked in the room. "How are you feeling?"

"Well, I could be better, but I'm happy to be alive."

"Is there anything you need me to take care of at work? Mr. Cross is still in the hospital."

"Nah, you can just take off, Daniel. We'll still pay you for a full day, though."

"You don't have to do that," Daniel said, feeling a little guilty about taking Everett's side at the restaurant.

"No, I want to pay you. So, have you talked to Everett? I heard he was in jail."

"Nah, I haven't talked to him, but Kirsten is pretty upset about this whole thing."

Jason took a deep breath.

"Yeah, I bet she is," he said, staring off into space.

"Jason, I know you're my boss and I don't mean any disrespect, but why would you do that to Kirsten?"

Jason shook his head.

"I really don't know, man. I just got so excited when I saw her. I miss her so much. I don't know what came over me. If I would have known that she didn't want me to kiss her, I would have never done it. I thought she missed me as much as I missed her," he said, sorrowfully.

"But, she's married, man. You've got to respect their union."

"I had her first!" he snapped. I feel like she's still mine."

"Nah, man! She's not. Everett wanted to kill you! She's his wife. Now, he's sitting in jail and you're sitting in the hospital. You've got to let her go before things get totally out of hand."

Jason let out a huge sigh of disappointment, then he went back to staring into space.

"Well, I'm going to go see Mr. Cross before I head home. Am I allowed to return next month?" Daniel asked, half grinning.

"Yes, definitely!" Jason responded, still sounding sad and disappointed that Kirsten was someone else's wife.

Daniel quickly made his way to Mr. Cross' room,

which was filled with all of his family members.

"Hey, Mr. Cross," Daniel said, as he walked in.

"Hmmm," was all Mr. Cross said in return.

"Is this the man who tried to make Daddy have a heart attack?" one of the ladies asked.

"Yes," another one whispered and everyone gave Daniel dirty looks.

Daniel decided that he wouldn't come in any further.

"I just wanted to say bye. I'm heading home now. I hope you feel better and if it's any consolation, I'm sorry about everything," Daniel said, trying to make amends with Mr. Cross and his family, who all looked like they wanted to throw him out of the window.

Mr. Cross didn't respond, so Daniel turned to walk out.

Mr. Cross looked over at his wife, who was giving him a dirty look.

"I'm sorry too, Daniel," he heard Mr. Cross say. He made an abrupt turn.

"Huh?"

"I'm sorry too. I would like us to have a fresh, clean slate when you come back next month, okay?"

"Uh, okay," Daniel said, not knowing whether to believe Mr. Cross or not, but he was still very glad to hear the words.

"Have a safe trip home," Mr. Cross' wife said to Daniel.

"Thank you," Daniel replied. "Good-bye, everyone," he said, waving and quickly closing the door before they all decided they hated him again.

As Daniel was driving back to the hotel to get Melah, he gave Kirsten a call.

"Hey!" he said, when she answered the phone.

"Hey," she responded, sadly, as if she was still crying.

"Have you talked to Everett?"

"Yeah. He's doing okay. The pastor called and the judge agreed to set bail for him, so he can come home, but the bail is twenty thousand dollars.

"TWENTY THOUSAND DOLLARS? Do you have twenty thousand dollars?"

"Well, yeah, but that's pretty much all of our savings. It doesn't matter. I'm headed to the police station now to pay it. I need my husband home."

"But this is his first offense. That should count for something, shouldn't it?"

"Yeah, and that's why the pastor was able to at least convince them to allow him bail, but the judge isn't convinced that Everett didn't purposefully try to kill Jason."

"Well, Kirsten. I was there and I'm not convinced either."

"I just hate I even told him what happened. I should have known he was going to go after Jason."

"No, you did the right thing. He needed to know. Besides, Jason is going to be fine, and like the pastor said, I'm sure he won't be putting his hands on you anymore. Well, let's just hope not anyway," Daniel said.

"I sure hope not too. I don't know what he was

thinking."

"I guess he doesn't want to believe it's over."

"Well, it is!" Kirsten said, sternly.

"So, do you need me and Melah to go with you to the police station? Well, it will probably just be me. I left Melah at the hotel sleeping. She does a lot of that these days," he said, laughing.

Kirsten let out a small laugh too.

"Nah, I'll be fine. Hopefully, I can just pay the money and get my husband."

"Okay, well Melah and I are going to hit the road then, but we'll wait to hear back from you before we leave, okay? Just call us and let us know that everything is okay."

"Alright, I will. Thanks Daniel," she said as they both hung up.

When Kirsten got to the police station, Everett was already sitting there waiting for her.

"Hey, baby!" she said, running and giving him a big hug. "I missed you so much!"

"Hey, I thought you were already here. They came and got me like ten minutes ago and told me I was free to go; my bail had already been paid."

"What? No! I just got here. I haven't paid anything, yet."

"Well, maybe the pastor paid it then."

"Yeah, probably. Well, let's just go before they change their minds," she said laughing. "We'll call and thank the pastor later," she added.

"Yeah, and we'll definitely pay him back."

"Yeah, for sure."

"Kirsten, my car has been impounded, so we have to go and get it. They had it towed from the restaurant," Everett said, as they were walking out.

"Oh, okay. I just need to get outta here! This place is giving me the creeps," she said, hurrying to the car and driving away.

CHAPTER

"Whewwww! Now, this was some trip," Daniel said to Melah, as he opened the hotel room door.

"And I am very ready for it to be over," Melah said, sitting on the bed fully dressed and all her bags packed.

Daniel laughed.

"Gee whiz, Mel, I figured you would still be sleeping."

"Who can sleep with all of this drama going on? Daniel, maybe we should rethink moving to Atlanta."

"We? So you're planning to move with me?"

"Do you really think you're going to get rid of me that easy? Of course I'm moving with you!"

"Okay, but we'll have to get married, eventually, ya know."

"Okay, that's fine," she said, smiling.

"Good, now, let's hit the road and get out of this crazy place."

He and Melah gathered up all of their things and jumped in the car. They were thirty minutes down the road before he remembered he wasn't supposed to leave until they heard back from Kirsten.

"Dangit! I was supposed to wait in Atlanta until I found out if Everett was out of jail."

"Oh, they're letting him out? That's great!"

"Yeah, can you call Kirsten and see if everything is okay?"

"Sure," Melah said, dialing Kirsten's number.

"Hey, Melah," Kirsten said, excitedly.

"Hey, girl! You sound happy. Does that mean your baby is back home?"

"Yes, girl, and no one tried to make him their girlfriend when he was locked up. Thank goodness!"

"That's only because I was locked up at the police station." Everett chimed in. "If they would have sent me downtown to the real jail, I would have been irresistible."

"That's not funny, Everett. You shouldn't be joking like that," Kirsten said.

Melah laughed.

"I'm just glad you were able to get him out."

"Me too. The pastor had already posted the bond for us, so when I got there, Everett was just sitting there waiting on me."

"That is wonderful!" Melah said, then she turned to Daniel. "Daniel, their pastor posted the bail bond for them. Isn't that cool? Kirsten, I really love your pastor. I will definitely be visiting the church when we come back. He wasn't judgmental at all, and I love that!"

"Yes, he's an awesome pastor, Melah. He's more than just a spiritual father; he's like a natural father too.

When Everett and I got married, I couldn't wait to join his church. There are so many great people there. It's truly like one big family. Yes, you still have those who stir up mess in the church, but you have people that stir up mess in your family too," Kirsten said, laughing. "As long as the pastor and his wife are good people and I feel like I can trust them, then I can look past the rest," Kirsten added, getting caught up in her own story, but Melah didn't seem to mind.

"That's great, Kirsten. I want to hear more about God. Maybe I'll give you a call later this week."

"Okay, that will be awesome," Kirsten said.

"Well, we're heading back home, so we'll talk to you guys later, okay?"

"Okay, bye."

"Bye."

"I'm glad that worked out," Daniel said.

"Yeah, me too," Melah said, drifting off and thinking about how she would handle Mr. Jack if he ever did to her what Jason did to Kirsten.

"YUCK!" she screamed.

"What?" Daniel asked, disturbingly.

"Oh, nothing! I'm just glad I don't have to deal with Mr. Jack again."

"Oh, you will when you get back to work, then I'll have to come punch him in the face."

"That's not funny, Daniel. Besides, he never comes down to where I work. I've only talked to him once since I've been there and that was for two minutes in the hallway when he asked me if I was—"

Melah stopped in the middle of her sentence.

"If you was, what?"

"OMG! Daniel, he set this whole thing up! He asked me if I was coming to this conference. I told him I didn't know anything about it and he said he would talk to my supervisor because it would be a good experience for me. I totally blew it off. When my supervisor told me that she wanted me to go, I didn't give a second thought to the conversation he and I had. It all makes sense now. I believe he was trying to get me alone with him from the beginning," she said, then she proceeded to tell Daniel everything that happened that day and all the things Mr. Jack had said to her.

"Melah, that is sexual harassment! You've got to report him."

"Daniel, he's my head boss and I'm the new kid on the block. I can't report him! Everyone is going to think I'm a trouble maker."

"And that is the reason why so many people get abused every day, because they're afraid that people are going to blame them. This man is clearly saying inappropriate things to you and you're afraid of how folks are going to view you? I'm going to turn him in!"

"Daniel, no! Don't do that. I'll lose my job."

"Melah, if you don't report him, it's only going to get worse."

"He has no reason to come to my department, Daniel. He's not going to take that risk."

"Oh, he's going to take it, Melah!"

"Please just let me handle it, okay? I don't want

you getting involved and going to jail, like Everett. I'll take care of it. I promise."

"You better, or I definitely will," he said, turning on music to try and clear his head.

Meanwhile, back in Atlanta, Kirsten and Everett had finally come down from their natural high of being reunited long enough to call and thank the pastor for posting bail for them.

"I didn't post your bail," he said, surprisingly. "The only thing I did was go down and talk to the judge to see if I could get him to agree to a bail. I honestly don't know who posted the bail, but just consider it a blessing. God works in mysterious ways, ya know? Anyone who's able to put down twenty thousand dollars and doesn't want any recognition in return, should definitely have a place in heaven," the pastor said, laughing, but neither Kirsten nor Everett was finding anything funny about this mysterious "blessing."

"Okay, thank you for everything, Pastor. We'll talk to you later, alright?"

"Sure, and Minister Larson, I would like us to sit down sometime this week if possible, so we can chat a little about what happened, okay?"

"Okay, Pastor," Everett said, as if he was embarrassed.

"Just take your time and take care of everything you need to do and when you're ready, just stop by the church."

"Alright, I will," Everett said to the pastor before hanging up.

"I wonder who would post my bail, Kirsten,"

Everett said, suspiciously.

"It doesn't matter. It is a blessing and it's money we don't have to pay back. Let's just be happy. People love you. They know you would never intentionally harm anyone, so don't worry about who posted it. So what do you want to eat for lunch?" she asked, trying to get Everett's mind on something else.

"I'm not hungry," he said, as if he was in a daze.

Great! Now, he's going to sit here thinking of every person in the universe who could possibly afford to spend twenty thousand dollars on a complete stranger. Hmmm, that is kinda weird when you think about it, though, Kirsten thought.

"Jason posted my bail, Kirsten. I can feel it," he said, turning red.

"Everett, you don't know that! You could have killed him. Why would he turn around and post your bail, like y'all are best friends?"

"I don't know. Maybe he wants me to come back and try to finish him off, so he can kill me and claim self-defense."

"Stop it, Everett! Just stop! That doesn't make any sense. I'm not listening to this. You need to go pray or read your Bible or something."

"Yeah, maybe you're right," he said laughing. Okay, I'm not going to worry about it. I'm just glad to be home with my wife," he said, subtly brushing himself up against Kirsten and unbuttoning her blouse.

"I missed you so much," she said, as he kissed her and laid her on the living room floor.

"The living room, Everett?"

"Yes! In every room in the house," he whispered, kissing her neck.

"Oh! Okay," she said, excitedly, as she happily relinquished herself and gave full and complete control of her body into the hands of her loving and devoted husband.

CHAPTER

When Saturday came, Daniel gave Melah a call.

"Hey, Mel. Today would be a great day to go to Fountainwater to meet my parents, don't you think?"

"Yay! I would love to meet your parents today!" Melah said, excitedly. "Do you think they'll like me?"

"Yes, I already told you, they will love you."

"Daniel, I'm so excited! I have butterflies in my stomach! How far away is Fountainwater from here?"

"It's about forty minutes. Will two hours give you enough time to get dressed?"

"Only two hours? Daniel, I'm meeting your parents for Pete's sake. I need to do my hair and my nails. I need new makeup and I don't have anything to wear. I need at least five hours."

"Oh, okay. Well I'm going to go visit my parents today and I'll see you when I get back, alright?"

"Daniel! That's not funny! I want to go with you. I just want to look perfect."

"Well, try to look perfect within two hours, okay?"

"Three?"

"Two and a half?"

"Three and a half?"

"I'll be there in three hours, Mel. Please be ready."

"Okay! I'll be ready! Gosh! I'm so excited. Daniel, did I tell you how excited I am?"

"Yes, you did. See you in three hours."

"Okay, bye, babe."

"Bye."

When he arrived three hours later, he figured Melah would not be dressed, but not only was she dressed, she was sitting on her porch waiting for him.

"Wow, well look what we have here! Someone is ready to go. Hair done, nails done, outfit banging! Turn around and let me see how those jeans are fitting you in the back."

"Stop it, Daniel!"

"Mmmm, let's go in the house for a minute so I can make sure you're ready to go."

"What? I am ready!"

"No! I mean, let me see if you're ready. It'll only take a few minutes."

"DANIEL, NO! You are not about to mess up my hair and makeup!"

"C'mon, babe. You look so good. I'll be quick."

"No!" Melah said, running past Daniel and hopping in the car.

He must be crazy! It took me three hours to look this fabulous. His parents are going to see ALL of the effort I put into looking good for them.

"It was only going to take a minute," Daniel said, sounding like he was brokenhearted.

"Boy, please! Get in the car and let's go."

Daniel got in the car, still trying to convince Melah that it wasn't too late to go back to her place for a little rendezvous, but she just stared at her phone like she was really into a text her friend, Anna, had sent her.

"Hahahaha, Anna is so funny," she said, laughing very loudly, and ignoring Daniel.

He looked over at Melah and said, "I met Anna, and she's ain't that funny."

"Daniel, can we please leave? We're not going back inside. You're wasting time. Besides, it might hurt the baby," she said, laughing.

"Oh, okay, so now you're concerned about sex hurting the baby? You're so full of it, Mel."

"I know, now can we go?"

"Fine!" Daniel said, driving off.

When they arrived at his parents' house, only his mom was there.

"Hey, baby son," she said, giving Daniel a big hug. "Oh, you must be Melah. I've heard so much about you," she said, giving Melah a hug too.

Oh! Wow! I didn't even have to work at impressing her. This is awesome! Melah thought.

"Your dad will be home in a minute," she said to Daniel. "And Roslyn may come over later with the kids.

They're all excited about seeing you and meeting Melah."

"Roslyn is coming over here with them bad kids? Dang, momma! Why?"

"Now, Daniel, don't you act like that about my grandbabies. They can come over here anytime they want and you should be happy to see your nephews and niece. When was the last time you saw them, about a year ago?"

"Nah, about nine months ago, but momma, those kids are bad! They get into everything."

"Well, that's what kids do, so maybe you'll keep that in mind before you go getting someone pregnant," she said, pointing to Melah. "Kids are a lot of responsibility. That's why you need to make sure you're ready to be a parent before you bring them into this world."

Melah just looked down at the floor like she didn't hear Daniel's mom talking.

"Mrs. Sarah, these are some really nice pictures you have in here," Melah said, trying to change the subject.

"Oh, yeah! Daniel's dad got them when we were stationed overseas in the military. We love that antique look."

"Yeah, I like it too," Melah said, which was all it took to get his mom distracted, and talking about her entire overseas experience, which Daniel was too young to even remember.

"Hey, Ma!" Roslyn yelled, as she came through the back door with her three kids.

"Hey, grandma!" They all yelled, running in behind their mom like a stampeding herd of cattle.

"Yay! Uncle Daniel is here," Roslyn's oldest son,

Leon shouted.

"What's up, lil man?" Daniel said, giving Leon a high five. Then Jeremy, the middle son came up and gave Daniel a high five too, but Mikayla, the baby girl held up her hands so Daniel could pick her up.

"Hold you, hold you!" she said, looking up at Daniel.

"Oh, you want me to hold you?"

"Mmmm hmmm," she said, nodding her head yes.

Everyone laughed.

"She says hold you instead of hold me; how cute," Melah mentioned.

"Hi, you must be Melah. I'm Daniel's sister, Roslyn. I'm very happy to meet you. Please forgive me for being rude. Whenever I take the kids somewhere, our introduction is like a whirlwind."

"Who's the black lady, mommy?" Jeremy asked.

"What's black?" Mikayla inquired.

Daniel's face turned totally red from embarrassment, and if Melah's skin wasn't brown, she would have turned red as well.

"Oh, I'm so sorry, Melah. I'm so, so sorry," Roslyn declared. "These kids say the first thing they think. I promise we're not racist. We have no problem with you dating Daniel. We love black people. We grew up with blacks, didn't we, Daniel?"

Daniel and Melah both sat there staring at Roslyn like she had lost her mind. Melah wanted to give Roslyn some comforting words, so she wouldn't feel so bad, but nothing comforting was coming to Melah's mind. She just sat there listening to Roslyn as she tried to convince her that brown skin was totally acceptable in the Stine family.

"Enough, Roslyn! Dang! You're making it worse," Daniel said.

"Oh, ok, but I am sorry, though," she said, one last time to Melah.

"I like black people," Mikayla said, looking up at Daniel.

"Oh, gosh!" Daniel said, shaking his head as he put Mikayla down on the floor, and headed towards the refrigerator. "Momma, do you have anything to drink?" he asked.

"Melah, can I tell you something?" Leon whispered.

"Yeah, sure," Melah said, with a smile.

"I don't like all black people. I just like some of them. There's this guy named Matthew in my class. He's black and I don't like him at all. He always wants to use my pencils and when I say no, he says he's going to take them. I told him I would tell if he does. He makes me sooooo mad! My pencils have cool pictures on them and his don't. I don't like him!" Leon emphasized. "But there's this other boy. I think he's black, I'm not sure. I like him a lot and then there's this girl; she's has really pretty barrettes in her hair. I like her a lot; I don't think my parents want me to like her, but I do. Then there's another boy that's black. I like him. My librarian is—"

"Leon, what are you doing? Leave Melah alone," Roslyn said.

"I was just telling her about all the black people I like. She was listening, ma. She wanted to know," Leon said, with a Southern accent.

"It's fine. I'm always interested in all the likable black people in the world," Melah said, laughing and giving Daniel an *I think I'm ready to go* look.

Daniel was so humiliated. If he could, he would have turned into *I Dream Of Jeannie* so he could blink and make himself and Melah disappear from his family.

Just then Daniel's dad came through the front door.

"HEY, GRANDPA!" all the kids screamed as loud as they could, running out of the kitchen and into the living room to greet him.

"Daniel's girlfriend is black," Jeremy whispered, like it was a secret.

"BLACK? Daniel better not be bringing home no Bla—" his dad said, abruptly stopping in the middle of his sentence as he looked right in Melah's face.

This day is going to be a blast, thought Melah.

"I think we should go, Daniel," Melah whispered.

"No! We're staying! Dad, this is Melah. Melah, this is my dad," Daniel said, introducing them and giving his dad a hug, hello.

"Hey, Melah. I'm sorry you had to hear that, but nobody told me that you were black. I didn't mean nothing bad by it. I just wasn't expecting it, that's all. Please try to make yourself at home."

"Thank you, Mr. Stine. It's nice meeting you," she responded, solemnly.

"Daniel, come help me get this stuff off of my truck," his dad commanded.

"Yes, sir! I'll be back," he said, giving Melah's

hand a slight squeeze.

"Melah, would you like to help finish cooking?" Daniel's mom asked.

"Sure," Melah responded, giving Daniel a crooked grin, as he left to go help his dad.

Since Roslyn was now somewhere running behind her three children, Melah and Daniel's mom had a chance to be alone.

"Melah, I know this visit isn't going exactly how you had imagined, but we really are good people. This whole interracial dating thing is just an adjustment that we're gonna have to make."

"But, Mrs. Sarah, you already knew that I was black. I just figured Mr. Stine would have already known by now as well."

"Yeah, but I didn't think you and Daniel were going to stay together, so there was just no need for me to get his father in an uproar over nothing, ya know."

Melah gave her a weird look.

"So, you were thinking that Daniel and I wouldn't make it?"

"Well, you know how kids are. They see something new and they just want to try it out. I figured the two of you were just intrigued with each other. I didn't think he would be bringing you home to meet us or anything, and then when Daniel called this morning to tell us you all were coming, his dad had already left. There was no way for me to reach him to tell him. Besides, I knew you had to be a lovely girl if my Daniel wanted you to meet us, and I'm glad you're here, Melah. Really, I am."

"But you're mixed with white and Italian, so I don't understand the difference," Melah said, sounding upset.

"Well, yeah. That's true, but it is kinda different, sweetheart."

"Mrs. Sarah, you don't want Daniel to date me either, do you?"

"It's not that I don't want my son to date you, but it just looks better if everyone in the family is the same color, you know what I mean? Lord knows what my friends are going to say, and God forbid if y'all get married and have kids—oh! I'm sorry! I didn't mean it like that. You understand what I'm trying to say, don't you, honey? It's nothing against you, really it isn't. You're just as sweet as pie, and I can tell by the way my son looks at you, you make him happy. He's protective of you, Melah. That's very nice. Very nice indeed," Daniel's mom explained with an empty look on her face.

Melah looked down at the floor and burst into tears.

"Oh, no! I didn't mean to make you cry. Come, come, dear! Don't cry. That wasn't my intent. Here, dry your face with this," she said, giving Melah a dish towel from the drawer.

Just then Roslyn and the kids came in.

"Hey, Melah, are you okay?" Roslyn asked. "Why are you crying? Is it what my dad said? Please don't mind him. He's old fashioned, that's all. It's just how he grew up; he has a small-town mentality. Momma and I don't think the way he does and when we gang up on him, he doesn't know what to do with himself. We'll have him eating out of your hands in no time," Roslyn said, giving

Melah a wink.

"I think I should go," Melah said.

"No! No! Please don't leave," begged Daniel's mom and Roslyn. "Please stay."

"Yeah, stay, Melah," Leon said. "I haven't told you about the shows that I like to watch on television and I want you to play with the games I have here at grandma and grandpa's house!"

Melah smiled.

"Stay, Melma," Mikayla said.

Everyone laughed.

"It's Melah, Mikayla. Mel-la."

"Stay, Mel-la," Mikayla said, mimicking her mom.

Melah let out a small giggle.

"Okay, I'll stay," she said, looking at Leon and Mikayla.

Daniel's mom gave Melah a bowl of potatoes and a knife.

"I would still love your help, Melah," she said, smiling.

"And I'll help too, momma," Roslyn added.

Melah went to the bathroom to wash her face and hands, then grabbed the bowl and they all began preparing for dinner.

Meanwhile, things were getting pretty heated outside between Daniel and his dad.

"Laying up with a black woman is fine, but for goodness sakes, don't make her your girlfriend, Daniel. Do you know how this is going to make me and your momma look? I know we raised you better than this and what's with all them twisty things in her hair? She doesn't fit in with us, son."

Daniel gave his dad a repulsed look.

"I think it's time for me to go, dad! I'll see you guys later."

"C'mon, son! I'm just trying to look out for your own good, can't you see that?"

"No, dad. I think you're trying to look out for your own good, so you can continue to be accepted by your friends at the Lodge. You don't care about what's good for me!"

"Don't be getting no smart mouth with me now, boy. You're still in my house and I won't be disrespected!"

"I'm sorry, dad, but I will be leaving your house now," Daniel said, walking off and into the house to get Melah so they could go.

"Bye, momma," Daniel said, giving his mom a kiss on the cheek. Come on, Mel. Let's go," he said to Melah.

"Okay," Melah said, putting the bowl of potatoes down and grabbing her purse, not bothering to ask any questions.

"Now, Daniel. There's no need to leave just because you don't like what I said," his dad argued, as he came into the house behind Daniel.

"What's going on? Daniel, please don't leave," his mom begged.

Roslyn could see the anger in Daniel's eyes, so she didn't say a word.

"Nah, I think it's best if we leave, ma," Daniel said as he and Melah headed for the front door. "And, by the way, Melah is three months pregnant. I'm really sorry for the embarrassment your brown grandchild is going to cause you. Once your perfect friends find out, you two probably won't ever be able to recover from it," he said walking out the door and closing it behind him.

"DANIEL, COME BACK HERE!" his mom screamed. His dad stood there like he was in disbelief and so did Roslyn. Thank goodness the kids had gone into the den, and were making so much noise, that they didn't hear anything going on in the kitchen.

"DANIEL!" his mom yelled again, as she ran to the door, but Daniel had driven off and didn't bother to look into his rearview mirror.

For Daniel and Melah, the ride home was like riding in a hearse from a funeral. Not only was it melancholy, but they both knew that something had just died between Daniel and his family. Melah couldn't help but feel it was somehow all her fault. She sat in the passenger seat, silently crying, while staring out the window. Daniel knew she was crying, but he was too upset to do anything about it. Never in a million years did he think his family would act this way about him dating someone black. He grew up around black people, his mom was best friends with a black woman, Roslyn had black friends all her life. His dad worked with black people and seemed to get along with them just fine. He never knew race was that big of a deal with them until now.

They are hypocrites! They go to church every Sunday and talk about how God loves everyone. They don't mean any of that! What they mean is, God loves everyone who looks like them.

"That's not real love," he said out loud, as they were pulling into the parking lot of Melah's apartment building.

"What are you talking about?" Melah said, turning towards Daniel, hoping he wouldn't notice her watered eyes.

"I'm talking about people who go to church every Sunday and sing songs about how great God's love is towards all mankind, but then turn around and treat people like they are substandard because their skin color is different. Did God not die for everyone? Who decided that certain colors and races are of lesser value? Do we serve a God who doesn't love everyone equally? Is that the kind of God we serve, Mel?"

"No, Daniel. That is not the kind of God we serve," Melah answered, sounding like she knew everything there was to know about God.

"Well, how can someone proclaim to know God and to love God, but they can't even love people who look different than them? They didn't even give you a chance! All they saw was your skin. Is it really a disgrace that I fell in love with a black woman? And why do you have to be a black woman? Why can't you just be a woman, Mel? You're a really wonderful woman who makes me very happy. What is so embarrassing and disgraceful about that? Why do my parents care about what their stupid friends will say about my love life, anyway? True friends would never make you feel bad for your children's choices. They would be there to love and support you, just like they've always done. The real disgrace is to find out that you don't have any true friends! Now, that's what's disgraceful," Daniel said, angrily.

"I know you're upset, but I need to be honest with you," Melah said, hesitantly. "My friends and family don't like you either and when they find out that I'm pregnant, they're going to hate you. As horrible as I felt at your parents' house, things are going to be equally bad at my family's house. When you first met them, they were all excited and proud of me for graduating, and they didn't want to ruin my day, but if the truth be told, they don't want us together any more than your family does."

Daniel gave Melah a disappointed glance.

"Well, I'm not going anywhere!" he said, staring straight into her eyes. "I have my child to raise and my woman to take care of. You two are my family now."

Melah smiled and gave Daniel a kiss.

"And you are my family now," she said, "So, let's go take a family nap because I am dog tired."

Daniel laughed and they got out of the car.

"Sounds good to me, momma," he said, tapping her on the butt, as they went inside.

CHAPTER

Back in Atlanta, Everett had finally gotten up enough nerve to go and talk to the pastor about what he did to Jason.

"Hey, Pastor!" Everett said, knocking on the pastor's office door at church.

"Hey, Minister Larson! Come on in. Believe it or not, I was just thinking about you. Have a seat."

"I actually do believe it, because I couldn't rest at all this morning. I knew I needed to stop avoiding you," Everett said laughing.

The pastor let out a big chuckle.

"There's never a need to avoid me. We're family. Do you avoid your family?" the pastor asked, laughing, then he corrected himself. "Well, okay, sometimes we do avoid our family, but there's no need to avoid me," he added, letting out a rowdy laugh.

"Yeah, I avoid my family a lot, Pastor," Everett said, smiling.

"Minister Larson, I'm really glad you stopped by, though," he said, giving Everett a serious look. "Some, definitely not all, but some of the congregation said I should ask you to step down from preaching for a few months, because of what you did."

Everett looked at him like he was horrified, but the pastor continued, as if he was unsympathetic to Everett's pitiful facial expression.

"They said they can't listen to a minister who has no self-control and who go out and start fights with people."

"Pastor, I—"

"But, do you know what my response was?" the pastor said, cutting Everett off.

"No, what?"

"I handled it the way I felt Jesus would handle it. I said to them, 'Go find someone in the church who's always had self-control and self-discipline. Someone who's never acted out of anger or did anything that they shouldn't have done, and when you find this person, tell them that I said go to Minister Larson and tell him to step down from preaching.'"

Everett looked up at the pastor.

The pastor continued, "So, my question to you is, who has come to you boasting of their righteous deeds of discipline, willpower, and self-restraint? Has anyone called? Text? Wrote you a letter or emailed you? Anyone, Minister Larson?"

Everett shook his head.

"No, sir," he said.

"You see, this kind of thing has been going on since the Bible days. People always want to run to the pastor or religious leader and tell them what someone did wrong, so the person can be punished for their sins. Jesus, and Jesus alone, is the one who died for all of our sins, so how can I punish someone for something Jesus already died and forgave them for? A pastor's job is simply to show people the way to Christ."

"Wow!" Everett said.

The pastor continued. "Minister Larson, the Bible says 'All have sinned and fallen short of God's glory.' So, if I declare myself as the punisher of sins and ALL have sinned, then shouldn't I punish everyone, including myself? But the fact is, no one will know you're sinning unless you get caught, so then it becomes about who gets caught and not the sin itself. Do you see how warped this can become?" the pastor asked Everett.

"Yeah, actually I do," Everett responded.

"This is only the way I see it, Minister Larson. I know some pastors temporarily remove folks from whatever ministry they're in to show the congregation that sin won't be tolerated, and I understand what they're trying to do, but I just don't believe that's my job. Now, do I talk to my people about what they did? Yes! Do I tell them that what they did was wrong? Absolutely! But I don't punish them, because sometimes people need help. I choose to show them a better way to handle the situation, and ultimately, I just point them back to the person who already endured the punishment for all sins, and that is Jesus."

"Wow! Pastor, that's deep. I have never thought about it like that before. I always thought that you're setting a bad example for the church if you let someone who's sinned continue to do things in the church."

"Well, don't get me wrong. If someone is using their position in this church to manipulate, control, prey on or abuse others, I will put a permanent stop to that; there won't be anything temporary about it. God holds me responsible to protect his people from wolves in sheep's clothing and He doesn't put people in positions of leadership so they can abuse their power. That is wrong and it won't be tolerated, but I'm not talking about those types of people. I'm talking about people who make mistakes; people who get caught up in a situation and end up doing the wrong thing. Punishing these people only causes them to be humiliated and I don't believe it brings them any closer to God. God doesn't want us humiliating His people into living holy. To me, showing love, mercy, and compassion is what bring people to Christ; God will do the reprimanding as He sees fit." Then the pastor gave Everett a stern look and said, "Minister Larson, I really don't think you're a wolf in sheep's clothing. I think you just made a mistake, so until God shows me where I need to issue out punishment, then this is how I'm going to handle it, okay?"

"Okay," Everett said, nodding his head in agreement.

"So, now that you know how I feel about punishing people for their sins, let's talk about what possessed you to go to that man's restaurant and try to kill him?"

Everett gave the pastor a half smile.

"I don't know, Pastor. I just lost it. He's been trying to get Kirsten back and—"

"Oh, an ex-boyfriend, huh?"

"No, an ex-fiancé."

"I see."

"I was trying to deal with it the best way I could, but when Kirsten told me that he kissed her, I felt like I was having an out of body experience. I didn't think about anything else, but making him pay for putting his hands on my wife. I wasn't trying to kill him. I promise, I wasn't trying to do that, but I just wanted him to leave her alone. Looking back on it, I probably wouldn't have gone to his restaurant, but Pastor, I had to do something."

"I agree," the pastor said. "You had to let him know that what he did was unacceptable, and it wasn't going to keep happening. The Bible tells us that it's okay to get angry, but it also tells us to not allow our anger to make us sin. So, in saying that, couldn't you have just filed a restraining order against him?"

Everett laughed.

"Yeah, I guess we could have, but I wasn't really thinking about a restraining order at the time," Everett said, laughing some more.

"Yeah, and maybe I wouldn't have thought about one either, but there will always be other avenues that we can take that will keep us from getting into trouble. All I'm saying is weigh your options before you react. Minister Larson, I've known you for a very long time and I know you have a good heart. You're not an evil person who hides behind the title of a Minister just so you can manipulate and wreak havoc in the lives of others. I'll be very happy to speak on your behalf when you go to court."

"Thank you, Pastor. I appreciate it.

"But you know you're going to have to face Mr. Glaznyte again, so you probably should pray and ask God to help you forgive him for what he did."

Everett gave the pastor a distressed look.

The pastor smiled and said, "You're not forgiving him for his sake, you're forgiving him for yours. Do you know how much energy it takes to harbor bad feelings towards someone? In order for you to move on with your life and be mentally and spiritually healthy, you have to forgive those who have wronged you. Now, that doesn't mean you need to put yourself back in a position for them to keep hurting you and it doesn't mean you have to trust them again, or continue hanging out with them. What it means is that you no longer hold a grudge against them. You no longer cringe when you see their face. You no longer want to run them over with your car," the pastor said, laughing. "If you dislike someone to the point where you cannot pray for them, then you haven't forgiven them. It may not be easy to forgive Jason for what he did, but—"

"I've got to do it," Everett said, finishing the pastor's sentence.

"Yep!" You've got to do it for yourself and for your relationship with your wife, or else, every time you turn around, you're going to be talking about Jason and eventually, it'll take a toll on your marriage. Just forgive him, and let it go."

Why Keep Us Divided?

"You're right, Pastor. I need to forgive him. So, do you think I'll go to jail?" Everett asked, nervously.

"No, I sure don't, but let's just pray and ask God to intervene in this situation. Remember to do your part, though; forgive, let go, and stop trying to handle situations your way."

"Okay," Everett said, as the pastor prayed a very long prayer; longer than Everett had ever heard him pray before. Everett knew he needed God to help him out of the mess he created. If convicted, he would be facing some serious jail time and Everett knew that prison life was not something he wanted to experience. He joined in with the pastor and asked God to forgive him for what he did to Jason and he even asked God to help him forgive Jason for what he did to Kirsten.

Afterwards, Everett felt like a load had been lifted off of him.

"Thank you, Pastor. I know that everything is going to be alright."

"Yes, it sure is. Oh, did you ever find out who bailed you out?" the pastor asked.

"No, I didn't. Did you?"

"No, I don't know who could have done it, but I'm sure glad they did."

"Yeah, me too," Everett said, walking to the door. "Pastor, I appreciate you taking the time to talk and pray with me."

"That's what I'm here for," the pastor responded. "Take care of yourself, Minister Larson."

"I will, Pastor," Everett said, as he opened the door

and left.

"About three weeks later, Everett and Kirsten were sitting on the couch when Everett decided he wanted some ice cream; Kirsten was all for it. They jumped in the car and rode across town to the year-round ice cream shop.

"I can't believe this shop stays open all year!" Everett said. "They have the best ice cream here!"

"Yeah, they do! I love this place too. I used to—"

"Why did you stop? What did you used to do?"

"Nothing."

"Kirsten, don't do that!"

"I was just about to say that I used to bring Ryan here every Friday. It was our little mommy/son time."

"Oh, okay. That was very nice of you. I bet you're going to be a perfect mom. Do you want to start trying to have kids when we get back home?"

"What? Are you serious?"

"Well, why not?

"Okay, I would love to start trying to have kids," Kirsten said.

"I actually got butterflies when you said that," Everett admitted. "Well, how about we go eat some ice cream and celebrate becoming parents," he said, as he pulled into the shopping center where the ice cream shop was.

"Fabulous idea!" Kirsten said, in some foreign accent.

When they walked into the ice cream shop, they looked right in the faces of Jason, his son, Ryan, and his ex-wife, Lacey.

Why Keep Us Divided?

NOOOOOO! THIS CANNOT BE HAPPENING! Kirsten screamed with her inside voice. Everett just shook his head. Jason was the last person he wanted to see, but then he remembered his talk with the pastor a few weeks ago, so he knew he had to man-up and face the situation the right way this time.

"Ms. Kirsten! Ms. Kirsten!" Ryan yelled, leaving his parents and running up and giving Kirsten the biggest hug ever.

"Hey, Ryan!" she said excitedly, returning his hug.

For a moment, Kirsten and Ryan were caught up in their own little world and nothing else seemed to matter. Ryan told her all about school and how he had a birthday coming up soon.

"A birthday!" Kirsten said. "How old will you be?"

"Seven."

"Oh my gosh, Ryan. I can't believe you're going to be seven."

"Can you come to my birthday party?" he asked.

She looked up at Everett and Jason, who were both giving her awkward stares, then at Lacey, who looked like she was sick to her stomach at the thought of being near Kirsten.

"Well, I don't think I can come to your party, honey."

"Aww! I want you to come. My mommy and daddy can come pick you up."

"Well, I have a ride and I would love to be there, sweetie, but I just don't think I can. Can you please forgive me?"

"Yeah. Well, can we come back here and eat ice cream together?" Ryan asked, excitedly.

"Well—"

"Ryan, please let Ms. Kirsten sit down and eat her ice cream. Maybe we can work out something later, okay, honey?" Lacey said to Ryan.

Jason and Kirsten both looked at Lacey like she was crazy and Everett gave her an *over my dead body* stare.

"Come on, Ryan. We're about to go, okay?"

"Okay, mommy!" Ryan said, walking back to the table, then he turned back to Kirsten. "Ms. Kirsten, my mom and daddy are getting married again," he said.

Kirsten and Everett's eyes got big.

"Oh!" she said, trying to maintain her composure. "I think that is wonderful, Ryan. I'm very happy for them."

"You should come to the wedding! I'm going to be the ring—"

"Ryan, let's go," Jason interrupted.

"Bye, Ms. Kirsten. I'll see you later."

"Okay, bye Ryan," Kirsten responded, then he, Jason, and Lacey got up to leave.

As they were passing by, Jason stopped in front of Everett. Kirsten's heart started pounding. Everett could still see some cuts and bruises on Jason's face.

"For what it's worth, I'm sorry that all of this happened," Jason said. "I was wrong, and I'm working with my lawyer to try and get the charges dropped against you," Jason said.

"I really appreciate that, man."

"No problem," Jason said, walking off.

"Jason," Everett called out. "Did you pay my bail bond?"

Jason took a deep breath.

"No!" he said, then walked off.

Without a doubt, Kirsten knew that Jason had paid Everett's bail bond and Everett knew it too, but for some reason it made both of them feel better to hear him say that he didn't.

CHAPTER

Two more weeks passed and Melah was now four months pregnant.

"Mel, you are huge!" Daniel said. "Wait! I don't mean huge in fat, I mean huge in pregnant."

"Yeah, yeah! It's all the same."

"No, actually it's not and you are still as beautiful as the first day I met you."

"Okay, what do you want?"

"I don't want anything."

"I'm just checking, because you wanting something is what got me here in the first place."

"Give it a rest, you enjoyed it!"

"Whatever! Hey, I meant to tell you that I finally got around to reading the story about Samson and Delilah."

"You read the Bible, Mel?"

"Yes, heathens read the Bible too, ya know."

Daniel laughed out loud.

"You're not a heathen, Mel. So what did you think?"

"I really enjoyed it. I've decided to pick out a few stories here and there to read up on. You should read with me."

"Absolutely! I'd love that. Oh, by the way, you know it's time for me to head to Atlanta again. I really don't want to go, Mel. There was just way too much drama last time."

"There sure was! I definitely do not want to go with you this time."

"I don't blame you, but I will miss you," he said.

Just then the phone rang. It was Melah's mom.

"Hey, ma! I haven't talked to you in a while."

"No, you have not. That's why I'm calling to see how you're doing."

"I'm good. How are you?"

"I'm fine. Your father wants us to come visit you next week."

"Ummm, why?"

"Well, he feels like we need to talk to you about you and Daniel and where you guys are trying to go with your relationship. When we first met him, we were so consumed with your graduation party that we really didn't have time to think about him being white and the implications that will have on you. We think you need to understand all the things that come with interracial dating. People are not always nice to interracial couples, Mel."

Daniel looked at the phone and raised one of his eyebrows.

"Where is this coming from?" Daniel mouthed to Melah. Melah shrugged her shoulders.

"Okay, ma!"

"We'll come in a few days, okay?"

Melah looked down at her bulging belly and Daniel shook his head.

"I'm getting ready to go out of town, so I won't be here in a couple of days," Daniel said.

"Oh, is that Daniel? Why is he at your house so late? Y'all aren't living together, are you?"

"Nooooo! No ma'am. We're not living together," Melah said, shooing Daniel away like he needed to head home.

"I'm not going anywhere," he whispered.

Melah rolled her eyes.

"So, we'll see you in a few days, okay?"

"Ma, why do we need to have this talk again? Daniel and I are already aware of what we're getting into. I just don't think you guys need to come way over here, just to talk."

"Well, your daddy wants to come, so we're coming."

"But, Daniel is going to be out of town. Don't you want him to be here?"

"No, not really. We mainly want to talk to you. You're daddy doesn't really like Daniel, anyway, so it's probably best that he's gone."

Daniel threw his hands up in the air and gave Melah an *I thought he loved me* look.

She threw her hands in the air too, like she was just

as surprised as he was, although she wasn't surprised at all.

"Well, ma, I gotta work."

"That's fine. We can stay at your house until you get off."

"And where is Patricia gonna be? She's gonna let daddy come here with you by himself?"

"Girl, please! She doesn't trust him like that; she's coming too."

"Ma, I just don't know about this. I live in a small apartment. Please try to convince daddy that this talk isn't necessary!"

"I tried, honey. You know how stubborn your daddy is. Besides, we're not going to spend the night or anything. We'll only be there for a few hours. Just leave your key under the mat."

Melah rubbed her hands over her face.

"Ma, please don't come over here," she blurted, desperately.

"Melah, if I didn't know any better, I'd think you don't want us to come see you. We haven't seen you since graduation. I would think that you would want to see your family."

"Tell her I'm your family now," Daniel mouthed to Melah, then let out a laugh.

"Shhhh! You're not helping," she mouthed back.

"Melah? Are you listening to me?" her mother asked.

"Sorry, ma! I'm listening."

"Why don't you want us to come see you? You haven't gotten yourself pregnant, have you, because we will kill you if you have," her mom said, without hesitation.

"Ma! Where did that come from?"

"Well, you've never tried to keep us from coming to see you before."

"It's just that I'm working full-time now, so I don't have as much free time anymore, but of course I want to see you."

"Okay, good! We're just a little worried about you, that's all. You will always be our little girl."

"I know, ma."

"Well, I'll try to talk your dad out of coming, but I can't make any promises. I'll give you a call later and tell you what he says."

"Okay. Thanks, ma!"

"Bye, baby."

"Ma?"

"Yeah?"

"I ummm."

"You what?"

Melah looked over at Daniel, who was shaking his head and whispering, "No! Don't do it, Mel."

Melah looked away.

"Ma, ummm."

"What's wrong, Melah?"

"Ma, yeah, I have gotten myself pregnant. I'm four months," Melah said, closing her eyes really tight, then peeping out one of them, as if she was trying to see the expression on her mother's face, but all she saw was Daniel with his head down.

"Not over the phone, Mel," he said.

"Ma, please don't be mad," Melah said to her mom, but the phone went completely silent. Then she heard the dial tone.

"You shouldn't have done that over the phone, Mel."

"Well, she asked if I had gotten myself pregnant and I didn't want her to think I lied to her."

"So, did she hang up?"

"Yeah, I guess. Should I call her back?"

"Yeah, see if she'll answer."

When Melah called her mom back, she heard a deep voice.

"Hello," a man answered.

"Hey, who is this?"

"This is Jonathan. Who is this?"

"Oh, hey, Jonathan," Melah said to her mom's boyfriend. "I'm trying to reach my mom."

"Well, you might need to start packing your bags and try moving to a new city instead, because she just jumped in the car with Corey and they are about to head your way."

"Oh, no! You couldn't stop her?"

"I didn't even know what was going on. All I heard was her screaming, "Melah's pregnant, then all of a sudden Corey started screaming, "Let's go," then she, Corey, and all of your cousins jumped in the car and drove off. I don't even know how all of those guys fit in that car, but they piled in there. She didn't say bye or anything. She just left me standing here looking crazy."

"COUSINS?" Melah bellowed, as if that's the only

Why Keep Us Divided?

part she heard. "They were over there too?" Melah asked, in a frightened tone.

"Yeah, they were all outside playing basketball and now they're all headed to see you, so you and your white boyfriend might wanna leave, and don't tell your momma that you talked to me, okay?"

"Okay. Thanks, Jonathan. Bye."

"Bye, Melah."

"Mel, why are your hands shaking?" Daniel asked apprehensively, as Melah hung up the phone. "What did he say?"

"He said momma, Corey, and all of my cousins are on their way here."

"Oh," Daniel said, quickly packing up his things and heading towards the door.

"Are you coming?" he asked, looking back at Melah.

"No, go on. It's you that they want to kill, not me," she said, trying to smile through her shakes.

"Stop shaking. They're not gonna kill me, okay?"

"Oh, they might, Daniel. They might."

"Well, it's going to take them at least fifteen minutes to get here. Maybe we can have a little fun before I die, ya think?"

"Daniel, this is serious! If my brother and cousins catch you here, they will kill you."

"Oh! Well in that case, I better hurry and get outta here, huh?"

"Yeah, you should. Bye, baby."

"Bye! I'll call you later, if I'm not dead," he said,

closing the door.

She tried to smile, but she couldn't find anything that was funny.

As Daniel was riding through town, he saw a car full of people. He knew it had to be Melah's family, but he did not make any eye contact whatsoever. If they would've spotted him, he knew he would have been a dead man.

"There's no way all of them are in seat belts. Where are the cops when you need them?" he said, to himself.

Just in case someone noticed him and tried to follow him, he decided not to go home. Instead, he went to his cousin Jake's house. Jake was a good, ole country boy, who loved to hunt. He had tons of guns, so Daniel knew he would be in good hands.

When Daniel pulled up, Jake was outside pulling a deer up on his truck.

"Hey, man! You just killed this deer?" Daniel asked.

"Yep! And I'm about to take him to the processor. You wanna ride?"

"Ummm"

"Why are you so red and sweaty, man?" Jake asked, as he went into the house to get his keys.

"Well, Melah is pregnant and her family just found out, so they're looking for me to kill me," Daniel said, walking in the house behind him.

"HAHAHAHAHAHAHAHAHA!" Jake leaned over, laughing so hard that he was holding his side. "Please be for real, man! What's wrong?" he asked, still

Why Keep Us Divided?

laughing.

Daniel looked at him with a straight face.

"I'm serious, dude! She's pregnant and they're looking for me! I wouldn't lie about something like that."

"You got her pregnant? C'mon, man! How dumb can you be? Black people don't want no white people in their family and white people don't want no black people in theirs. I thought I told you this already, so why would you have a baby with her? You're dumb! That's all there is to it. I thought you were smart, but you're not; you're a dummy!" Jake said, taking a deep breath. "So, do Uncle Dan and Aunt Sarah know?"

"Yeah, I told them about a month ago."

"What? And nobody called and told my parents?"

"My dad probably won't tell anybody. I don't think he's going to even claim the baby."

"Now, that's not true! Uncle Dan isn't that bad."

"I don't know any more, man. I totally misjudged his reaction to this entire thing."

"Well, you should have known he wasn't going to be happy, but you're his only son and you carry on his name. He loves you, man. He may be upset, but he's not going to destroy his relationship with you over this; you should know that much about your dad. He'll come around, but first things first. Let's go get some of these guns, go over to your place, and wait for these nig—"

"Whoa! Don't do that, man! That's not necessary. Don't call them that!"

"Oh, wow! They're trying to kill you, but you don't want me to call them names? Don't you think they're calling you names right now?"

"Yeah, probably."

"Probably? Would you like me to tell you some of the words they're probably calling you, because I have a list of things they've called me, and some of them are not even in the dictionary."

"Nah, I've heard the list before."

"So what exactly would you like us to do, Mr. Stine, paint signs of love and peace and post them all over town?"

"Stop it, man!"

"Whatever, dude! If I wasn't your cousin, I'd leave you to fend for yourself, but instead, I'm going to go call some of the boys and we're going to your house and wait on them to show up."

"Her family doesn't know where I live."

"Ummm, I bet they will before the night is over. We'll just crash at your place tonight and if they show up, then it's on like popcorn," Jake said, like he was ready to fight.

Daniel just walked off, then went and sat on the couch, while Jake made phone calls to tell all the guys to meet him at Daniel's house. Daniel sat there in a daze, wondering how things had gotten so out of hand.

"All I want to do is love the woman I'm with. I don't understand why that is so hard to do," Daniel said to himself.

When Jake hung up the phone, he responded, "It's hard because you're going against the natural grain of relationships. If you stuck with your own kind, this wouldn't have happened."

"SHUT UP!" Daniel screamed. "JUST SHUT UP!"

"Hey, hey, now! Let's not forget that I'm your only hope of survival, so you might wanna be nicer to me," Jake said, giving Daniel a buck-eyed look. "Now, get in the truck. The rest of the guys will meet us at your place in a few minutes."

"So, what did you tell them?"

"I told them you invited us over to get drunk and play cards. If someone shows up at your house, those guys will be ready to fight," Jake said, laughing. "I hope you have some money because you're gonna have to buy us some beer and food."

"Really, man?"

"Well, would you like me to send you out to the wolves to defend yourself alone, big dog?"

"Fine! Fine! Let's go!" Daniel said.

When they got to the truck they saw the deer still lying there.

"Aww! My deer! See what you made me do?"

"Man, it's January; that deer is fine out here on the truck. Besides, I thought hunting season had ended by now."

"It ends today. You used to know when hunting season began and ended. You've become too corporate, Dan. You gotta come back to the country where you belong."

"Whatever, man!" Daniel said.

He and Jake went to drop the deer off at the processor, then to the store to get all the beer and food Jake could stand, then on to his house for a party that he was already regretting. He really didn't think Melah's family was crazy enough to come to his house, but then again, he'd only met them once and once was not sufficient timing to make a "They are not that crazy" judgment call. Although Daniel would never say it out loud, he had to admit that he felt safer with Jake and the boys there and for that reason alone, he gave them whatever that asked for, and Jake was asking for a lot.

While the guys were drinking and eating everything in Daniel's house, he snuck away to answer a phone call from Melah.

"Hey, babe. How are things going?" he asked her.

"Fine, I guess. They're finally gone. They ransacked my apartment looking for you. Even my mom couldn't get them to stop. I had to eventually tell them that I was going to call the cops. Then, of course, Corey told them it was time to go. He had the nerve to give me a kiss good-bye when he left."

"They're all gone? Thank goodness. I can come out of hiding now."

"Daniel, is that all you heard? They ransacked my apartment like maniacs!"

"Yeah, I heard you, but I'm just happy about being alive right now. If I'm alive, I can help you clean your apartment up, but if I'm dead, I can't do anything for you."

Just then, Jake passed by Daniel's bedroom.

"Hey, Jake! They're all gone, so you guys can pack up and leave if you want," Daniel said excitedly.

Jake let out a laugh.

"Not so, my sweet cousin of love and peace. I already told the boys that we were going to crash at your place tonight, so they are getting drunk as skunks in there. We're not leaving, but please tell Melah we all said hello."

Melah laughed.

"Sounds like you have company for the night," she said, still giggling.

"Yeah, sounds that way. So, what all did they say? Were they saying racial slurs about me?"

Melah laughed even harder.

"And you call me naïve? Did you expect them not to use racial slurs? That's the first thing people use when they want to fight someone of a different race. It's like second nature."

"Yeah, I guess. I hate this place, Mel. Everyone's mentality is so warped, but do you know what the funny part is?"

"No, what?"

"The way blacks and whites think around here is exactly the same. Their hatred is towards each other, yet, their mentality is the same for how they handle each other. I bet if you took a poll, white men would think that the world would be a better place if black men didn't exist and I guarantee black men would feel the exact same way about white men. Unbelievable! Yet, they think they're so different. Mel, sometimes I wonder if this world is ever going to get better."

"I don't know, Daniel. I hope it does because I don't know how much more I can take."

"What do you mean?"

"If you were black, yes, my family would have still been upset with you, but I know they wouldn't have destroyed my apartment looking for you. Sometimes I wonder if the struggle is even worth it. I'm tired, Daniel. I'm just really, really tired."

"Mel, we'll get through this, okay?" Soon, we will be moving to a city that accepts us just the way we are."

"But why do we have to run away just to be accepted?"

"I don't know, Mel," Daniel responded, unhappily.

He and Melah just sat on the phone, silently wondering how much more they would have to endure before being able to live a peaceful life together with their unborn child.

CHAPTER

Over the next couple of weeks, things seemed to be on an even keen. Neither Daniel's nor Melah's family was talking to them anymore, which was fine because that meant no drama and they were both very happy to be living drama-free. However, unfortunately for them, it would not last long.

One day, while at work, Mr. Jack showed up, unannounced at Melah's job.

"Hey, Melah. I was just in the neighborhood and decided to drop by to see you."

Oh, no! Not him!

"Hey, Mr. Jack," Melah said, trying not to sound disappointed to see him.

"Did you enjoy the conference?"

You mean that conference that took place a month and a half ago? Is that all he could come up with to talk to me about?

"Yeah, it was very informative."

"I figured you would like it. I thought it was very informative as well."

Melah's supervisor looked over at Mr. Jack.

"Sir, I didn't know you attended the conference with Melah," she said, suspiciously.

"Oh, yeah! It was a last minute decision. I figured it may be good to go up and do a little networking," he responded.

Melah's supervisor gave him a weird glare, as if she didn't believe him, then she glanced over at Melah, who was looking very uncomfortable.

"Oh, okay!" she said, going back to what she was doing.

"So, was that really your boyfriend or were you guys just pulling my leg?" he whispered to Melah, trying to make sure her supervisor couldn't hear him.

"Yes, he is my boyfriend," Melah said, loud enough for everyone to hear.

"Well, he was a real nice guy. I'm glad I had the chance to meet him." Mr. Jack said, loudly, as well.

"Melah, here are the papers you need," her supervisor interjected.

"Oh, thanks," Melah said, getting up and grabbing the papers.

Mr. Jack looked down at Melah's shirt, that was long and flowy and then at her belly that was slightly protruding through the shirt.

"Melah, are you pregnant?"

Melah was so startled that she dropped the stapler

that was in her hand onto her foot.

"Ow, ow, ow!" she yelled, trying to take the attention off of her belly and onto her foot.

"Melah, are you okay?" her supervisor asked as she ran over to see what happened.

Mr. Jack was totally unmoved by the incident. He asked the question again, "Melah, are you pregnant?"

"Yes, sir!" Melah said, hesitantly.

"You are?" her supervisor chimed in. "How did I not notice that? Why didn't you tell me?"

"I'm having a hard time adjusting to it myself. I just wasn't quite ready to discuss it," Melah said, still holding her big toe.

Mr. Jack was standing there looking at Melah like he was disgusted.

"Well, y'all have a good day," he said, abruptly as he left the office.

"That was weird," her supervisor said.

"Oh, you should have seen—"

"He's never come down here before," Melah's supervisor said, interrupting Melah just as she was about to tell her everything Mr. Jack was doing and saying at the conference.

"He hasn't?" Melah replied.

"No, sure hasn't," she responded, like she was jealous that Mr. Jack came to see Melah. "I wonder why he would come to see you?" she said, giving Melah a slightly envious glare.

"He only came to ask me about the conference, that's all. I hate when big wigs come down and try to talk to us little peons," Melah said, giving a fake laugh and going back to her desk, pretending to be busy.

From that day forward, Melah noticed that her supervisor changed towards her. She didn't know why, but for some reason she acted like she didn't like Melah anymore. Mr. Jack, on the other hand, couldn't seem to get enough of Melah. As each month passed, he found more and more reasons to come by and make small talk with her, but his talks always lead to some type of sexual innuendo. It was sickening to Melah, but she felt that there was nothing she could do. He was the head honcho of the company and everyone loved him. If that wasn't enough, her immediate supervisor now acted like she hated her.

One day Mr. Jack called Melah.

"Hey, Mel," he said, sounding like Daniel.

"Who is this?" she asked.

"This is Luis Jack. You don't know my voice by now?"

"No, I guess not."

"Well, that's a shame," he said, laughing. "So what do you think about us going out for drinks or something, virgin of course, and discussing where you would like to go in your career? I feel you have great potential and a lot to offer this company."

"Ummm, that's sound great, but I just don't think it would be appropriate for us to be seen together. It just doesn't look right."

"Okay, that's fine. Would you like to come to my place for dinner and we can discuss it there?"

"Sir, I can't do that. I'm sorry."

"Melah, let's be real about this. That white boy is not going to marry you. You'll be a single mother and you're gonna need some help, so let me take care of you. We'll just keep it between us, alright?" Mr. Jack assured.

The words "single mother" immediately sent Melah into a tailspin.

"I AM NOT GOING TO BE A SINGLE MOTHER AND I DO NOT NEED YOUR HELP, SO PLEASE LEAVE ME ALONE!" she screamed, hanging up the phone in Mr. Jack's face.

The whole office looked over at Melah like they were afraid she was about to start shooting up the place. She put her head in her hand, trying to hold back tears, then her phone rang again.

"Don't you ever hang up on me. You must not know who I am," Mr. Jack said, angrily. "I've done nothing but try to provide you with a better life and you've spit in my face. I don't take too kindly to someone who doesn't know what side their bread is buttered on, Ms. Thompson. You're just an entry-level employee, so you might wanna learn your place, or you can quickly be unemployed. Do you understand? Goodbye, Ms. Thompson," he said, hanging up the phone.

"I need to go home," Melah said to her supervisor. "I don't feel good."

"Make sure you put your leave in the system before you go," her supervisor responded, unremorsefully.

While Melah was about to leave all of her troubles for the day, Daniel was just about to walk into some troubles of his own.

"Daniel, do you have a minute, so we can talk?" his supervisor said.

"Yeah, sure. Please have a seat," Daniel responded.

"Nah, I'd rather stand," he said, sternly, looking down at Daniel.

Daniel pushed his chair back so he could still feel a little power against his boss, who was hovering over him.

"Okay, what can I do for you?" Daniel asked.

"Well, you've been missing a lot of work lately, gone for days at a time. The head boss seems to think that you're involved in some illegal activities."

"WHAT? WHOA! Illegal activities, just because I take off for a few days each month?"

"Well, we looked back at the records and saw that it was at the same time each month, so it kinda looks suspicious. We just wanted to make sure you understood our policy against drugs?"

Daniel shook his head.

"I can't believe you're accusing me of being involved with drugs. I've never used or sold drugs, ever."

"Well, your acquaintances have changed, Daniel, and with that may have come other associates that could have introduced you to activities you normally wouldn't have been associated with."

"Say what? Are you trying to say that since I started dating a black girl, she's exposed me to people who sell drugs?"

"Well, now, don't get all bent out of shape, Daniel. We know that her people are typically drug dealers and we just don't want any part of that in this company."

"ARE YOU SERIOUS?" I'm going to the Human Resources office to file a complaint. This is ridiculous!" Daniel said, getting up from his desk.

"I wouldn't do that, Daniel," his supervisor said, grabbing his arm.

"Don't touch me!" Daniel said, snatching away.

"If you file a report, I will have no choice but to fire you."

"Well, do what you gotta do. My drug and thug life will have to support me, I guess."

"I never said that, Daniel. I just merely wanted to remind you of our poli—"

"Oh, I heard what you said, loud and clear," Daniel said, walking off.

By the time he had gotten to the Human Resources department, his supervisor had already called them and told them that Daniel was being terminated for suspicious activity and he was looking for ammunition to use against the company. He told them that a full investigation was being conducted and he advised them to not get involved.

"Hi," Daniel said, walking into the office. "I would like to talk with someone about a work complaint."

Everyone in the office just looked at him like he was crazy.

"Sorry, Mr. Stine, an investigation is being conducted on you and we are not allowed to discuss anything with you."

"An investigation? What kind of investigation?"

"Well, I'm not sure exactly, but we are not allowed to get involved," the lady said, sorrowfully. "I'm really sorry this happened to you. You were a great worker," she whispered.

"Were a great worker? What does that mean?"

"Oh! I've said too much. Mr. Stine, I'm going to have to ask that you leave the office, now. I don't want to be involved."

"Oh, I see. Okay."

When he got back to his office, a termination letter was already typed and laying on his desk.

He ran into his supervisor's office and started screaming, "YOU'RE FIRING ME? FOR WHAT? I HAVEN'T DONE ANYTHING WRONG!"

"We ain't looking for no trouble, Daniel. Just pack your things and quietly leave the premises before we have to get the law involved. I've done everything I could to try and protect you, but you wanted to get HR involved, so there's nothing else I can do for you now," he said, looking up at Daniel with a cold demeanor.

"You haven't tried to protect me!" Daniel said, staring him in the eyes like he wanted to punch him. Then he thought about Everett and decided that going to jail wasn't worth it.

He went back, packed his things and quietly left the premises as he was instructed.

When he got home, he laid on the bed and wondered if it could get any worse. Just then, Melah called and told him that she was quitting her job. She told him how Mr. Jack had done nothing but sexually harass her for the past two months, and when she finally stood up to him, he threatened to fire her.

"He can't do that, Mel," Daniel said, angrily. Then he thought about what they had done to him at his job.

And they can't do that to me, either, he thought. *God, I really need your help.*

"I got fired today, Mel."

"What? They fired you? Why?"

He told Melah everything that happened.

"That's absurd!" she said, sounding very upset and offended. "No one in my family is involved with drugs!" she added.

"Yeah, I know. I'll give you a call back later, okay? I need to take some time to clear my head," he said.

"Me too," she agreed, and they both hung up.

CHAPTER

The next day, Daniel called Melah.

"Hey, Mel, let's go to church on Sunday. I think it will do both of us some good."

"Yes, I so need God right now."

"Yeah, me too. I'm stressed out, babe."

"Why are you stressed?" Melah asked.

"Nothing. We'll talk about it later."

"Okay," Melah said, being too caught up in her own stress to pressure Daniel into telling her about his.

When Sunday came, Daniel called Melah to let her know he was on his way to come get her.

"Okay!" she said, excitedly.

When he pulled into the parking lot, Melah didn't even let him come in. She ran outside and jumped in the car.

"Whoa! Somebody is excited to be going to the

house of the Lord," he said, smiling.

"Daniel, I need this so bad. I feel so drained. I want to feel what I felt when the pastor was praying at the police station. Did you feel it?"

"Yeah, I sure did."

"AAAAAAHHHHHH!!!!!! Did you see that?"

"Ummm, yeah, Mel. I said I felt it and saw it."

"No, silly. The baby kicked."

"Oh it did? Let me see!"

Melah pulled up her shirt and she and Daniel watched the baby who was seemingly turning flips in Melah's stomach.

"I can't believe you're six months, Mel. I can't wait to see what this little person looks like," Daniel said. "Mel, I really think we should find out what we're having. I wanna know."

"No, let it be a surprise! Let's wait until he or she gets here."

"Mel, we've got to get on the ball. We don't even have a name picked out. We barely have any clothes, no bottles, no bibs—"

"And no jobs," Melah added.

"Don't say that! We'll be just fine. Now, let's go to church and get our praise on," Daniel said, driving off and heading to church.

When they arrived, they were so excited. As they stepped into the church, a lady at the door greeted them with a nice smile.

"Welcome to Chapel Hill Worship Center," she said.

"Thank you," Melah and Daniel both said, simultaneously.

As they walked in, they noticed another lady staring at them with a weird look on her face.

"Why is she looking at us like that?" Daniel asked.

"I don't know! I don't care. Let's not let anything ruin our time with God," Melah said, grabbing Daniel's hand and leading him inside the church.

During the entire praise service Daniel and Melah were totally oblivious to anything else going on around them. All they could focus on was praising God and singing along with the choir.

♪ ♪ ♪ How great is our God. Sing with me, how great is our God and all will see, how great, how great is our God. ♪ ♪ ♪

For Melah not to know much about God or about church, she caught on pretty fast and was singing right along with Daniel, who had been in church all of his life.

After praise and worship service was over, the pastor spoke on the Power of Love. He talked about how God wants us to love every human, because we are all His creations.

"AMEN!" Daniel shouted, while Melah just sat there nodding her head in agreement.

When the sermon was finished, the pastor asked if there was anyone who wanted to come to the altar to give their lives to God. Melah leaped out of her chair and ran to the front of the church where the pastor was.

"Give God a hand for this new soul that will be entering his kingdom," the pastor said, and everyone started clapping for Melah. A lady came up beside her and gave her a hug and welcomed her into the family of God.

"Thank you!" Melah said excitedly, with tears running down her face. The lady stayed by Melah and even grabbed her hand to comfort her.

"Will there be another?" the pastor asked and a few more people came up, including Daniel.

"My heart rejoices that all of you want to know more about the Lord. He's been waiting on this day," the pastor said to everyone who came down to the altar.

The pastor looked over at Melah and she smiled.

"If you are sorry for all the sins you've committed over your lifetime, then this is the time to let God know that you're sorry, let Him know that you want His forgiveness and you want to live for Him. Thank him for His mercy and His grace, for if it wasn't for Him then some of us wouldn't have been able to endure all the things we've endured. Let's thank Him for taking care of us and protecting us and loving us enough to give His life," the pastor said, and the whole congregation joined in with loud uproars and hand clapping.

"Salvation is a relationship between you and God, only. It has nothing to do with me, nothing to do with your spouse, your friends or your loved ones. It is personal and it's only something you can decide on your own. Are you ready?" he asked.

"Yes," they all said, with excitement, but Melah screamed, "YES!"

After everyone was done praying and asking God for a clean slate, they went back to their seats, then the pastor ended the service.

After church was over, the lady that was standing with Melah came up to her and Daniel, with her husband and introduced themselves. They told them that if they needed to talk about the decision they made or anything else to please give them a call.

"Oh, thank you! That is very nice," Melah said, giving the lady a hug, but as she was hugging her, she noticed two other ladies looking over at them with uneasy looks on their faces. Daniel noticed it too, but they were so excited about their new commitment to God that they did not give it a second thought.

"Our names are Janice and John, okay?" the lady said, as she and her husband walked off.

"Okay," they responded.

A couple of weeks went by and Melah and Daniel were becoming pretty involved in church. Since they weren't working, they had a little more time on their hands to help out. Daniel was helping with the music and Melah was helping with the food ministry for the homeless. One day, her team met at church to review how they were going to distribute the food. Melah was very eager and had a lot of ideas. Most of the group welcomed her input, but she noticed that one lady seemingly got agitated every time she spoke. After the meeting was over, the lady pulled Melah to the side.

"Melah, is the guy in the music department your husband?"

"No, he's my boyfriend."

"And y'all are having a baby?"

"Well, yeah. I'm six months."

"Can I be honest with you, Melah?"

"Yeah, sure!"

"People here don't particularly like mixed couples, ya know, then on top of that, y'all are having a baby and you're not married. That's just not right in the eyes of God. None of it is right. Now, I'm not trying to be mean, but I need you to understand what the Bible says about this. Okay, honey? Now, you have some great ideas about feeding the homeless, but I think you should keep them to yourself until after you've gotten your personal life situated and in alignment with God, alright?"

Melah just stood there speechless, with tears in her eyes, as the lady walked off like she had just done some heavenly deed for God.

Melah ran out of the church and got in her car and left. She called Daniel to tell him what the lady said. He was livid.

"I'm so sick of this, Mel! Everywhere we go, it's the same thing over and over and over again. If you can't find love in the church, then please tell me where can you find it?"

"I don't know," Melah said, still crying. "I don't want to go back to that church, Daniel. I felt so humiliated."

"Okay, but, Mel, there are good and bad people in everything you do. The church is no different. We've met some really nice people while we've been there. Don't let one person keep you from going back."

"But, Daniel, they know that we're having this baby

and we're not married. They feel like we're heathens."

"Janice and John also know that we're having a baby and we're not married and they've been nothing but nice to us."

"Yeah, but—"

Just then Melah's phone rang; it was Janice.

"Daniel, this is Janice. Let me give you a call back, okay?"

"See. They're not all bad, Melah," Daniel said.

"I guess. Bye, babe," she said clicking over to the other line to talk to Janice.

"Hi, Melah. This is Janice. How are you?" Janice said.

"I'm okay, I guess," Melah responded, trying not to sound too upset.

"What's wrong?" she asked, but Melah didn't want to tell her because she didn't want Janice to think she was trying to start mess in the church.

"Melah, I want to be your friend. You can talk to me, okay?" Janice said, reassuringly, so Melah told her everything that happened at the church meeting.

"Oh, Melah. I'm so sorry. Please don't hold that against the entire church. As much as the pastor talks about love and kindness, some people are just mean-natured. I don't even know why they come to church. I know that's bad to say, but it seems like they only come to try to destroy the church members. I'm so very sorry this has happened to you."

"But maybe she's right. Daniel and I are having a baby out of wedlock and God is not happy about that."

"Melah, you've already asked God to forgive you for all of that, it is water under the bridge, now. No one can make you feel bad for that. And you were already pregnant when you came to the church. It's a nine-month process, Melah. You can't just make the baby come out, just because you've asked God for a clean slate. You still have to carry the baby until it's ready to come. She should not have tried to make you feel bad for something you have no more control over."

"Yeah, but Daniel and I really should get married, so it won't look so bad."

"That is never a reason to get married, sweetie. Do you love Daniel and want to spend the rest of your life with him?"

"Yeah. I do."

"Well, then that's the reason you get married, okay?"

"God has forgiven you, so don't you let anyone make you think he hasn't."

"Well, what about what she said about mixed couples not being right in God's eyes?"

"You should have told her to show it to you in the Bible. It's so ridiculous how people use God's word to try and make people do what they want them to do. I truly believe that they will have to answer to that. Melah, if you and Daniel are happy together, maybe he is actually the one that God has chosen for you to be with. Have you ever thought about that?"

Melah smiled really big.

"No, I've never thought about that."

"Well, you should. You both came to church and gave your lives to God, so why wouldn't he be the one for you? God can go to another race to bring you the person he has for you, ya know? He doesn't put himself in a box. He'll put together any two people he wants and there is nothing anyone can do about it. I think you are a beautiful couple. The Bible says, 'What God has joined together, don't let anyone tear apart.'"

"The Bible says that?"

"Yes, it does," Janice said, smiling.

"I'm gonna go find that scripture and show it to Daniel. He knows the Bible pretty well, so he's probably already heard of it before."

"Sounds like you have a good man, Melah."

"Yeah, I do. Thank you, Janice."

"So, you won't leave the church, right?"

"No, I won't leave."

"Good! I'm very glad to hear that. Okay, well call me anytime you need to talk, okay?"

"Okay, I will."

"I'll talk to you later then."

"Okay, bye Janice."

As soon as Melah hung up with Janice, she called Daniel back.

"Daniel! Did you know that the Bible says, 'What God has joined together, don't let anyone tear apart?'" Melah said, before Daniel could get, "Hello" out of his mouth.

"Ummm, well hello to you too. I see you're in a much better mood."

"Yes, I am. So did you know that?"

"Yeah. I've heard it before."

"Daniel, that scripture is for us. I think we should quote it to each other whenever we're going through rough times."

"I'd like that, Mel. I think that will be nice."

"Me too."

"I think I'm going to give Jason a call and ask if I can start work early. Although my time off has been wonderful, I need to get back to work. Besides, my 6-month probation will be up in two weeks anyway and I don't see any reason why I shouldn't get the job permanently."

"So, you're gonna go ahead and move to Atlanta?"

"I don't have a choice, Mel. I don't have a job anymore and we have a baby coming in three months."

"Well, I'm going too!"

"What about your apartment lease?"

"I don't know, but I don't have a job either, so I can't pay them if I'm not working. Maybe they'll work with me on the lease."

"Well, let me give him a call and I'll call you back, okay?"

"Okay, bye," Melah said.

Daniel immediately called Jason.

"Hey, Daniel. I'm very glad you called," Jason said, sounding like he was really upset.

"You don't sound good, boss. What's going on?" Daniel asked.

"Mr. Cross died this morning. The whole office is

in bad shape. He's been with us from the beginning and I—"

"Oh, no! I'm so sorry to hear that. I know he never came back to work from when he was in the hospital, but I didn't know he had gotten sicker. Was it related to the heart attack or was it his liver disease?" Daniel said, hoping that he was not the cause of Mr. Cross' death.

"It was his liver disease. It had already turned into cancer. That's why he passed out that day. The hospital told him that he did not have a heart attack. It was just the cancer eating his insides up and he collapsed."

"Oh, he didn't have a heart attack at all?"

"No, not at all."

"Oh!" Daniel said, sounding relieved. "So when is the funeral service?"

"It's this Saturday. That's why I'm glad you called. I have so much going on this week and I could really use your help. I know your probation isn't up until a few weeks from now, but do you think you can start work early? I know I'm throwing this at you at the last—"

THANK YOU, JESUS!

Daniel tried to gather his composure.

"Absolutely!" he said, cutting Jason off. It's no problem at all. When do you need me to come?" he asked.

"Well, I would like you to come as soon as you can. I know you need to put your two-weeks' notice in at your—"

"Already done," Daniel said, cutting him off, again.

"Oh, good! And don't worry about a place to stay. I'll put you up in a condo for a few months until you get settled and figure out where you want to live."

"You're gonna do what?"

"I'll put you in a condo. It's really nice and in a nice neighborhood. You'll like it. So when do you think you can come?"

"I can come today," Daniel said, in a serious tone.

Jason let out a small laugh.

"Nah, tomorrow morning will be fine. Just relax today and think about what you want to bring with you. Pack up enough things for a few days and after the funeral, I'll give you some time to pack up your house. The secretary will have a moving company to give you a call tomorrow and set up a time to pick up the rest of your things."

"You're moving me to Atlanta?"

"Yes, of course I'm moving you. You thought I was going to let you move yourself? That's not how I do business, Daniel. I take care of my people, because when they start working I expect them to take care of me."

Daniel thought about how he did not take care of Jason the night Everett came to the restaurant. He still felt very guilty about that, but he didn't know what else he should have done. Well, he definitely shouldn't have told Everett that he could go back and finish the job, but other than that, he didn't know what else he should have done.

"Well, I have to go, Daniel. I'll see you tomorrow, okay? Thank you for doing this for me on short notice. I really appreciate it."

"Oh! No problem," Daniel responded.

"Wait!" Jason said. "You called me. What did you

need?"

"Nothing. I was just checking in. That's all."

"Well, it was good timing," Jason said.

"Yes, it sure was," Daniel said, before hanging up the phone. Then he immediately called Melah and told her to pack her bags, because they were moving to Atlanta.

CHAPTER

"HONK! HONK! HONK! HONK! HONK!" was the sound Melah heard outside of her apartment window early the next morning. It sounded like someone's car alarm was going off, but it was just Daniel, ticking off all of Melah's neighbors.

"What are you doing? Stop blowing the horn like a wacko!" Melah said to Daniel as she came out onto her balcony.

"YEAH! STOP BLOWING THE HORN LIKE A MANIAC!" a little old man said, angrily, as he was sitting on his porch, reading the newspaper and sipping on coffee. "These young'uns act like they ain't got no cotton-pickin sense no more," the man added, giving Daniel some more choice words, then going back into his apartment and slamming his door.

Melah and Daniel both laughed!

"Mel, you have no idea how ready I am to leave this place," Daniel yelled from the parking lot.

"Oh, yes I do, because I am just as ready as you are, but we're never gonna make it if you get beat up by that little old man."

"Yeah, right! I can take him with my eyes closed. Now, come on. Let's go!"

Melah grabbed her bag, locked up her apartment, and rushed outside.

"I can't believe how this worked out," she said, hopping in the car.

"It was nothing but God that did this for us. There's no other explanation," Daniel said.

Daniel gave Melah a serious look.

"Mel, I'm pretty bummed that Mr. Cross had to die. I was hoping he would survive this thing, but I'm really glad I wasn't the reason for his death, though. I wouldn't have been able to live with myself."

"Huh? Why in the world would you think that you had anything to do with Mr. Cross' death?"

Daniel told Melah everything that happened the day Mr. Cross passed out.

"Oh, my gosh, Daniel! Why didn't you tell me that you like to kill people?" she said, staring at him like he was the Grim Reaper.

"That's not funny, Melah Thompson. I was planning to tell you all about it, but so much was going on that day, it just slipped my mind."

Melah laughed.

"I think that's the first time you've ever called me by my full name, Daniel. I kinda like it."

Daniel gave her a faint smile.

"Yes, there was a lot going on that day," she said. "But, you should have never felt responsible for Mr. Cross' death."

"Yeah! You're right."

"Daniel, do you think we should call Janice and John to tell them we won't be coming back to church?" Melah asked, changing the subject. "They've been so nice to us. I'd hate to just leave and not tell them anything."

"Sure! If we stop coming, they're gonna be worried about us."

"Yeah, they will," she responded, dialing the number.

"Hello," John answered.

"Hi, John, this is Melah. Hold on, I'll let you speak to Daniel," she said, tossing the phone into Daniel's lap, like she was afraid to hold a conversation with John.

"Thanks for trying to make me have a wreck," Daniel said to Melah, grabbing the phone out of his lap.

"What's up, John!" he said.

"Hey, bro. How's it going?"

"Everything is great! I just wanted to call and let you know that I got a job in Atlanta, so I'll be moving up there."

"For real? Man, I sure do hate that you guys are leaving, but sometimes you gotta do what you gotta do," John said.

He asked Daniel a few more questions about what he was going to be doing in Atlanta. Then he said, "I would like to say a quick prayer for you over the phone, if you don't mind."

"Sure, but I'm driving."

"Don't close your eyes!" Melah whispered.

Daniel looked at her out of the corner of his eyes.

"That's okay," John said. "I can pray while you drive; you just keep your eyes on the road, though."

Daniel laughed and looked over at Melah, thinking she heard what John had said, but she was busy looking out of the window at her dream cars as they passed by.

John prayed a very quick prayer for safe travels, blessings, and God's will to be done over Daniel's life.

"Thank you, man," Daniel said, as John finished the prayer.

"Daniel, you will do right by Melah when you get to Atlanta, won't you?"

"Yeah, but what do you mean?"

"Well, she's having your baby and you love her, right?"

"Yeah," Daniel responded, hesitantly, trying to see where John was going with the conversation.

"Have you given much thought to marrying her?" John asked.

Daniel looked over at Melah, who seemed oblivious to the entire conversation.

I'm no fool. I know Melah always eavesdrops even when she looks like she's not, Daniel thought.

"Well, kinda," he said, to John. "It's definitely something I want to do, but so much has been going on that I haven't actually made any plans, but yes, I will do it."

"Well, whenever you decide, please let us know. We'd love to come. I mean, if you decide to have a wedding, that is; I know some people don't have wedding ceremonies. Anyway, I'm not trying to get all in your business or anything," John said, laughing. "I was just wondering how you felt about getting married, that's all."

"Nah, you're good! Y'all are good people! I don't mind you asking me that."

"Good! So, how long have you guys been dating?"

"Okay, now you're just being nosey, bruh," Daniel said, laughing.

John laughed too, then Daniel started counting dates in his head.

We were dating four months when she got pregnant. She's six months pregnant now, so—"

"Ten months," he said, catching Melah's attention. Melah turned to Daniel and started listening to see what they were talking about, but when Daniel saw her glance over at him, he figured it was time to cut the conversation short.

"John, I have to run, but I'll keep you posted on everything."

"Alright, bro. Y'all take care, okay?"

"Okay, sure will," Daniel said, hanging up.

He knew Melah was about to ask him what he and John were talking about, but instead, she started telling him about a white convertible Audi R8 that just passed.

"Daniel, did you see that car? Do you know how good I would look in that?" she said, excitedly.

"Well, one day I'll buy it for you."

"Awwww, that's so—wait a minute! Did you even see what car I was talking about?"

"Nope, but when I'm ready to buy it, I'm sure you will tell me," Daniel said, laughing.

Melah rolled her eyes, then she laughed and said, "You're right about that! I sure will tell you."

Melah glanced at Daniel with a serious look on her face.

"What's wrong?" he asked.

"Daniel, do you think we should tell our family we're moving to Atlanta together?"

"Nope!"

"Daniel! We have to tell them."

"Yeah, I guess, but let's do it next week, okay?"

Melah frowned, then said, "Well, okay, but I really miss talking to my mom."

Daniel glimpsed back at her.

"Yeah, me too, Mel. You know I'm a momma's boy, but my mom hasn't even tried to call me."

"Well, mine hasn't tried to call me either. I don't understand why they're so upset about us having a baby. Anyone can see that what your mom said isn't true."

"What do you mean? What did my mom say?"

"Uhhhh! Nothing. She and I were just talking. It was nothing," Melah said, trying to backtrack her words.

"I want to know what my mom said to you," Daniel responded, like he was getting upset.

"She didn't mean anything by it, Daniel. She said she thought we were just intrigued with each other and wanted to try something new, but she didn't think we would actually stay together and she didn't expect you to ever bring me home to meet them."

Daniel rubbed his eyebrow.

"I can't believe she said that to you. I can't believe

she even felt that way. I thought she supported me. She acted like she was happy for us. What else did she say?" he asked.

Melah saw how upset Daniel was getting and there was no way she was going to tell him the rest of the things his mom said to her. Mrs. Sarah was still Daniel's mother and Melah knew Daniel loved his mom more than life itself; she was not going to cause an even bigger gap between them than what was already there.

"Nothing. That's pretty much it," Melah replied.

"Well, that was definitely enough. It still wasn't as bad as the stuff my dad said to me, though."

"What did your dad say?"

"It doesn't matter and it doesn't change how I feel about you," Daniel said, turning on the radio to listen to music.

Melah decided to not push the issue because she knew it was only going to get her upset and she was too excited about moving to Atlanta to let anything upset her.

When they got to Atlanta, Daniel stopped by the office to pick up the key to his condo.

"I gotta drop some things off first," he said to the secretary. "But, I'll be right back," he added. He didn't bother to mention that the things he had to drop off included Melah.

Daniel found the condo, which was only about a fifteen minute drive from his job.

"Oh, my! Look at this place," Melah said, with her mouth wide open.

"This place is beautiful!"

"Yes, it is. I can't believe he did this for you," Melah said.

"For us," Daniel said, correcting Melah.

Melah almost let out a loud giggle, but she didn't want to seem too excited about Daniel using the word "us," so instead, she just smiled.

When Daniel went back to the office, Melah made herself comfortable in their new condo, which was already fully furnished. Once they moved to Atlanta permanently, the company was planning to give them an unfurnished apartment, so they could bring in all of their furniture, but until then, Melah was busy getting lots of decorating ideas from the lovely décor already in place.

That upcoming Saturday was Mr. Cross' funeral, which Daniel and Melah both attended. Mr. Cross' family was very distraught, but as they were getting into the hearse to leave the grave site, his wife walked up to Daniel and gave him a hug.

"My husband really did like you," she said. "I know he didn't show it, but he used to come home and brag about how smart you were. He was just a little jealous, that's all; he knew the company's accounting books were going to be in good hands. After he got out of the hospital he decided to just enjoy his remaining three months. He went sky diving!" she said, letting out a big laugh. "Can you believe that? I thought I was going to have a cow, but he survived and so did I, I guess," she said, laughing again and wiping away tears. "He said he got the idea from you," she added, giving Daniel a sideways look and grinning some more.

Daniel laughed.

"I just told him that there was a lot that he could do in six months. I didn't give any specifics," Daniel explained.

"Well, he did them, Daniel and he had a blast."

She gave Daniel a serious look. "Thank you," she said, wiping the flow of tears that had started to run down her face. "Thank you so much! He was so depressed until you came along. You gave him his spunk back. You gave him a reason to live before he died and I just want to say thank you."

Daniel was trying to hold back his tears, but Melah was standing beside him balling like a little baby and so was the rest of Mr. Cross' family.

Mr. Cross' wife gave Daniel another hug and told him good-bye.

"Bye, Mrs. Cross," he said, as he wiped a tear from his eyes.

The rest of Mr. Cross' family gave Daniel and Melah hugs too, then they all got in the hearse and drove away.

As the hearse drove down the street, Daniel looked over at Melah and gave her a hug.

"It's a beautiful day, Mel. Let's go to this park over here," he said pointing to a park right across from the cemetery.

"The park?" she asked, still wiping away tears. "But we're in funeral clothes.

"It doesn't matter. Let's go," he said, grabbing her hand and leading her across the street, to the park.

CHAPTER

When Daniel and Melah got to the park, they sat down on one of the benches.

"You are so very beautiful to me," Daniel said to Melah.

She gave him a strange look because Daniel really wasn't the sentimental, romantic type.

He put his arm around her and they reminisced about the day he got up enough nerve to talk to her in math class…

I would really like to get to know her, Daniel thought as he stared at Melah, sitting across from him in Business Calculus class.

"Melah Thompson, I know you're trying, but you're not doing so well in this class," their teacher, Mr. Lloyd, said, walking up to Melah and handing her a math test with an 'F' on it.

"Ugggghhhh! I don't understand any of this foreign

disarray of utter confusionology," Melah said, in an aggravated tone.

"It's called math, Ms. Thompson and it's been around for ages; nothing foreign or utterly confusing about it," Mr. Lloyd responded, walking over to Daniel and handing him his test.

"Very good, Mr. Stine, as always," he said.

"Grrrrr, I hate math," Melah grumbled, like a two year old, about to throw a tantrum.

"Well, I suggest you be a big girl and pay someone to tutor you," Mr. Lloyd responded, nonchalantly.

"I suggest you be a big girl and pay someone to tutor you," Melah's friend, Anna chimed in, mocking Mr. Lloyd. "It's okay, girl, you'll get the hang of it. I can help you if you want," she added.

"What did you make on your test?" Melah asked Anna.

"Girl, I made a 'D' plus."

Daniel let out a small giggle; Anna looked over at him and gave him a death stare.

Melah twisted up her lips at Anna.

"You made a 'D?' You can't help me with nothing," said Melah.

Anna laughed.

"It was a 'D' plus, thank you very much."

"Whatevvvv."

"Okay, I cannot help you, but maybe we could have a study party tonight at your place. If you're willing to cook, I'll buy all of the ingredients."

"Why do I have to cook?" Melah asked.

"Because, no one else can cook as good as you and we can't afford to go out to eat, so tell me what you want to cook and I'll pick up all the stuff this afternoon when I get out of class."

"I'm cooking a math casserole. Maybe that'll help us pass this stupid class."

Anna gave Melah a perplexed frown.

"That was such a corny joke, Melah. Please don't try to make anyone else laugh with that. Besides, a 'D' is passing, so, I really don't have to study, ya know," Anna said, as if she was trying to do Melah a favor.

"Ummm, you're barely passing, hun, but maybe I can cook some lasagna," Melah said, trying to redeem herself from the bad math casserole joke.

Daniel's wheels started turning, trying to figure out how he could interject himself into their conversation.

"I love lasagna," he blurted, without even thinking.

"AND? Who asked you?" Anna said to Daniel, but Melah just looked at him and smiled.

After class was over, Daniel walked up to Melah.

"Hey, Melah," he said.

Anna looked at him like he had lost his mind.

What does this white dude want? He ain't getting none of our lasagna! Anna thought.

"I'm very good at math," Daniel continued. "But I hate cafeteria food, so if you're willing to cook for me from time to time, I'll help you become a straight 'A' student in Mr. Lloyd's class. Deal?" Daniel asked, smiling and extending his hand towards Melah, so they could seal the deal with a handshake.

"Oh! Uhn Unnn! We don't trust you," Anna said, pushing Daniel's hand away from Melah.

"ANNA!" Melah yelled.

Before that moment, Melah and Daniel had never said one word to each other, mainly because they were in two totally different circles and never had a need to communicate. Of course they knew each other from some of their classes, but Melah had never thought about having a conversation with him and she definitely never thought about cooking for him or being tutored by him. One thing she had thought about, though, was how she desperately needed help with Calculus.

Just then, Daniel's cousin, Jake, walked up. "C'mon, man! Let's go," he said, wondering why Daniel was talking to Melah.

"Okay, hold on," replied Daniel. He looked back at Melah and said, "Just think about it and let me know, okay?" then he and Jake began to walk off.

Melah took a deep breath.

"Yes! I'll do it!" she yelled to Daniel, "But you have to help buy some of the food."

He turned around and smiled.

"Great! What's your number? I'll give you a call when I'm ready for dinner," he said, with a sexy grin.

"Ummm, she's having dinner with me tonight!" Anna interrupted.

"We will let Melah be the judge of that," Daniel said, then he took out a ten dollar bill. "This should help with the food," he said to Anna.

"I don't want your money. Don't pay me like I

work for you."

"Okay, I get to eat for free; even better," Daniel replied, putting his money back in his pocket.

Anna looked at Daniel like she wanted to give him a back-handed slap.

"How about we all meet at my place around 6:30? Lord knows you could use some tutoring too, Anna," Melah said.

"I don't need any tutoring and I honestly don't think he's interested in any tutoring, either," Anna professed, staring at Daniel.

"You're right, Anna. I really just want some food, but I'll throw in the tutoring for free," he said, giving her a sarcastic wink.

"I don't think I like you," Anna said to Daniel.

"Many people don't," Daniel replied. "I consider it a gift," he added.

Melah laughed really loudly, as if Daniel had just said something worthy of an Oscar Award.

"Oh, isn't he just a bag of laughs?" Anna said, giving Daniel an evil-eye glare.

"Here, Melah," he said, giving her a piece of paper that he wrote his phone number on. "Call me and give me directions to your place."

"Okay, I sure will. Thank you for your help; I really appreciate it," Melah responded.

"It's not a problem. I'll see you ladies at 6:30," Daniel replied, then he turned back to his cousin, Jake.

"And please leave your knives and strangling materials at home," Anna added, as Daniel walked off.

"I only have enough strangling materials for one person, Anna. I guess you'll be the lucky girl," he said, as he kept walking.

Melah let out another loud laugh.

"That guy is creepy, Melah. He may be a straight 'A' student, but it's the smart ones that build bombs and start blowing up everything, ya know. You better watch out for him," Anna said, suspiciously.

"I think he's funny!" Melah replied.

"What was that all about?" Jake asked Daniel.

"Nothing, I'm just going to tutor her in math and she's going to give me home-cooked meals."

"What? Are you serious?

"Well, she's flunking math, dude. Somebody needs to help her and that cafeteria food is growing a fungus in my belly. I don't know how much more I can stand! If I can get her to cook for me a few times a week, then I might be able to survive college."

"You're just a picky eater. You can find something edible in that cafeteria."

"That food is nasty and you know it. She and I are just helping each other out, that's all."

"I don't know about this set up, Dan. If people start seeing you hanging out with a black girl, they're gonna start talking and there goes your love life, down the drain of no repair."

Daniel shook his head.

"It's not that serious, man."

"Okay, suit yourself, but she got an 'F' on that test, so you've got your work cut out for you. Even I got a 'C' and you know I don't know a thing about math."

"Well, everyone isn't good enough to make 'C's' in math like you," Daniel said, sarcastically. "I have her in two of my other classes and she's as sharp as a tack, so I know math is just her weakness."

"How do you know so much about her? Why do you even care?" Jake asked.

"I'm a very caring person. You should know that about me," Daniel said, laughing

"Yeah, right. Well, I'm sleepy," Jake said, changing the subject.

"Yeah, me too. I'm definitely gonna crash when I get to my room," Daniel responded, as they walked back to the dorm.

Later that evening, when Daniel arrived at Melah's apartment, Anna was there waiting for him, ready to pick up where they left off.

"Hey, Daniel!" Melah said, excitedly, opening the door and letting him in. "I'm so glad you're helping me! This is the first time I've ever felt a glimmer of hope towards Calculus."

"It's my pleasure; I love math, so I'll have you in tip top shape in no time," he replied, smiling. Then he glanced over at Anna, who looked like she was sickened by his and Melah's sweet and cordial interaction.

Anna could see right through Daniel's plan. She knew he liked Melah, but she felt that he only wanted to use her to find out what it was like to have sex with a black girl and for that, she was not letting him get anywhere near Melah.

Daniel didn't care about Anna's opinion of him. The only person he wanted to impress was Melah and that's exactly what he did.

They all sat and ate dinner, while Daniel showered Melah with his jokes and charm, then he jumped right into Calculus, giving Anna very little time to pick a fight with him. He brought in an easel and went over each problem just like Mr. Lloyd would do, except with Daniel, it wasn't as complex. Matter of fact, he made it look extremely easy. Even Anna had to admit that she liked the way Daniel explained things. With each problem that Daniel solved, he became more and more fascinating to Melah. She began to notice everything about him; his jet black hair, his olive skin, his pretty eyes and even his pink lips.

This guy is really handsome, Melah thought. *I wonder if he's all white or if he's mixed with something else. Most white people don't have olive skin.*

"Daniel, what race are you?"

Daniel laughed; Melah noticed his perfect teeth, but the only thing Anna noticed was how these two were thoroughly getting on her nerves.

Daniel responded, "My grandmother was white and my granddad was Italian, so my mom is mixed, but my dad is all white. I just happen to have a lot of my granddad's traits."

"Oh, that explains why your skin—"

"Ummm, excuse me. Although I would love to continue hearing about his Italian heritage, I'm getting sleepy and would like to finish this tutoring sometime before midnight," Anna mentioned.

"Hush, Anna. If he's going to be tutoring us, we should try to get to know him, don't you think?"

"No, I don't think! This is all business; we don't need to get to know him," Anna responded, and Daniel went back to explaining Calculus on the easel.

He then instructed Melah and Anna to try to do the problems on their own. When he came over to look at Melah's paper, she got a whiff of his cologne.

"Daniel, what is that you're wearing? It smells good," Melah said.

Anna just threw up her hands.

"Is this about learning math or about Mr. Peabody's cologne over here?" Anna asked.

"Anna, Mr. Peabody is a dog," Melah said, cynically.

"Well, if the ruff fits, let him wear it," Anna replied.

Daniel laughed so hard that he almost choked on the glass of water he was sipping. Anna looked at Daniel and she started laughing too, then Melah joined in.

"Well, I've had enough of you and Daniel," Anna mentioned. "I'm going home. Goodnight," she said, packing up her things and leaving.

"Bye, Anna. I'll see you in the morning."

"Yeah, yeah! I'll call you later to make sure Romeo doesn't put you under his spell with all of that cologne."

"Anna! Stop it!"

When Anna left, the attraction between Melah and Daniel was so strong that, although they tried, neither of them could concentrate on math anymore. Every time they looked at each other, they pictured themselves in bed, having sweaty, passionate sex. They tried very hard to deny the chemistry that was brewing between them. All they could think of was ripping each other's clothes off, but they didn't. At least not that night.

When Daniel got ready to leave, Melah walked him to the door.

"Thanks again for all your help," she said, smiling.

"You're very welcome. Have a good night," he responded, then she closed the door as he left.

As Daniel walked to his car, Melah stood at the window watching him, then all of a sudden he made an abrupt stop, turned around, and came back to her apartment.

"BAM! BAM! BAM!" he knocked.

She opened the door.

"Did you forget something?" she asked.

"Yeah, I forgot to kiss you," he said, pulling Melah into him, not waiting for her response, which was fine because there wasn't much of a response for Melah to give, other than to return his kiss, and that's exactly what she did. He leaned her up against the door, while tasting every part of her lips. Then he stopped.

"Okay, see you in class tomorrow. Goodnight," he said, walking off again.

"Ummm, oh, okay! Goodnight," Melah responded, still standing there panting like a hungry lioness. She closed the door again and went back to the window to watch Daniel as he drove off.

"Bummer! Now I've got to go take a cold shower to cool myself off," she said, so that's just what she did, then she got into bed and went to sleep.

The next day, Anna anxiously waited for Melah to arrive at school so she could question her about what happened after she left, but Melah's lips were sealed.

In class, Anna watched how Melah and Daniel kept giving each other weird glances and subtle grins.

I knew I shouldn't have left those two alone.

She reached over and pinched Melah's arm.

"Ow! What did you do that for?"

"You better not have slept with him," she said, looking back at Daniel and rolling her eyes.

Daniel shrugged his shoulders like he didn't know what Anna was talking about.

"Oh, don't play dumb, Daniel. I saw right through your sneaky little plan," Anna whispered to Daniel.

Melah just sat there smiling like she was still on cloud nine from Daniel's kiss, not paying a bit of attention to Anna.

"Anna, I don't know why you decided to come to class today because all you've done so far is talk," Mr. Lloyd said. "Would you like to go home and try this again tomorrow?" he asked.

"No, sir!" Anna said, as if she was embarrassed, but obviously not embarrassed enough to stop giving Melah and Daniel dirty looks.

After class, Anna still tried to pry information out of Melah, but Melah wasn't saying a word and neither was Daniel. Matter of fact, Melah didn't even let Anna in on the next tutoring session, if one would call it a tutoring session. It was more like a tutoring and make-out session, but nevertheless, Melah ended up with a 'B' in Business Calculus, and for that, Melah was very grateful to Daniel.

There was no doubt that Daniel and Melah had an undeniable bond, and to them, that was enough reason to disregard the many obstacles they would face for believing that love should never be bound by color.

CHAPTER

After Daniel and Melah finished reminiscing about how they fell in love, Daniel looked over at Melah, who was still blushing about their first kiss.

"You mean the world to me, Melah," he said, getting down on one knee and grabbing Melah's hand.

She gave him a strange look.

Is he about to—

"And I want to spend the rest of my life waking up next to you," Daniel added, interrupting Melah's thoughts. "I would be so honored if you would become Mrs. Stine," he said, as he placed a ring on her finger.

"UUUUAAAAAAAHHHHHHH!" was all Melah could say.

Daniel waited patiently for her to come out of shock and give him a yes or no answer, but instead, she just gave him a big hug, then danced around the park singing, ♬ ♪ ♬ I can't believe we're getting married, married, married, married, married. ♬ ♪ ♬ I can't believe we're getting married. I'm the happiest girl in the world ♬ ♪ ♬

Daniel took that as a yes and started rocking his head back and forth to Melah's music, then all of a sudden she kissed him.

"Yes, Mr. Stine. I would love to marry you," she said, then went back to her "married" song and dance.

Daniel didn't want to ruin the mood, but there was something he really needed to discuss with Melah before they went any further.

"Mel, I want my family to be at the wedding," he said, looking up at Melah, who was still twisting and twirling around to her made-up song.

"Wait! What?" she said, abruptly stopping in her tracks.

"I don't want to get married without my family being there," Daniel said. "I know they're not happy about us, but I still love them and I want them to love you too."

"Oh, okay. Well, let's call them. I'll invite my family too," Melah said. "I think enough time has passed for them not to be angry anymore, right?" she asked, unconvincingly.

"I don't know, Mel. I sure hope so, though."

"Well, let's call them now and see," Melah suggested.

Melah called her mom first.

"Hey ma! This is Melah," she said waiting for her mom to start screaming.

"Hey, Melah. How have you been?" her mom responded in a calm tone.

"I'm great. Really great! Momma, Daniel and I are

getting married and moving to Atlanta. I know you guys don't really care for Daniel, but I love him and we would love for everyone to come to our wedding."

"Oh! I see. Are you sure you—"

"I love him, momma and I'm sure about everything."

"Well, okay! I'll be there. When is it?" her mom asked.

"Daniel, when is the wedding?" Melah whispered to Daniel.

"I don't know. I guess our anniversary will be a good day to get married."

"That's only two months away, Daniel!"

"Melah, are you still there?" her mom asked.

"Yes, ma. Hold on for one minute," Melah said, putting her mom on mute. "Daniel, you're the only one working right now. Are we going to be financially ready to have a wedding in two months? Besides, I'm going to be eight months pregnant. I'll look like a sacred cow in all of that white. Lord knows I shouldn't even be wearing white."

"We'll be fine, Mel. Tell her we're getting married on our one-year anniversary, May 10th."

"I'm sorry, ma! I'm back now. Our wedding will be on May 10th, our one-year anniversary date."

"One-year anniversary? Well, I guess y'all were sneaking around way before you brought him to meet us, huh? That's not a good sign, Melah."

"Momma, please! I really want you and daddy to be there. It's my special day, so please don't try to make me feel bad."

"I said we're coming, didn't I?"

"Okay, but it'll be really small, so just tell Corey and daddy, grandma, Aunt Sue, and Uncle—"

"I know who to invite, Melah."

"I don't want everyone to come, ma. I want to keep it small, okay?"

"I got it, I got it. I'll call and tell your dad now. Just call me back and let me know where it's going to be."

"Well, can you please just get everybody's address for me? I want to send out invitations."

"Just send your invitation to me and I'll make sure everyone knows how to get there," her mom demanded.

Melah let out a deep sigh.

"Ma, I really want to do this the right way."

"Melah, you're six months pregnant and you're getting married in less than two months, so you're obviously not that set on doing things the right way."

Daniel's eyes got big.

"Hang up!" he said, loud enough for her mom to hear. "She's trying to be hurtful."

"DID HE JUST TELL YOU TO HANG UP ON ME?"

"No, I think he was talking about something on television," Melah said, telling Daniel to shush. "Okay, well, I'll send all the invitations to you and you can pass them out to everyone, okay?" she said, trying to get her mom back on track.

"I know he was not talking to the television, but that's fine, send me the invitations."

"Okay, bye, momma."

"Bye," her mom said, slamming the phone down.

"Melah, I don't think this is a good idea," Daniel said, shaking his head. "I have a bad feeling about this."

"About us getting married?"

"No, about us inviting our families to our wedding; your mom has not forgiven you for getting pregnant and she clearly hates my guts, now. She was the only one in your family who genuinely acted like she liked me. Now, I don't even have her in my corner."

"Hey, you will always have me in your corner, so it doesn't matter who else likes you or not, okay?"

"Well, I guess. So, are you ready to go into the next lion's den?" Daniel asked.

"What does that mean?"

"It means are you ready to call my parents?" he asked, laughing.

"Oh! Sure, let's do it and get it over with. Hopefully your mom will treat you better than mine treated me."

"Don't hold your breath," Daniel responded, as he dialed his parents' number.

"Hello! Daniel is this you?" his mom asked, noticing the number on caller ID.

"Yes, it's me. How have you been, ma?"

"Oh, I'm doing good. Just missing my baby son."

"I miss you too, momma!"

"Things really got out of hand, Daniel and I'm very sorry. I like Melah and if she makes you happy, then I'm very happy for you, okay?"

"I'm so glad you said that because I was calling to let you and dad know that Melah and I are getting married in two months and we're mov—"

"TTTAAAPPPAAHHHH!" Daniel heard, as if something hit the floor.

"Momma, what was that?" Daniel asked, but his mom didn't answer.

"Sarah! Sarah! What's wrong, what's wrong?" Daniel heard his dad yelling.

"DAD! DAD! WHAT HAPPENED?" Daniel yelled, hoping his dad would hear him on the phone, but he didn't. The phone went dead and when Daniel called back, he couldn't reach either of them. He called Roslyn and told her what happened (minus the part about him and Melah moving and getting married.) He asked if she'd go check on their mom and let him know if she was okay.

Daniel and Melah went back to their condo while they waited for Roslyn to call back. By the time they got there, Roslyn was just calling. She told him that their mom fainted, but no one knew what caused it. She said she was doing fine now and was at home resting.

"Wow! Oh! Okay. I'm glad she's fine," Daniel said, like he was in shock.

"Yeah, me too!" Roslyn responded.

Roslyn tried to make small talk with Daniel, but there was definitely something missing. They finally just got off the phone. Daniel wanted to call and check up on his mom, but he figured he should let her get some rest.

"Melah, do I have a knack for making people pass out?"

"No, babe! Don't beat yourself up about that. You didn't know your mom or Mr. Cross were going to respond that way. It's not your fault," Melah said, trying to offer him comfort.

"I don't know, Mel. I think we should just get married with maybe a few friends and leave our family out of it."

"Okay, we can do that or we don't have to have anyone there but us; just you and me."

Daniel smiled.

"Okay, let's just have you and me, then."

"But I still want it to be at a lake, though, and I still want to be in a wedding dress."

"Absolutely! Whatever you want," Daniel said.

"Yay! I'm so excited," Melah said, kissing her ring, then leaning over and kissing Daniel.

A month and a half had passed and Daniel and Melah's cozy wedding for two was only two weeks away. Everything was in place. It was going to be held on Lake Belize, the most beautiful lake in Georgia. They even found a dress to stunningly accommodate Melah's eight-month pregnant belly. Everything was wonderful and perfect.

"Daniel, wait! We don't have anyone to officiate our wedding," Melah said.

"Oh! Well, I guess we do need that, huh? Maybe we can ask Kirsten and Everett's pastor."

"Daniel, our wedding is only two weeks away; he's going to think we're crazy. Maybe we can just ask Everett," Melah suggested.

"That'll be cool. He is a minister, so he should be able to perform weddings."

"Let's call him and ask!" Melah said, excitedly. "Daniel, can we invite Janice and John too?"

"Yeah, sure. That would be great. Matter of fact, John told me to invite them."

"He did? When did you talk to him?"

"While we were on our way—" Daniel said, cutting off his sentence. "It was right around the time we got engaged," Daniel answered, not wanting to tell Melah that John asked him if he was going to marry her. He knew she would think that John was the only reason he proposed to her and that would not go over well.

"Oh, okay," Melah said, not sounding suspicious. "And maybe Anna?" she whispered, timidly.

"Huh?"

"Anna is my best friend and I want her—"

"No! No, Anna! She's too ghetto! If we're gonna invite her, we might as well invite the rest of our crazy family. No! I'm not dealing with Anna," Daniel said, harshly.

"Daniel, don't be like that. Anna likes you."

"You don't have to lie to me, Mel. Anna has hated me since the day I asked for some of your lasagna," Daniel said, with an evil grin.

"Don't be mannish, Daniel, as my grandma would say," Melah said, laughing.

"Well, I did ask for some of your lasagna, didn't I?"

"Yeah, and eventually, you got more than that. I bet you won't go around asking for lasagna any more, will you?"

"Nope, because I have all the lasagna I need."

Melah smiled and figured she would use Daniel's flirtatious mood to try and ease Anna back into the conversation.

"So, can I ask An—"

"No! No Anna and no crazy family," Daniel responded, as his phone rang. It was his mother.

"Hey, ma! How are you doing?"

"Hey, baby son. Have you gotten married yet?"

"No, not yet. We're getting married in two weeks, May 10th."

"Oh, good!" His mom said, enthusiastically. "I talked to your dad and Roslyn and we all want to come. By the way, I didn't tell them about what happened the last time we talked. We'll just keep that between us, okay, son?"

"Okay, sure."

"Daniel, we're all very sorry about how we acted and we want to be there to support you. We told your uncle and aunt all about Melah and they wanna come. I'm sure Jake is going to ride up with us too, so you may wanna count on six of us coming. Oh, and Roslyn's three kids. Goodness! I'm forgetting all about my grandkids and son-in-law. Roslyn's husband may come; he's had a hard time adjusting to it, though, so I'm not sure about him. Just plan for ten people. Well, make that twelve, because I told Kirsten's mom, Jan about it and you know she wants to come. Also, my friend Edna was totally fine with you marrying a black girl. I really thought she was going to give me a hard time. As it turns out, her niece married a black man and he is fitting quite nicely in their—"

"Ma, the wedding is only two weeks away and we only planned for two people; just me and Melah."

"That's okay, we'll help you with all the food and decorations and stuff. Is her family paying for anything?"

"Nah. They weren't planning to come."

"What a shame. I can't believe they're not coming to see their little girl get married. No worries, we'll be there and we'll pay for everything, okay?"

"Well, ma—"

"I won't take no for an answer, Daniel. As your mother, I have not been there for you and I'm going to make things right. You are my only son and I don't care what color my grandbabies are, they are still my grandbabies and I'm going to love them just like I do my other grandbabies."

It meant a lot to Daniel to hear his mom say that. He had tears in his eyes and there was no way he could tell his mom that she couldn't come to his wedding. He glanced over at Melah, who was giving him a dirty look.

I can't believe him! A few minutes ago, he was adamant about family not coming, now he's on the phone, under his momma's magic spell, crying like a baby.

Daniel got nervous. He knew Melah was not happy and he also knew this meant that ghetto Anna would be attending their wedding, and there was nothing he could say about it.

"Okay, ma! I will check with a caterer to see how much they will charge per plate."

"Wonderful!" his mom said. "Call me back and let me know and we'll send you the money.

"Alright, thanks, ma."

"I love you, baby son. I really, really do."

"I know, ma! I love you too."

"Okay, talk to you later."

"Alright. Bye, ma."

"Bye."

Daniel got up off the couch. "Call Anna and the rest of the world and tell them they can come, okay?" he said to Melah, hanging up the phone and walking off.

"Oh, you think you're gonna get off that easy?" Melah asked, following Daniel down the hallway.

"I have to use the bathroom, Mel. You can't follow me in here."

"Boy, I've seen everything you got. Nothing is going to surprise me."

"Okay, suit yourself," he said, as he sat down on the toilet.

"Uggghhh! You didn't say you had to do all of that."

"So what do you want to talk about?" Daniel asked.

"Daniel, what you did wasn't right. You know I wanted my friend and my fam—Oh, gosh! This is so stinky, I don't think I can stay in here," Melah said.

"No, don't go! Let's talk," Daniel said, laughing. "I said you can invite Anna."

"Yeah, but only after your mom called and—Uhhh, I think I'm about to die. You smell like rotten skunk eggs."

"Well, go on and leave if you want, Mel."

"No, because then you'll come up with some other reason to not talk about this."

"Talk about what? I said invite whomever you want. My parents are going to pay for themselves to come and we'll pay for whoever else you want to invite, okay?"

"They're gonna pay for themselves? Aww, that's so sweet," Melah said, covering her nose. "But, I'm still not gonna invite my family. I'll just invite Anna," Melah said, sounding like she couldn't breathe.

"Why are you torturing yourself? We can talk about this when I'm done. Just go ahead and call Anna, Everett and Kirsten, and John and Janice. Don't forget to ask Everett if he'll officiate the wedding or I can call him when I'm done blowing up the bathroom," Daniel said.

"Okay, good. I'm going to go call Anna and Janice. Bye," Melah said, running out of the bathroom and gasping for air. "I don't think I can marry someone who stinks this bad," she mentioned, as she shut the bathroom door.

"Well don't come in the bathroom with me and you'll never know you're married to this side of me."

"Deal!" Melah said, walking back into the living room, with her hand still over her nose. "Ewww, I think the smell has gotten on me! I gotta go change clothes. I better wash my hands too, just in case he contaminated me while I was in there."

After Melah changed her clothes and washed her hands, she immediately called Anna, then Janice, but neither answered their phones. She left a message telling them about the wedding location and date.

When Daniel was done in the bathroom, he grabbed

the phone to called Everett.

"Did you wash your hands?" asked Melah.

"Ummm, yeah!"

"Did you make bubbles with the soap?"

"I know how to wash my hands, Mel."

When he called Everett, he asked him if he would officiate their wedding.

"Yeah, sure! Are you planning to get any pre-marital counseling?" Everett asked.

"Huh? What's that?"

"Well, it's basically couples counseling. It goes over what couples should expect in a marriage and it gives some tips on how to handle things the right way. To be honest, I've never counseled any couples before, so I'll probably ask my pastor to help out."

"That'll be great. Melah and I won't mind if he's there."

"Okay, I'll get everything set up and let you know when we can start. It will probably be several times a week because we only have two weeks to cover everything and normally it's a month long."

"Oh, wow! That's a long time!"

Everett laughed. "Well, it's not every day, but there is a lot of information the pastor wants to go over. It's the best, though. Kirsten and I decided to go through it ourselves. It was really worth it."

"Okay, well, we're ready whenever you are."

"Okay, great," Everett said, then hung up.

Over the next week, Melah and Daniel were totally engrossed in pre-marital counseling and loving every minute of it. Janice had called to confirm that she and John would be attending the wedding, but Melah never did hear back from Anna. She knew Anna didn't like Daniel so she wouldn't be surprised if Anna didn't come, but she figured she should at least be there for her. As Melah was making dinner and thinking about her, Anna called.

"Hey, girl! I was just thinking about you," Melah said.

"Oh you were? Well, I just called to let you know I'm coming to your wedding next weekend. I ran into your mom at the store and she said I can ride with her or someone else from the family since so many people are coming."

"WHAT?" Melah said, putting the phone on speaker, so Daniel could hear what Anna was saying.

"Yeah, I think they're renting a bus or something."

"Who's renting a bus?" Daniel asked Melah.

"My family, to come to the wedding!"

"Oh, no!" Daniel said, but Melah looked at him like she was insulted. Not that she wanted her family there any more than Daniel did, but he didn't have the right to say anything about her family coming.

"I didn't know my mom was coming," Melah said to Anna.

"You didn't?" She said you called her a couple of months ago and invited her."

"Oh, yeah! I guess I did, but I didn't think she was really coming."

"Well, she's definitely coming, Melah."

"But I never called her back to tell her where the

wedding was going to be."

"She asked me if I knew, so I told her. Either way, they are all coming."

"Do you know who 'they' are?" Melah asked, nervously.

"Yeah, 'they' are as many people as they can fit on a bus."

"Oh, no!" Melah said, sounding like Daniel, but Daniel didn't say a word. "Okay, thanks. I'll see you next weekend."

"Well, me and your mom will be up on Thursday, so we can help you get everything ready."

"Oh!" Melah responded.

Daniel was sitting at the kitchen table frantically shaking his head, no.

"Okay, see you guys on Thursday," Melah said, trying not to sound unappreciative.

She hung up the phone and went straight into the bedroom and cried.

Daniel walked in the room behind her.

"This is going to be a disaster! A horrible, horrible, disaster!" Melah said.

"No, it won't!"

"Stop kidding yourself, Daniel. We're not talking about our immediate family members, we're talking about cousins and aunts and uncles and nieces and nephews. Everybody from both sides of our families, Daniel! Picture it! This is not going to end well."

"Well, let's just try to stay positive, okay?"

"Positive about what? We only have one more

week before our wedding and everyone wants to come. What happened to it just being the two of us? I want to go back to the two of us, Daniel," Melah said, like she was about to have a panic attack.

"Mel, calm down. You're eight months pregnant, remember? You can't get all worked up. It's not healthy for you or the baby," Daniel said, kissing her on the forehead, then lying beside her, staring up at the ceiling, and dreading the thought of having his cousin, Jake and Melah's brother, Corey in the same room with each other.

CHAPTER

When Thursday morning came, Daniel got up and got dressed for work.

"Are you going to be okay, Mel?" he asked, looking at Melah, who had been stressed out since she talked to Anna.

"I don't know, Daniel. I don't feel good. I can't believe my mom told the whole family about the wedding. I made it clear that I wanted a very small wedding. Why would she do this to me and how are we going to feed all of my family, Daniel?"

"Don't worry about it. God will take care of it, okay?"

"Daniel, are we still going to get that cat I said I wanted for my graduation present?"

"A cat?"

"Yeah, remember the day of my graduation, I told you I wanted a cat?"

"Yeah, but why are we talking about a cat right now? Besides, I got you a baby instead," Daniel said, laughing. "Speaking of which, we still have to go shopping for."

"I'm eight months pregnant, Daniel. We have nothing for our baby and that is horrible!"

"Well, maybe someone will buy us some baby clothes as a wedding gift."

"Well, that's not the ideal wedding gift, but I definitely won't complain."

"Me either," Daniel said, giving Melah a kiss on the forehead as he left for work.

As soon as Daniel left, Melah started having chills, then hot flashes, shortness of breath, dizziness, and nausea.

"God, what is wrong with me?" she asked.

She knew she was stressed about the wedding and she tried hard to calm herself down. When her mom and Anna arrived, she looked like she was going to faint.

"Melah, what is wrong?" Anna asked.

"Come and lay down," Melah's mom said, walking Melah to her bedroom and bringing her a glass of water.

"I'm just stressed over the wedding, that's all."

"Well, stress no more, because Anna and I will take care of everything," her mom said, as if she wasn't the cause of Melah's worry in the first place.

As the day went on, Melah seemed to have been much calmer and everything was going great. When Daniel came home from work, Anna and Melah's mom did their very best to be nice to him; he gave all three of them hugs and asked Melah how she was feeling.

"I'm feeling much better. Thank goodness."

"Good! So do you ladies want to go out to dinner tonight?" Daniel asked, noticing that nothing was on the stove cooking.

"No! Anna and I are going to cook," Melah's mom answered.

"Ms. Sharron, I can't cook!" Anna responded.

"No, momma. Anna doesn't even know how to boil water," Melah agreed.

"How are you planning to get a husband and you can't cook, child?"

"It's not a requirement for women to know how to cook anymore, Ms. Sharron, a lot of women don't know how to cook and they still got a husband," Anna mentioned.

Daniel wanted so badly to chime in but he resisted the urge and just kept quiet.

"And a lot of women's husbands leave them for women who know how to cook too, Anna."

"Ms. Sharron, I can't believe you said that. No man is going to leave me."

No man is going to even marry you, Daniel thought.

"C'mon, child. Hush all of that foolishness. I'm going to teach you how to cook," Melah's mom said to Anna. Anna gave Melah a dirty look like it was her fault.

"What did I do?" Melah asked, as Anna was walking out of the room.

"I'm very proud of you," Melah said to Daniel.

"For what?"

"For not saying what you were thinking when Anna talked about cooking not being a requirement."

Daniel laughed.

"It was indeed, a very difficult moment for me, Mel."

Melah smiled.

"Daniel, we're getting married in two days."

"Yep! Are you ready?"

"Yes, are you ready?"

"I've been ready," he said, winking at Melah. "But I need you to not stress. It's not good for you or the baby, okay?"

"I'm feeling great right now, babe, so I'll be fine."

"Okay. Good!" he said, turning on the television and watch Jeopardy.

"You're such a nerd," Melah said.

"You're just noticing that?"

"No, not at all. I knew you were a nerd a long time ago."

"But you fell in love with me anyway. You're a smart girl!"

"Yes, I sure did and I have no regrets," Melah said, as she watched Jeopardy with Daniel.

After dinner, everyone played a board game. They had so much fun that all of Melah's apprehensions about the wedding were gone. She was now very glad that her mom and Anna were there and so was Daniel. It kept Melah from stressing over the wedding and Daniel was very happy about that.

The next day, when Daniel came home from work, Melah's mom met him at the door.

"Sorry, it's the day before the wedding and you

cannot see the bride," she said as soon as he walked in.

"Excuse me?"

"You heard me."

"Where's Melah?"

"She's out with Anna, so please pack up a few things, because you will not be able to stay here tonight."

"Ms. Sharron, you can't be serious!"

"Oh! I am serious. It is very bad luck to see the bride the day of the wedding, Daniel. I cannot let you do it."

"But the wedding isn't until tomorrow."

"Yes, but you guys are living in the same apartment, so if you stay here tonight then you will see each other in the morning, won't you?"

"Yeah, I guess so, but—"

"And for the record, I think it's very wrong for y'all to be living in the same apartment. You're not even married, yet."

"Well, what were we supposed to do? It didn't make sense for us to move up here and for Melah to get an apartment, knowing within two months she was going to move in with me."

"It didn't make sense for you to move her away from her family when you hadn't even proposed to her."

Daniel wanted to tell Melah's mom that Melah invited herself to Atlanta, but he knew that was not going to come out right and it would be taken totally out of context.

"Would you feel better if I told you that Melah and I haven't had sex since we've been in this condo?" he said, trying to offer her some type of consolation.

"No, what would make me feel better is if y'all would have never had sex in the first place."

"Ms. Sharron, I'm sorry for how things turned out, really I am, but we can't do anything about that now. I love your daughter and I want to spend the rest of my life with her. For Melah's sake, I would like us to try and get along."

"I'm trying to like you, Daniel, but Melah is my only girl. I just don't think you're the right one for her."

"Why? Because I'm white? Is that why I'm not the right one?"

"Well, yes! If you want me to be honest about it, but even if you weren't white, I wish she would have stayed in the apartment her dad and I got her when she started college. It bothers me that as soon as you moved, she just hopped right up and moved with you, leaving her job and terminating her apartment lease.

MELAH QUIT HER JOB, SO THAT MEANS SHE HAD NO MONEY TO PAY HER LEASE AND Y'ALL WERE GETTING ON HER NERVES. THAT'S WHY SHE MOVED, SO CHILL OUT! Daniel wanted to scream to Melah's mom.

"She paid the termination fee! Everything has work—"

"It doesn't matter. It's still wrong. Y'all are still wrong for each other. This is never going to last, ya know?"

"Well, we'll be married tomorrow. You can attend if you want, but if you don't, then that's fine too," he said, walking down the hallway and climbing into bed to take a nap.

"Daniel! What are you doing?" Melah mom asked, walking into the room behind him.

"Ms. Sharron, can we establish some boundaries, here?"

"You can't stay here, tonight. I told you it was bad—"

"FINE!" he said, hopping out of the bed. "Can I please have five minutes to pack my things?"

"Yes, that's what I've been trying to get you to do."

"Alone, Ms. Sharron. I need five minutes alone!"

"Oh! Okay. I'm leaving," she said, walking out of the room. Daniel hurried and locked the door behind her, since she obviously didn't know that bedrooms were off limits.

What happened to the sweet lady I met a few months ago? Daniel thought. *I really wish I could have that lady back as Melah's mom.*

Daniel happily packed up some things for the night because there was no way he wanted to spend the night in the same place as Melah's mom anyway.

He called Everett to see if he could crash at their place.

"Hahahaha!" Everett laughed. "You let your future mother-in-law kick you out of your own house? I should have your man-card pulled," Everett joked. "I'm just kidding, man. Kirsten and I didn't see each other the night before our wedding or the morning of. I was missing her like crazy. I wanted to tell the pastor to just pronounce us husband and wife, so we could get to the kissing part, but yeah, you can crash here."

"Thanks, man. I appreciate it. Oh, and have you found out when you go to court for your altercation with Jason?"

"Never!"

"Never? What do you mean?"

"Jason got his lawyer to drop the charges."

"What? Man, that's cool. I'm really glad he did that. I told him that he—alright, I'll see you in a few," Daniel said, cutting off his sentence.

"Don't try to change the subject and think I won't notice. What did you tell him?" Everett asked.

Daniel gave a slight chuckle.

"It was nothing really. I just told him that he had to let go because Kirsten is your wife. That was pretty much it."

"Oh, yeah? What did he say?"

"He didn't really say anything. He kinda acted like he was in a daze. It was when he was in the hospital. I don't know if he even remembers the conversation," Daniel said, trying to down play the situation.

"Oh, I'm sure he remembers. Alright, well I hope this is not just another one of his ploys to try and get Kirsten back. By the way, Kirsten and I ran into him, his ex-wife, and son a while back. Their son said they're getting remarried."

"Really? Well, there's this lady who doesn't work for the company, but she is always in his office. She has the biggest butt in the Guinness Book of World Records. I wonder if that's her?"

"Yep! That's definitely her. It is hard not to look when she passes by, but for the sake of my relationship with Kirsten, I just stared at a picture on the wall until she was out the door," Everett said.

Daniel laughed loudly.

"Daniel, can you please hurry it up in there? Melah will be home in a minute," Melah's mom yelled out.

"Dang, man! I better let you go before she takes your phone away."

"That's not funny, man. She's acting like a nut case," Daniel whispered, hoping she wasn't at the door eavesdropping like Melah would be doing.

Daniel packed his things and headed to Kirsten's and Everett's for the night. When Melah and Anna returned, Melah's mom told her where Daniel was and reminded her that enough bad things had already happened and she didn't want to bring on more bad luck.

"You're right about that," Melah agreed and decided not to make a big deal over Daniel not being there. Later that night, she and Daniel did manage to sneak away and talk to each other, though. Daniel told her how Everett took him out to eat and they talked about life. She told Daniel how Anna wanted to take her to a strip club for her bachelorette party. Daniel laughed so hard that he was crying.

"It's not that funny, Daniel" Melah said. "I bet if I wasn't as big as a horse right now, you would not think it was funny."

"I'm sorry, Mel. No, it's not funny, but who takes an eight-month pregnant woman to a strip club for her bachelorette party?"

"Apparently, Anna does," Melah said, laughing. "Well, I need to get my beauty rest, so I'll talk to you later."

"Okay, goodnight, and for the record, I don't think you need any beauty rest."

"Aww, that's so sweet, but let's see if you still say that when I'm looking like an old hag walking down the aisle tomorrow."

"Okay, well in that case, go rest up. Darn it! Mel, I left my tuxedo at the house."

"Aww, babe! You did? Well you should come get it."

"And have your mom waiting at the door with an ax? No thank you." Your mom is not as nice to me as she once was, ya know."

"I'm sorry, babe, but if it's any consolation, she's not as nice to me as she once was either. I'll bring your tux with me in the morning, okay? If you decide you want to sneak out of the house later, I can meet you in the moonlit park for a little—"

"Ummm, good night, Mrs. Stine. I'll see you tomorrow."

Melah laughed.

"I can't wait! Goodnight, Mr. Stine."

CHAPTER 29

"WAKE UP, MELAH! WAKE UP!" Anna was screaming at Melah.

"Huh? Why are you yelling?"

"Girl, the parking lot is filled with all of your family. There are people and buses everywhere!"

"Oh, no!" Melah said, staring out of the window. "Anna, I can't deal with this! I don't even know if we're gonna have enough food to feed everyone."

"Girl, your mom already did a head count and called the caterer."

"She did what? How did she know who my caterer was?"

"She got it out of your book that was labeled *My Wedding Stuff*."

"Well, yeah. That's a dead give away."

"Anyway, she paid for everybody. She tried to pay for Daniel's family, but someone had already paid for twelve plates for them."

"Wow! I'm impressed," Melah said.

"So, what do you need me to help you with?"

"Anna, I need you to help me get rid of all of these people, so Daniel and I can have a private wedding."

Anna laughed.

"No can do!"

"Well, okay. Can you please make sure I get Daniel's tuxedo out of the closet and take it to the lake? Then I need to go get my hair and makeup done."

"Okay, let's go, but you're gonna have to at least say hi to your family."

"Why are they here so early? So much for the stereotype that black people are always late," Melah said.

Anna laughed so hard that she fell onto Melah's bed.

"Move out of the way, so I can say hi to my family," Melah said, pushing Anna and going into the bathroom to wash her face.

"Hey, everybody!" Melah yelled, stepping outside into the parking lot where her family was.

"HEY, MELAH!" Everyone started yelling and giving Melah hugs.

"I can't believe so many people came!" Melah said, looking around at everyone.

"Of course we came," her brother, Corey said. "We are family! Family sticks together, no matter what!"

Melah looked at Corey.

"Thank you, Corey. That means a lot to me," Melah said with tears in her eyes and everyone responded in agreement with Corey.

"Okay, well, I'm going to the lake so you guys can follow me there. There's not a whole lot to do there, but at least you can get off of your feet."

Everyone agreed to follow Melah and began to get back on the bus, while Melah ran in the house to take a quick shower. She grabbed Daniel's tuxedo and jumped in the car with Anna.

After she got her family settled at the lake, she and Anna left to go do her hair and makeup, while her mom stayed at the lake trying to entertain the family. Her mom had rented a karaoke machine to keep the kids company during the reception, but the adults decided to sing songs while they waited for Melah to come back.

Soon, Daniel, Everett and Kirsten arrived.

"OH MY GOODNESS! Who are all of these people and why are they doing karaoke?" Kirsten asked.

Daniel just shook his head.

"These are my in-laws. I hope Melah doesn't see this. She's gonna freak out!" he said.

"Oh, boy!" Everett said.

About twenty minutes later, Daniel's family pulled up in a van. They were peeping out of their windows like they were afraid to get out.

"Daniel, your family is here," one of Melah's cousins yelled. "You better hurry and let them see some white skin before they turn around and go home," he added.

All of Melah's family laughed and Daniel and Kirsten ran out to meet them.

"Momma!" Kirsten yelled, giving her mom a hug.

"Hey, baby! It's so good to see you?" her mom said. While Kirsten and her mom got caught up, Daniel was trying to coax his family to get out of the van.

"There are so many of them," Roslyn said.

Daniel's dad just shook his head, as he thought about the black people that were about to become a part of his family.

"Come on. I'll show you where you're going to be sitting," Daniel said.

He took them to the front row, then he asked Melah's parents if they could come up so he could show them to their seat as well.

"Corey, can you tell them to turn the karaoke machine off?" Daniel asked. "The wedding is going to start in twenty minutes and I really don't want Melah to see them doing karaoke."

"Sure," he said, as if they were the best of friends.

Daniel didn't want to offend Melah's mom by seating her after Melah's dad and her stepmom, so he just escorted all of them to their seats and let them figure it out themselves.

Corey was able to get all of the family settled down, then he looked at Daniel's shoes, or lack thereof, and said, "Bruh, why don't you have on shoes?"

"Long story. I left my tux at the condo, so Melah brought it to me this morning. I forgot to tell her to get the socks and shoes. I just got dressed ten minutes ago. Luckily, I still had on my black socks from yesterday. There was no time to run back home to get the shoes, I guess socks will have to do."

"Melah isn't going to be happy; I hope you know that," Corey said.

"I'm hoping she won't notice."

"Ha, ha, ha! You must not know Melah very well," he said, walking off and taking his seat beside his mom.

Daniel went around the long way to get back up to the front in hopes that no one else would notice he wasn't wearing shoes.

Soon, Anna came in to let everyone know that Melah had arrived and the wedding could begin.

When the music started playing and Melah walked in, Daniel swore she was an angel. Her dress hugged her belly, so beautifully showing off her God-given curves.

"God! She is so beautiful," Daniel said, as Melah walked closer to him.

Her dad sat there pouting because he felt deprived for not being able to walk her down the aisle, but Melah was very content to walk down the aisle all by herself.

"Where are your shoes?" she whispered to Daniel.

"It's a long story. Just pretend that I have them on," he said.

Everett did his opening speech, then he turned it over to Melah and Daniel who wanted to exchange their own vows.

"Melah, a year ago today, I got up enough nerve to speak to you. It was one of the happiest days of my life. From the moment I met you, I knew there was something special about you. On days when I feel like I can't take another step, you give me the strength to go on. You are beautiful in so many ways. I know God gave you to me and what God has joined together, we will let no one tear apart," Daniel said, leaning down to kiss Melah's hand.

Melah smiled.

"You remembered our relationship motto," she said to Daniel.

"Of course I remembered," he responded, then Melah attempted to graciously say her vows through her flow of tears. When she was done, she too ended with their motto. She looked him in the eye and said, "What God has joined together, we will let no one tear apart."

He smiled.

"I love you, Melah Stine."

"I love you too, Daniel Stine."

"Well, on that note," Everett chimed in. "I now pronounce you husband and wife. Daniel, you may kiss your bride."

Daniel gave Melah a big kiss and all of the family clapped, as if they were all okay with Melah and Daniel being together.

As soon as the wedding was over, the music started and everyone moved over to the pavilion where the food and dance floor were.

Melah and Daniel were out on the dance floor and everyone seemed to be having a good time. That was until Corey overheard Jake talking to Roslyn.

"I don't know what Daniel was thinking marrying into this ghetto family. I told him he was making a huge mistake."

Corey didn't even give Roslyn a chance to respond before he ran over and pushed Jake in back.

"WHAT DID YOU SAY ABOUT MY FAMILY?" Jake turned around.

"I said y'all are ghetto. I don't bite my tongue for no—"

Just then, Corey punched Jake in the face and they went tumbling down, taking the food table with them, and sending food flying everywhere. People were rushing over to try to break them up, but it seemed as if there was pinned up tension that they were determined to take out on each other. As folks tried to pull them apart, one of them bumped into the table that had the cake and punch on it, which caused their beautiful wedding cake to flip over onto the floor.

"STOP IT! STOP IT!" Melah started screaming at the top of her lungs. "WHY DID Y'ALL HAVE TO RUIN MY WEDDING? THIS WAS MY SPECIAL DAY!" she said, running out of the room. Daniel ran behind her, stepping on the train of her dress and almost making her fall.

"I'm so sorry!" he said, trying to keep her from falling.

"JUST LEAVE ME ALONE! I HATE THIS DAY!" she said, pushing Daniel back and jumping into the car where Anna was sitting and talking to her boyfriend.

"TAKE ME AWAY FROM HERE!" she screamed to Anna.

Anna didn't ask any questions, she just drove off as fast as she could, leaving Daniel standing there in the dust.

CHAPTER

"What happened? Where are we going?" Anna asked, trying to get some answers from Melah.

"I DON'T KNOW! JUST SHUT UP AND DRIVE!" Melah screamed.

As Anna was driving to the land of nowhere, Melah started hyperventilating and sweating.

"Melah, are you okay?"

"Ohhhhhh! My stomach hurts Anna. It really hurts," Melah said, trying to catch her breath.

"Anna, I can't breathe. I can't breathe."

"AAAAHHHHHH! I'm hurting, Anna! Please help me."

"I'm taking you to the hospital, Melah. Try to stay calm."

Anna called 911 and asked where the nearest hospital was.

The dispatcher happened to have an ambulance crew that was near the lake and she told Anna where to pull over to wait for the ambulance to come.

Anna called Daniel and told him what was going on and told him to meet them at the hospital. Daniel was so upset that Everett and Kirsten had to drive him there. Janice and John followed behind them and as soon as Melah and Daniel's parents got wind of what was going on, they all jumped in their cars and went to the hospital as well.

When the ambulance picked up Melah, she was sitting in a puddle of blood and still in a lot of pain. They rushed her to the hospital; shortly after, Daniel arrived.

"I'M LOOKING FOR MY WIFE, MELAH STINE. WAIT! MELAH THOMPSON! I DON'T KNOW WHAT NAME SHE'S UNDER!" he screamed, frantically.

The lady at the front desk gave him a weird look, but she told him what room Melah was in. When he got to the lobby, he saw Anna; he didn't have time to ask her any questions, he just wanted to get to where Melah was. When he walked in the room, Melah looked like she was fighting for her life.

"Daniel, I'm so glad you're here!" she said, solemnly.

"Doctor, what's going on?" Daniel asked.

"Melah's stress level is way above safe levels and the baby's vital signs are very low. We're gonna have to deliver this baby tonight," he said to Daniel.

"Tonight? She's only eight months!"

"The baby is coming. There's nothing we can do about it. Our only goal right now is to try and deliver a healthy baby for you."

"Okay, Melah. I need you to push," the doctor said,

calmly.

"EEEEEEUUUUUUUUU!" Melah said, pushing.

"Okay, stop!"

After a few seconds, he told her to push again.

"AAAAAAAAAAAHHHHHHHHHHHHHHHH!" Melah screamed, pushing as hard as she could. Meanwhile the baby's vital signs were getting lower and lower.

"We've got to get this baby out of here," the doctor said.

"One last push, Melah. As hard as you can."

"EEEEEEEEEAAAAAAAAAAAUUUUUUHHH!" Melah said, pushing like her life depended on it.

"There we go!" the doctor said, pulling the baby out of Melah.

"It's a girl!" Daniel shouted. "It's a girl, Melah!" Daniel said, kissing Melah's forehead.

"It is?"

The nurses quickly grabbed the baby and immediately started hooking tubes up to her.

"What's wrong?" Melah asked, but the nurses didn't respond.

"WHY ARE Y'ALL DOING THAT TO HER?"

"Melah, your baby no longer has a heartbeat. We are trying to resuscitate her."

"No heartbeat?" Daniel asked. "What does that mean?"

Daniel looked at Melah; her skin had changed colors and she looked like she was about to pass out.

"Oh, no! I need someone over here," the doctor said, trying to get Melah to stay alert.

They were eventually able to get Melah stabilized, but after a few minutes of working on the baby, they pronounced her dead.

"MY BABY IS NOT DEAD!" Melah yelled. "MY BABY IS NOT DEAD! DON'T LET MY BABY DIE! GOD, WHY DID YOU LET MY BABY DIE?"

"Don't do that Melah," Daniel said, crying like a baby.

"DON'T TELL ME WHAT TO DO! I HATE THAT I EVER DID THIS WITH YOU! I HATE THAT I LET MYSELF GET INVOLVED WITH YOU. I HATE THAT I HAD THIS BABY WITH YOU! I SHOULD HAVE HAD THE ABORTION!" Melah screamed to Daniel, along with a few other hurtful words.

"You don't mean that, Mel," he said, still crying.

"I DO MEAN IT! GET OUT! GET OUT! I WANT NOTHING TO DO WITH YOU OR YOUR RACIST FAMILY! STAY AWAY FROM ME! STAY OUT OF MY LIFE!" Melah said, taking off her ring and throwing it at the walls.

"Mr. Stine," the doctor said, interrupting. "I'm really sorry to do this to you, but if we don't get her calmed down, she's going to go into shock and we may lose her. We can give you some time alone with the baby if you want, but we've got to ask you to leave so we can get her stable, okay? I'm really sorry."

"MY BABY JUST DIED AND MY WIFE IS ABOUT TO GO INTO SHOCK AND YOU WANT M E TO LEAVE?"

"I'm sorry, Mr. Stine. I just don't want you to lose

your baby and your wife, alright? The nurse will take you into the next room, so you can see your baby if you'd like."

While the doctor tried to stabilize Melah's blood pressure, Daniel was in the next room admiring his beautiful baby girl, who looked just like him.

"GOD! WHY? WHY DID YOU HAVE TO TAKE MY BABY?" he said, putting his head on the baby and letting out a loud scream, which his family could hear from the lobby.

After a few minutes, Daniel wiped his face and walked through the lobby to leave.

"Daniel! Is she okay?" the family asked.

Daniel looked around at everyone. All of his family was in the lobby, and as many as could fit from Melah's family was there too. They were all holding hands and praying like they were one big happy family. Melah's mom and Daniel's mom were hugging each other like they were old friends. Even Corey and Jake had somehow made peace with each other, even though their clothes were covered in each other's blood.

"Is this what it takes to bring you all together?" Daniel asked.

"Y'all have all made our lives hell on earth, with your racist attitudes and hateful words and then convincing yourselves that you did it for our own good. You have intentionally tried to sabotage our relationship and when that didn't work, you tried to sabotage our wedding. Now you're here acting like y'all love each other so much. You're a bunch of racist hypocrites! The mixed baby girl that y'all dreaded so much is now dead and Melah doesn't want anything else to do with me, so if that's what you were hoping for, then your wishes have finally come true" Daniel said, walking off.

"DANIEL, WAIT!" everyone began to yell.

"NO!!!!!! Y'all got exactly what you wanted, so please leave me alone and no one better follow me!" he said, coldly.

Shortly after Daniel left, the doctor came out to tell the family that they couldn't save the baby, but they were able to get Melah stabilized. "However," the doctor said, "I can't risk her getting upset again, so I cannot allow anyone to see her until tomorrow."

"WHAT? YOU CAN'T KEEP ME FROM SEEING MY BABY!" Melah's mom yelled.

"Ma'am, we almost lost her, so if you want to see your baby again, I suggest you allow her to get some rest, okay?"

Everyone began to cry; Corey more than anyone.

"Daniel was right!" Corey said. "We've made their lives miserable all because we didn't want them together! If it wasn't for our racist mentality and stupid way of thinking, Melah and that baby would be fine right now! We murdered that baby! That's all there is to it and I'm really ashamed of myself," he said, walking off in tears.

"He's right," some others agreed.

"You guys, Melah and Daniel really loved each other. They were very happy together. That's what should matter most," Kirsten said. "My husband's parents are an interracial couple and they went through a lot of heartache from the crazy people in this world, but the reason they stayed together is because their families stood by them and encouraged them to never see color. If a person doesn't have love and support from their family, then what do they have? Daniel is a great guy and Melah is a great girl. They were made for each other and a precious baby was created from this union. That baby girl had both of your bloodlines running through her. She was the single most innocent human being here because she didn't have any pre-conceived ideas that one side of her family was better than the other. She would have loved you both equally. Unfortunately, she was going to enter into a family who hated her mother or her father simply because of their skin color; she would have felt it, because hatred can never be completely hidden. As she grew up, your hatred for the other side of her family would have been unveiled, sooner or later, and that would have been one more person you're adding to your team so she can continue your legacy of racial injustice. Although I'm so sad that their baby has passed, I hope you all will use this tragedy to change the way you think. This world has got to find a way to get along with each other. We've got to find a way to stop being divided. That is my prayer," Kirsten said, walking out of the door, followed by Everett, Janice, and John.

When they got outside, they saw Corey sitting on the steps, crying.

"Hey, bro," Everett said. "It is clear that you are the leader of your family. If anyone can help things to change, it's gonna have to start with you."

Corey cried even harder.

"I know, man! I'm the reason my niece isn't here

anymore. I don't know if my sister is ever going to forgive me."

"Don't beat yourself up about something that has already happened, just decide to make a difference going forward," Everett said.

As they were standing there talking, Daniel's family came out of the door. When Jake saw Corey, he reached out to shake his hand in hopes of extending the olive branch of forgiveness and unity. Corey returned Jake's handshake.

"I'm sorry for everything, man," Jake said.

"Nah, I'm the one who should be sorry," Corey responded.

"We should all be sorry," Daniel's dad said, extending his hand to Corey as well. That was the first time Daniel's dad looked at black people as his equal. He knew his son was somewhere hurting and he felt that it was all his fault. He didn't know how he was going to rebuild his relationship with Daniel, but if it took the rest of his life to do so, then that's exactly what he was going to do.

"Change begins with us," Daniel's dad said to everyone. "We all have a part to play. If anyone sees my son, please tell him that we love him," he said tearing up.

"Okay," everyone responded, then they all left to go back to their homes.

Daniel was sitting across the parking lot watching the whole thing, but he was still disgusted that it had to take his little girl dying for their families to try to get along.

"What good is it now? I've lost everything. God, I don't understand why I had to lose everything that I loved.

I have always believed in you. I have always believed that things happen for a reason and you're in control of everything, but it's so hard for me to believe right now. If there's something you want me to learn from this, please show it to me, because I don't see the lesson that I'm supposed to learn from losing the people I love. I have to believe that you will help me through this," he said.

Daniel couldn't bring himself to go back to their house, so stayed in the car for the rest of the day and he slept in the car all night.

The next morning he went back into the hospital, hoping that Melah had calmed down enough to want to see him. He still had on parts of his tuxedo and some tennis shoes he found in the car.

"Hey," he said, carefully opening her room door.

She looked over at him. He could tell she had been crying a lot.

"Hey," she said glancing at him, then looking away.

"Can I come in?"

"Yeah," she said, still not making any eye contact.

He looked over at her ring that was sitting on the night stand.

"Oh! You got your ring back?"

"Yeah, the nurse found it and gave it back to me."

"So, does that mean—"

"No, Daniel. I can't live my life this way anymore. I can't deal with all the hurt and pain that being in an interracial relationship has caused me. I'm sorry. I just can't go on."

"Mel, don't throw away what we have."

"Daniel, I love you with all of my heart, but this is just too much for anyone to have to deal with. I can't do it anymore."

Daniel rubbed his face, then grabbed Melah's hand.

"C'mon, Mel!"

"Daniel, please! I don't want to get upset. Just go, okay? It was our baby that kept us together. She's gone now, so it's time for us to move on and find love within our own race. It's just easier that way. It's easier for everyone."

"You're wrong! Our baby is not what kept us together and you know it."

She touched his face and rubbed her fingers across the stubble on his jaw.

"I'm asking you to please let me go, Daniel."

His kissed her hand.

"Mel, please don't do this to us."

"I have no choice. Here you go," she said, grabbing her ring and placing it in his hand.

"Mel!"

She gave him another long kiss. "I love you, Daniel Stine," she said, with tears running down her face. "If you love me, you'll let me start my life over in peace, without all this unnecessary stress and drama."

He looked into her eyes.

"Is this what you really want?"

"Yes. This is what I want and need."

He kissed Melah's lips again. It felt just as passionate as the night he kissed her in her doorway, after their first tutoring session.

Tears were streaming down both of their faces. Melah could taste the salt from Daniel's tears.

There's no way she can kiss me like that and not still love me, he thought, but she seemed very adamant that she wanted him to leave; he kissed her one last time.

"Are you sure you—"

"Good-bye, Daniel," she said, softly.

Daniel let out a long sigh.

"Good-bye, Mel," he said, turning around and walking out of the door as calmly as he walked in.

Over the next couple of weeks they spent most of their days depressed and crying. They both tried very hard to move on with their lives. Daniel allowed Melah to stay in the condo until she got back on her feet and started working again; he rented a small furnished apartment down the street.

Soon, three months had passed and there was no communication whatsoever between Daniel and Melah. Melah had finally started working again and was diligently trying to get her life back on track. She went apartment hunting and found the perfect place for her new beginning. The bedroom had a bay window in it. "I LOVE BAY WINDOWS!" she screamed, when the lady showed her the apartment. It also had a sitting area, with a built-in book case, which was wonderful for all of the books Melah loved to read.

Daniel was also trying to move forward with his life. A girl from his job had made it very clear that she was interested in going out with him. He agreed to go out for drinks, but told her he wasn't sure when his divorce would be final, so he needed to keep things light until then. The girl seemed very understanding and was happy to be there for Daniel while he healed from the loss of his marriage and his child. She told him that it would do him some good to get out of the house; he agreed.

He met the girl at a restaurant and tried very hard to engage in conversation. She was beautiful and of course, she was white, just like his family would like. She was also very sweet and kind. He sat at the table, listening to her talk about all the fun things she like to do. She seemed to be just what he needed, but she wasn't Melah. He eventually cut her off and said, "Look, I'm really sorry, but my heart is just somewhere else. I don't want to waste your time. Here's a twenty dollar bill; that should take care of our drinks. I'm really very sorry," he said again, getting up and walking out without looking back.

Daniel left the restaurant, went to get Melah's ring and went straight to the condo where Melah was. He knocked and called her name. She heard someone fumbling at the door, so she got up to see who it was. She looked through the peep hole and saw that it was Daniel. She ran into her room to try to fix herself up a little, but she forgot that he had a key. She threw on some lipstick and perfume and ran back into the living room. He knocked again and then let himself in. When Daniel opened the door, Melah was standing there looking as beautiful as the first day he met her. He didn't say a word, he just grabbed her and kissed her.

"What God has joined together, we will let no one tear apart," he said, sliding the ring onto Melah's finger.

She smiled.

He squeezed her tightly and kissed her forehead.

"Tomorrow, we will go get you the cat you wanted, okay?"

"Okay," Melah said, and once again, these two soul mates made sweet, passionate love to each other, with no thoughts of birth control ever crossing their minds.

The End

Coming Soon

I am really excited about my upcoming novels and children's books: *A Will To Live, Why Do All Of My Friends Hate Me,* and *Easter Is About Jesus, Crazy Bunny.* Below, you will find a quick overview on what each of them are about.

A Will To Live

Life seemingly had a personal vendetta against Casper Rane. Even before he was conceived, the odds were against him. He somehow survived and became his parents' miracle baby. His childhood was filled with wonderful memories and a stable and loving environment, but when he turned sixteen, tragedy struck. From that day forward, Casper's life spiraled out of control, constantly being filled with agony, calamity, disappointment, and defeat. His only hope was in the comforting words of his father, "Son, as long as there is breath in your body, don't you ever give up."

Standing face-to-face with death, Casper knew the only way he could survive was by having a will to live.

Why Do All Of My Friends Hate Me?

Ellise Baker was a breath of fresh air. She was smart, pretty, and very popular. She never had a problem fitting in with the preppy kids, but unfortunately, she couldn't tell the difference between her friends and her enemies. One day, she asked her grandmother, "Grandma, why do all of my friends hate me?" Her grandmother responded, "Your true friends will never hate you, dear."

That day, Ellise had to reevaluate her idea of what friendship was all about and make the difficult decision of who should stay in her life and who should go.

Note: Because this book brings to light issues that children of all ages face, like bullying, peer pressure, betrayal, and low self-esteem, it has been written in two different formats; one for elementary school children and another for middle/high schoolers.

Easter Is About Jesus, Crazy Bunny

When the Easter Bunny learns that Easter is not about him, he is not very happy! He pouts, he stomps, and he kicks, but perhaps he will come to his senses when the children share with him the true meaning of Easter.

Meet The Author

I'm Colette Orr, founder of Orr Novels. I'm from a small, country town called Pelham, Georgia.

Words cannot describe how I have thoroughly enjoyed this journey as an author. I'm so grateful for all the support I received for my first novel, *It's Okay, You Loved Him...and you looked like a fool.* Your eager anticipation for the release of my second novel, *Why Keep Us Divided?* has definitely been fuel for me. It was very exciting to write about such controversial topics and I pray that you are not disappointed. I have two other novels coming: *A Will To Live* and *Why Do All Of My Friends Hate Me?* which is also written as a children's book. My second children's book is called, *Easter Is About Jesus, Crazy Bunny*, and it is simply adorable.

I hope you've enjoyed the book previews and will read them in their entirety when they are released. Thank you for all of your support in helping Orr Novels remain successful. I am forever grateful.

Love,

www.ingramcontent.com/pod-product-compliance
Lightning Source LLC
Chambersburg PA
CBHW020922090426
42736CB00010B/1000